Dream BIG!

Katrina Radke

Be Your *Best* Without *The* Stress:
It's Not About The Medal

By: Katrina Radke, MFT

Published by Motivational Press, Inc. | Henderson, NV 89074

ISBN: 9781935723615

Printed in the United States of America

First Printing: 2012

Disclaimer

Some names and facts have been altered to preserve people's privacy and to combine different stories into one to help illustrate a point.

This book does not prescribe treatment for any health problems. Seek the advice of a physician before starting any new exercise, nutrition, or wellness plan. The intent of the author is to offer general ways to enhance your overall well-being. It is up to you how you choose to use this information.

The author and publisher assume no responsibility for your actions.

Dedication

I dedicate this book to my wonderful husband, Ross, and my two children, Shanti and Sanjay, who fill me up with light, laughter, and love.

I also dedicate this book to all of you who aspire to feel alive, and to live from your heart.

Endorsement Quotes

Katrina teaches powerful life lessons, helping you make your everyday life that much more successful and fulfilling. Her journey and knowledge is a guarantee that she knows about what she speaks. Get the benefit of her experience and expertise."

John Naber
Olympic Hall of Fame, Four-time Olympic Gold Medalist,
Network Television and Radio Announcer

Trina offers a wonderful testimonial on how to enable your mind to unleash your body and achieve more than you ever thought possible. Her book is filled with sound and practical advice on how to live a healthier, less stressful and more successful life.

Gary W. Hall, M.D.
Vice President, US Olympians; Director, The Race Club;
Three-time Olympic Swimmer, Three Olympic Medals

"Katrina's inspirational book shows you how to go for success in all areas of your life, regardless of what obstacles show up along the way. Get started now."

Rowdy Gaines
Three-time Olympic Gold Medalist, NBC Sports Commentator

"Katrina has been at the top and is an expert at helping others to attain their peak potential and good health. Her inspirational book provides steps to help you get started now."

Jenny Thompson, M.D.
Twelve-time Olympic Medalist (eight golds), Four-time USA Olympic Swimmer

"Katrina's transformational book helps you find your true self as you listen within, discover your calling, and commit to fully living it."

Jeffrey M. Schwartz, M.D.
Best Selling Author, The Mind and The Brain, Leading Expert:
Neuroplasticity, Mindful Awareness, OCD; Author, You Are Not Your Brain

"Unlike many 'experts' whose counsel is based on classroom theory, Trina has walked the talk. Through determination and a never-give-up attitude, she has persevered through seemingly insurmountable obstacles to achieve her goals and fulfill her potential. Trina's story is one that is bound to inspire and motivate anyone who wants to get the most out of life."

Dennis Pursley
2012 British Olympic Head Coach, Swimming
Former USA National Team Director, 1989-2003
American Swimming Coaches Hall of Fame

This noble-hearted, talented teacher and coach has mastered the inner game— of life. If you wish to awaken and be all that you can (and are), then this inspiring and courageous book, by a top peak performer, is for you.

Lama Surya Das
Bestselling Author, Awakening the Buddha Within; Author,
Buddha Standard Time: Awakening to the Infinite Possibilities of Now

"All by itself, Trina's story is an amazing inside look at what it takes to be an Olympian. Her insights on how to be your best are pure gold. I wish I had this book when my career was just getting started."

Pete Cipollone
2004 Olympic Gold Medalist and World Record Holder
Three-time Olympian, USA Rowing

There are so many self-help books but seldom with such goodwill, and balance of expertise and heart. This is a book by someone I know who dances Tai Ji with me, and follows the "Watercourse Way" of TAO. I highly recommend it.

Chungliang Al Huang
Founder-president, Living Tao Foundation, and Tai Ji Master,
Author, Embrace Tiger, Return To Mountain

"Katrina's personal journey from debilitating illness to health, and her lessons and professional advice on health and potential, are a definite must read."

Gurkipal Singh, M.D.
Scholar and Expert, Immunology and Rheumatology,
Adjunct Clinical Professor of Medicine, Gastroenterology
and Hepatology, Stanford University School of Medicine

"Katrina's intimate and professional knowledge of world class athletics, mental power, health, and relationship training makes her the perfect guide to help you maximize your full potential."

Mel Stewart
Co-Founder, SwimSwam.com,
Two-time Olympic Gold Medalist, Swimming,
Director, Alumnae Relations, USA Swimming Foundation

Katrina's inspiring story and experience, as an Olympic athlete and therapist, provides practical guidance to make "healthy" choices for all of us who are striving to improve our lives in a complex and changing world.

Ira Glick, M.D.
A Founding Father, Sport Psychiatry,
Professor Emeritus, Psychiatry and Behavioral Sciences,
Stanford University School of Medicine,
Author, Marital and Family Therapy, American Psychiatric Publishing, Inc.

"Katrina's great book has the power to change your life. Get started now."

Jenny Potter
Four-time USA Olympic Hockey Player, Four medals

This is a story about Spirit and how a spirited girl achieved Olympian psycho-mental-physical success by disciplining the speed and intoxication of competition. It's also a story about how illness obligated a spirited woman to slow down and start examining her life, and accept, in ways previously unimaginable, a changed yet realistic potential. Katrina candidly shares her journey, insights, and spirit in a way that will inspire and guide you to fully live, experiencing life's challenges and opportunities.

Joseph M. Helms, M.D.
Founding President, American Academy of Medical Acupuncture;
President, Helms Medical Institute;
Author, Getting to Know You: A Physician Explains
How Acupuncture Helps You Be the Best YOU

"Katrina Radke is the most mentally tough Olympic swimmer with whom I have ever trained. If anyone can help you fulfill your potential (and find deep satisfaction in your life), she is the one!"

David Berkoff, J.D.
Two-time Olympic Gold Medalist and World Record Holder
Innovator, 35 Meters Underwater Dolphin Kick, Berkoff Blast-Off
Board of Directors, USA Swimming

Trina is a true example of excellence and perseverance. She walks the talk. Let her spirited book show you how to bring out the best in you.

Richard Shoulberg
USA Olympic Swimming Coach, Six-time Head USA Swimming Coach,
Head Coach, Germantown Academy Aquatic Club, Trina's coach

Katrina inspires all those who come in contact with her. She is charismatic, warm, and leads by example: A true Olympian with the Olympic spirit (Citius, Altius, Fortius) burning inside her. A must read.

Helen Mendel
Former Chairman of the Board,
American Cancer Society, California Division

In a society overly stimulated, Trina is able to instantly capture you to slow down, take a breath and utilize her wisdom and advice. Through her incredible adventure as an Olympic athlete, Trina helps you create a unique understanding that ANYONE can win in LIFE (love, sports, business, health)!

Chris Morgan
2008 Olympic Swimming Coach, Switzerland
Eleven-time Swiss National Team Coach

"Trina galvanizes her readers to action by encouraging us to go BIG with our own dreams. She provides proven strategies required for success."

Beth Rypins
Two Time Whitewater World Champion,
Owner, Wine Country CrossFit

"Each moment can be great. My friend, Katrina's wise and warm book shows you how you can start loving yourself and your life right now."

Jeff Prior
Four-time International Medalist for USA,
Owner, Water Wise Swim School

Finding peace in your own skin and loving yourself is the road to happiness. Trina has found that happiness. Her inspirational story and powerful tools will help you find this, too.

Roque Santos
1992 USA Olympic Swimmer and Entrepreneur

"*Katrina's ingenious book helps you master the art of taking care of your health while also performing your best, in all areas of your life.*"

Janel Jorgensen McArdle
Olympic Silver Medalist, Swimming
President, Swim Across America, Non-Profit benefitting cancer research

"*Stop looking out there. Happiness is an experience within and Katrina shows you how to BE here, now.*"

Ross Gerry, M.Ed.
Olympic Coach, Former Stanford University Women's Associate Head Swimming Coach, Won 6 NCAA Division I Championships in 7 years.

"*Katrina has a gift with helping others be empowered, be healthy, and reach their potential. Let her show you how in this inspirational book.*"

Karl Mohr, Ph.D.
Optimal Performance Coach Associated with Cal Men's Swimming and Diving Team for over 30 years

Let Katrina help you to uncover your true potential with the tools and inspiration she offers in this compelling book. A great read for young and mature adults.

Roberta Hladek
Co-Founder of EMC2, Energetic Balancing

"*Having known Trina since her childhood, it is no surprise to me she has compiled into a "how-to" book her thoughts on being positive, goal-oriented, and staying focused--character traits she has exemplified all her life.*"

Bruce Telander
CEO of Cobb-Strecker, Dunphy, & Zimmermann; "Dad 2"

"*Thanks to Katrina Radke for much needed advice to athletes, coaches, and parents on the motivation and science behind competitive swimming, commitment and excellence. Her book provides a nice balance on the elements needed for success in sport and in life.*"

Joseph F. Heyse, PhD
Vice-President, Biostatistics, Merck Research Laboratories;
Parent, Germantown Academy Swimmer (Trina's team)

Acknowledgments

I have been able to create wonders in my world because I could stand on the shoulders of many. Thank you to all of my mentors, teachers, coaches, parents, family, competitors, colleagues, and friends for helping to mold me into whom I am today. You all have been a gift in my life.

I feel blessed by everyone whom I have interacted with; for those who loved me, tested me, supported me, and stood by my side. Thank you for smiling at me when I needed it most, for acknowledging me as a human being who is worthy, for helping me stay on my path, and for allowing me to immerse myself in pursuits I loved.

Thank you to all of you who have supported me on my journey and in writing my book. I feel your love and appreciate you.

I particularly want to thank Coaches Richard Shoulberg, Graeme Brown, Teri McKeever, Karen Moe Thornton, Dave Storer, as well as my age-group coaches, who also inspired me and believed in me. To all of my teammates, friends, and training partners at Germantown Academy, Cal Berkeley, and the US Swimming National Team (and everywhere!), thank you for all of the fun memories and adventures, and for pushing each other to go beyond our limits!

I would like to thank all of my graduate school teachers and advisors, especially Barb and Ed Lynch, who taught me a lot about how systems work and how to help others heal emotionally. Additionally, thank you to Master Kim, Chungliang Al Huang, and to my Taoist Chi Kung Teachers for teaching me the healing art of energy work.

Many health professionals supported me as I was healing from CFIDS. I especially want to thank Dr. Joseph Helms, Dr. Michael Coomes, acupuncturist Stephen Birch, and Anneke Hogeland, MFCC. Your diligent love and care has forever changed me. Also, thanks to Karl Mohr, Dr. Mohsen Hourmanesh, Stephen Lewis, Evan Slawson, and Roberta Hladek, for your powerful energy and healing work.

Much gratitude to the families who opened up your homes to me, whether it was for two weeks or five years! Thank you to the Larsons, Dyes, Heaths, Samuels, Greers, Vollmers, and Shultzes. I especially want to thank the Stoebenaus and Telanders, who were very supportive and became like my second families.

To my dear friends Jeff Prior, Beth Rypins, Sallie Spignesi, Helen Mendel, and Caroline Paul, thank you for your continued faith in me and your support of my book. To Louise Hay and Reid Tracy: thanks for your support in the writing process.

To Mike Farris: Thank you. You are so much more than an agent. You first believed in the value of what I have to share. You also have been a wise teacher and mentor who helped me learn the art of writing. Thank you for helping me to edit much of my work. I appreciate your integrity and conscientious nature.

Thank you to my publisher, Justin Sachs, and Motivational Press for your dedication and commitment to excellence and in making this project a great gift for others. To my personal editor, Julie Coleman, thank you for helping me get my book into good shape!

To my loving parents, who gave me the opportunity to do what I loved and live my dream—thank you. To my two brothers whose footsteps I wanted to follow in; because you were both swimming, I began this fabulous journey.

To Wayne, Susan, Brenner, Benjie, Penny Freeman, and all of my extended family and stepfamily members, thank you for the love and kindness that we have shared. To Praveen and family—thank you for loving me and helping me to heal and reclaim my voice.

Most important, to my dearest husband, Ross who can always make me smile, laugh, and have fun—thank you for tirelessly reading, discussing, and reviewing my material. I love you, and I appreciate your support of allowing me to shine my light. To my two beautiful, energetic, loving children: Shanti and Sanjay. Thank you for reminding me of the miracles and magic in our lives.

Introduction

I knew I had to write this book, but that it would require the best of me to do so. As I examined my life, I didn't want to expose myself by sharing my accolades and joys or admitting my own pain, especially by articulating it to the world. Yet, a little voice within kept prodding me, reminding me that this is something I needed and wanted to do to help others strive to be their best and alleviate stress.

While I sought my dream of swimming in the Olympics, I learned and grew in ways that I wouldn't have expected, and I enjoyed experiences that I will treasure for the rest of my life. Throughout the process of training and performing, I gained tools and insights that later helped me cope with a debilitating chronic illness. Life threw me some unexpected—and seemingly insurmountable—obstacles, which allowed me to learn how to heal my mind, body, relationships, and spirit. From triumphant highs to heartbreaking lows, I eventually found balance, wisdom, and peace.

As my life drastically changed—I went from being an Olympic athlete to struggling with a chronic disease—I decided to pursue a career that focused on health, human potential, and relationships. I explored tools to understand what drives us to be our best and how to feel content in all areas of our lives. As I dug deep within, I found my truth. I discovered new depths within myself that I want to share with you.

By being honest with you, I hope that you will be encouraged to open yourself up and trust the process of exploring your personal journey—to be true to who you really are. This book will help awaken you to lost aspects of yourself, become more aware of your impact and importance, and commit to decisive actions that will help you live *your* best life, one designed and fulfilled by you. It will be an adventure: exploring the outer world while contemplating the inner world and learning what really motivates you.

Using my professional knowledge and examples from my personal journey, I'll help you realize your own power and how to maximize your potential. By offering steps and solutions to help you live your dream life, I will guide and challenge you to thrive rather than survive. My goal is for you to reclaim your spark, the spirit that knows who you are and what you want.

You'll be inspired to do what you always wanted but may have been afraid to try. As your bigger vision comes into focus and you find and commit to your true path, you will go deep within and attain *your* best, your true self. By altering how you choose to live, your life will be forever changed. You can live each day as if you had it all right now.

The caterpillar can't imagine the butterfly, but as he grows he learns how to live from a place of radiant beauty and magnificent power. As the sages knew long ago and the lucky ones still discover: Life, if you live it right, keeps surprising you, and the best surprise is yourself.

Table of Contents

PART FOUR: MAXIMIZING YOUR POTENTIAL AND FEELING CONTENT

PART ONE

CREATE YOUR DREAM LIFE

Chapter One

My Dream: Making the Olympic Team

Follow your heart and your dreams will come true.
                                        – Anonymous

Austin, Texas. August 13, 1988, 7:00 a.m.

I opened the door to the University of Texas's natatorium on the mark at 7:00 a.m. When the smell of chlorine hit my nostrils, I felt at home. I took a deep breath as I excitedly walked into the brightly lit pool area. I was there to try out for the 1988 Seoul Olympics.

I headed for the women's locker room, glad to find I was alone. I went straight to the second stall from the right. This was my pattern, my superstition; I always changed in this stall.

Once in my swimsuit, I walked out to the pool, dove in an empty lane, and began my wake-up swim. I started slowly, warming the aerobic engine. I didn't have to think. I just had to do.

By then, I had swum a couple thousand meters, a pattern of doing what science and success had taught me: forty laps of drills and easy warm-up, feeling the rhythm of my body loosening, of readying; then two or three "build 50s," increasing speed on each 50-meter lap. The water felt good, my body limber.

After tuning up my body, I rinsed off, changed back into my warm-up suit, and rode back to the hotel for breakfast. It was impossible not to think about the race and my dream. I had been imagining what it would be like to compete in the Olympic Games since the third grade, when I had written: "When I am 25 I will be a swimmer. I am going to go to the Olympics and win lots of medals. After that I am going to be a swim coach for a couple years. Then after I am a swim coach I am going to get a boyfriend and then get married."

I was determined to make that Olympic dream come true; it was my every-day intention. I focused on it. Trained for it. Ate for it. Slept for it. Hugged my parents for it. Coming from a small farming town, where only half of most senior classes went to college, our community spirit rallied around family, farming, and local sports. To consider making the Olympic Team from my hometown seemed impossible, yet I was determined to do exactly that.

As I relaxed in my hotel room, lying on the couch, ten years flashed by my eyes.

*****

I remembered being ten. My father was transferred to Adelaide, South Australia, for one year. My dad and brothers flew there earlier, and my mother and I followed on three planes across the United States and over the ocean to a new town, a new country, and—most important—a new coach. I was fortunate enough to swim with a top Australian coach, Graeme Brown. His personal aim was to put his swimmers on their National Team and Olympic Team. I loved that he synched with my focus immediately. I dove in and worked hard. He encouraged us to keep a journal. I handed mine in to him each week, and he wrote encouraging words back. He knew I really wanted to be as good as the best.

For morning practices, he picked up my brother Earl and I in his big Mercedes so we could start practicing at 5:00 a.m. The song "Rich Girl" often blared on his cassette player as we sang along. At morning practice, since I was younger than the more experienced group, Coach Brown let me watch top Australian swimmers do strength work. Among the group was Anna McVann, who swam for Australia in the 1984 Los Angeles Olympics. I loved watching these top-tier athletes, imagining I would get my chance to join their ranks soon.

A year later, I was sad to leave my friends and Coach Brown, but somehow I understood that I would find the right place to continue pursuing my dream. When we moved back to my hometown of Morris, Minnesota, I was an excited, anxious sixth grader. One morning, as my parents and I were having breakfast, I blurted out, "Where can I go to swim to make it to the Olympics?" I was nervous and already knew that there was no quick solution. Yet, the powerful experience of training in Australia had intensified my commitment. I had matched Coach Brown's expectations for willingness and pace of improvement. I knew I had it in me to become one of America's and the world's best. Good coaching was too far away from Morris to be realistic, but my mind was made up: I needed help in fulfilling my dream.

My parents decided to drive me to the Minneapolis area (three hours from Morris) on weekends the summer before and during my sixth-grade year so I could train with a team of competitive swimmers. During the car rides to and from Minneapolis, my father and I made up a game. If I matched a certain swim time, he would pay me five dollars; if I went faster, ten dollars; and so on. As the years went on and I got better, we added new categories and he chose the amounts: break the state record, twenty dollars; break a national record, fifty dollars. I didn't really care about the reward. I cared only about the times—they were getting faster. And I loved that my dad and I were having fun.

I kept swimming and winning those bets.

In seventh grade, my parents decided to let me stay with a family in the Minneapolis area so that I could go to school and train with a dedicated team. Later that year, my father transferred to Pennsylvania and then my parents separated. This family overhaul meant I also moved to Pennsylvania, to another new school, and to time split between my parents.

During the week, I stayed with a family close to the prep school, Germantown Academy, where I swam with Coach Shoulberg, a top American swim coach who later became an Olympic and USA Coach for international competitions (and a major figure in my life). On weekends, after a five-hour Saturday practice, I would see my father, who lived over an hour away. My mother would fly in from Minnesota every so often to spend time with me as well. I rarely saw my two older brothers during these years, since I lived away from home since seventh grade, and they now were in college.

This chapter in my life felt exciting, intense, and full of change. Even though I loved swimming and was given the opportunity to attend an elite prep school and swim with a top American coach, I was nervous. Yet, in the water, I felt peace—every emotion soothed, other than the will to improve. I recognized the value of attending an elite prep school (and did well), but my focus was on my two training sessions each day. I knew there were no guarantees, but I had to see what was possible.

I had been the National Age Group Record Holder, Junior National Champion, and High Point Winner, and I knew I had a lot of potential. Even though there was no rational reason to believe I could ultimately swim for Team USA, I knew I could keep living my dream. All I had to do was continue swimming. So I did.

In 1985, at age fourteen, I became the youngest member of the USA National Team and went to Japan for the Pan Pacific Games. I came home with my first American record and first international gold medal.

The next year, I was expected to make the World Team but I just missed it, thanks to a case of mononucleosis. While disappointed about not getting to compete in Spain, I took this as a warning sign to protect and value my health. I recovered somewhat, enough to get back in the water. I made another international USA squad in 1987 and went to Perth, Australia, for the Pan Pacific Games. I swam the 200-meter freestyle and the 4x200 freestyle relay, in which we broke the Australian Open record.

Long before the mononucleosis slowed me down, I had already received numerous medals and trophies. More than the need for medals, I had already discovered that I swam for the love of giving *my* best effort. For me, the drive came from inside, wanting to see what was possible as I challenged myself to be my best.

By 1987, I had been training with Coach Shoulberg for three years. He was tough and yet funny, with a widely accepted reputation for overtraining his athletes as he, like other top coaches, tried to keep up with the steroid-using East Germans. This didn't bother me. My training had become like an interesting science experiment. I loved being in the moment, focused on utilizing my mind, body, and soul to reach my maximum on any given day. I had moments where everything clicked, and my performances and practices were like dreams. I was immersed, my body and mind fully connected and engaged.

When I didn't perform my best, my instinct was to analyze the practice or race and to come up with new, creative ways to train as I took on the challenge of a new race, set, or day. The opponent was not in the other lanes; rather, the opponent was the opportunity itself. I didn't have to focus on others to pump myself up, and I didn't have to anticipate the glory I'd receive in order to swim fast. I just knew I needed to enjoy living my dream daily, and as long as I enjoyed the process of testing my limits, I knew I would gain more than I could ever imagine, regardless of the outcome.

Working through the ranks of my sport, I met a lot of athletes on the same path as I—first locally, then regionally, statewide, at the national level, and then internationally. Now, many of us were at the Olympic Trials. Training an average of five hours a day, six days a week, for ten years, I had swum enough miles to circle the globe. I knew all of the training and years of racing came down to this one moment on the blocks, at the Olympic Trials.

*****

In recalling my past ten years, I was proud of myself. I'd had many fabulous experiences, and I was hoping to have many more in the future. Yet, as much as I was aware that it's in the journey itself where the true fun lies, I also knew that I had built my life around a third-grade dream, hoping to become a United States Olympian.

During the previous day's trials, many candidates had swum their best races but few made it through. As I walked around the pool deck, I saw top athletes crying, some who had tried more than once to make the Olympic Team. Some swimmers who had been on the 1980 Olympic Boycott Team or on the 1984 Olympic Team (when the steroid-using East Germans and Soviets were not there due to a government political boycott) hoped to have another chance to partake in Olympic glory. Even some world record holders failed to make it.

Very few people get to experience the ultimate ecstasy of making the U.S. Olympic Team, getting to participate in the most universal sporting event in the world, the Olympic Games. The U.S. Olympic Trials were known for being the most intense meet that any U.S. swimmer would ever compete in. Only 0.4% (1 in 250) of competitive swimmers ever make it to this meet, and only forty to fifty swimmers make the Olympics. I knew I would have to swim close to my best time in the preliminary rounds in order to make the top eight for the finals. From the finals, only the top two would make the team.

I had to stay focused within myself and shut out all of the distractions around me. I started building my confidence. "I've been on the U.S. National Swimming Team several times in the 200-meter freestyle," I told myself. "I have held the American, U.S. Open, and Australian Open records. This is my event."

By noon, I knew the outcome. I missed making the finals by a split second. Many thoughts and emotions raced through me as I pondered my results and what they meant. "Gosh, how did I *not* make the finals? Does this mean I'm not rested enough? Maybe this is not my time, maybe four years from now is…." I had to stop ruminating, as I knew I would have plenty of time to review this race when the meet was over. For now, I had another event to focus on.

I still had a chance to make the Olympic Team. In five long days, my last shot to make the team would be in the 200-meter butterfly. My mind was whirling. If I didn't make it in my best event, how was I going to prepare differently, to think differently, and be ready for my second-best? Should I warm up more? Warm up less? Eat differently? Calm down? Get more excited? Remind myself of what I was capable of, that I could do this? Just enjoy each day for what it was? *I really wanted to make the team.*

It was easy to focus on all of the things that went wrong, or my struggles over the past several years, or wonder if I had overtrained and hadn't rested enough. I knew I would wear myself out if I spent five days reliving the last race or my past. At this point, all that mattered was the moment. *Relax,* I told myself. Relax, laugh a lot, give the body fuel, drink loads of water, and focus on being a brand-new me each day. I couldn't change the past or control the future, but I could be confident, relaxed, and happy.

And that's what I did. I stuck to my training regimen over the next few days, rested more than I normally would have, gabbed with friends on the telephone, and watched movies. Anything to relax!

My roommate, 1980 Olympian Karen LaBerge, and I made up a contest of super-hydrating, counting how many times we went to the bathroom each day to determine the winner. Twenty-eight was the record; Karen won.

The night before the race, I loaded up on carbohydrates and some protein at the Spaghetti Factory—one pound of fettuccine with Alfredo sauce and a half pound of chicken, with a massive green salad and a spare amount of Thousand Island dressing, my good-luck meal. That night, I was excited. Karen, another friend, and I dressed up for fun and danced around our hotel room. At 10:00 p.m., I forced myself to calm down and get some rest.

I arose at 6:00 a.m. the next morning, pulling myself out of bed. I began to focus on my race. I had done everything I could for my body. Now, anything within my control for this race was in my head. I looked down at my feet and smiled. I recalled June 9, earlier that summer.

∗∗∗∗∗

I had told myself that if I could break Karen LaBerge's record for climbing the thirty-foot rope above our pool at Germantown Academy, I could make the Olympic Team. I liked playing mental games like this, and it usually worked. She had climbed it thirteen times, and my goal was fourteen.

On June 9, 1988, at 6:00 a.m., Coach Shoulberg arrived to unlock the doors to the decorated pool area. As usual, we gave each other big smiles, and said "Hi." Flags from all of the countries to which any of his athletes had travelled for competition hung from the ceiling. I walked in, imagining Seoul, Korea's flag being the next one up there. I went into the smelly locker room and put on my swimsuit. I had told Coach Shoulberg, often called just "Shoulberg," that this was going to be the day that I wanted to get the team record on the rope. Our first practice outside in the sun since the previous summer had been just the day before. Though I had lathered myself up with sunscreen, I still got a minor burn. But since I had told Shoulberg that I was climbing the rope on this day, I was committed, sunburn or not.

There were two ropes, each about thirty feet high, hanging from the ceiling over the six-lane pool. I jumped into the cool water and shook out my body, giddy with nervousness and excitement. I had been climbing the rope all season, preparing myself to break the record. The most I had done in a row before today was eight. I lifted up my arms to the bottom of the rope, where a big knot rested about three feet above the water's surface. Grabbing the knot, I pulled myself up, placed my butt on top of the knot, and wrapped my legs around, just sitting there, taking in my surroundings. I looked up at

27

the ceiling. It was tradition that when people graduated from Germantown Academy, they signed the ceiling with their name and year. I was going to be a senior this coming academic year; next year would be my time to sign. But today, I knew I was ready to challenge myself to something even more special. Shoulberg leaned against the block and said "Rocky (my nickname in honor of how I trained), are you ready?" I said, "Yes."

I began my first climb to the ceiling. My arms reached up as far as they could, and then I pulled myself up to meet them as my feet wrapped around the rope to maintain my place. I climbed up the first time with ease, even though I could tell my body was slippery from all the sunscreen I had worn the day before. I reached the ceiling and touched it with my right hand as I held onto the rope with my left, indicating "one." I slowly lowered myself to the bottom of the rope by dropping my hands to my hip area and then lowering my legs. I looked like a monkey climbing a tree. I loved it.

By the fourth time up, I was tempted to tell Shoulberg that I was going to stop. I slipped constantly, and my already sunburned left foot was getting rope burn. I thought to myself, "I should just stop and do it another day." My forearms started to burn, and this was the turning point. Did I go for it or not? We reach that point in anything we do, where we have to decide to commit to going for it, even though the outcome is no guarantee. I looked up and got back to the present, moving my hands up the rope and using my full body to pull myself up one more time. I was determined. If there was ever a time I could do it, it was now. I was already in pain, but I decided to just focus on each pull up the rope. I was so aware of each second that nothing was going to stop me.

Somehow, by number six, my mind went quiet. I was in that peaceful place, doing what I loved most, testing my body and mind, just letting the universe take over and climb the rope for me. I was in a state of bliss. So much so, I had become oblivious to my left foot's skin getting torn.

On number eleven, I slid from close to the top of the rope all the way down to the bottom and had to start over. I then noticed how shredded my hands and feet were, but I just kept going. I thought to myself, "If I have forgotten about the pain up until now, I should be able to do three more." I pulled and pulled. My forearms burned beyond what I could fathom, but my focus was number twelve. By number thirteen, I knew I could do it. My focus was fourteen, and I did it fourteen times.

When I got to the bottom of the rope, I smiled with joy, pumped my fist in the air, and yelled, "Yes!" I looked up to Shoulberg, who had been watching me. He had a big grin on his face. Then I fell into the pool. Yeeouch! Not until then did I realize how much my foot was raw and burned. I had shut out the pain and knew I could do it—it had started off as a struggle, but I did it! I had persevered, gotten into the flow, and enjoyed one of the most amazing blessings of this life. I loved being immersed in this peak experience, pushing myself to see what was possible.

*****

Back at the Olympic Trials, I was feeling pumped, ready, and confident after recalling my rope-climbing experience. I knew I had only three things to do this day: believe in myself, give my best, and enjoy the experience.

I gathered my swim gear together—two pairs of goggles, two caps, two racing suits, my warm-up suit, and two towels—and headed to the pool. During warm-ups and behind the blocks before my prelim swim, I sang a song in my head that I had made up years before: "A is for aggressive, B is for bionic, C is for competitive, D is for dynamic, E is for electric, F is for fast, G is for great," all the way to "Z is for zest."

On the blocks, I felt pumped and ready. I looked down at my lane and loved seeing the clear, crystal-blue color. As the starter said, "Take your marks," I gripped the blocks with my fingers. I looked at the rope-climbing-record scars on my feet. I felt an inner calm, knowing that amazing things can happen when we believe. I leaped to a good start with the beeper and was cruising, repeating the alphabet song to myself. I won my heat and was ranked fourth going into the finals. "Yes!" I knew I could make the team.

After our lunch, Shoulberg rented the movie *Rocky*. I felt pumped as I thought to myself, "I can overcome the odds…yes…if it is meant to be, it is up to me."

The finals for the 200-meter butterfly were that evening around 7:00 p.m. Before having the top eight swimmers march out to swim the final, we congregated and waited in a room by the pool, known as "the ready room."

As I sat there, I felt calmer and more focused than before the 200-meter freestyle. Even though there were several top contenders in the butterfly, I knew it could be anyone's race. As the announcer paraded the final eight swimmers down the pool deck, past our teammates and friends to the starting blocks, I felt love and support. I was excited, yet calm.

I knew I would find the announcer's excited litany of everyone's accolades distracting, so I blocked it out, listening to the song, "Eye Of The Tiger" from *Rocky* with my big Sony headphones instead. All I had to hear was my name. When I heard that, I took off my headphones, walked to the block, and waved to the crowd. I shed my sweat suit. I made sure my goggles were on my head and ready to put over my eyes. I swung my arms one more time and kneeled down, placing my hands in the water. I splashed a handful of cool water onto myself before the whistle sounded for us to get on the blocks.

As the starter said, "Take your marks," I gripped the block as I kept my head down, looking at my scarred feet. The whistle blew; it was time to step onto the block. As the beeper sounded, I was off. I had a good start and felt I was at a good pace, but I was in last place after two lengths, the halfway mark. This was the decision point. *Do I commit to giving my best, even though it looks like I don't have a chance?* From my years of swimming, while being aware I needed to make a move, I knew I had to swim my own race. At the final turn, I could tell I still had to pass a few people. With one more length (of the four) to go, I was in sixth place, with several of us quite close. This was it. *Fly,* I told my body.

I sent my arms and legs into overdrive, as if I had to sprint only five seconds, not thirty. For the last fifteen meters, I put my head down and didn't breathe, focusing every ounce of strength on a totally fast finish. Kick, kick, p-u-l-l, REACH. Shift the gear into overdrive. I was in a zone, letting my body take over and fly.

As I touched the wall, I looked at the scoreboard and saw "6" and "2." Lane six, second place. I had made the Olympic Team! At age seventeen! I was going to Seoul! I thrust my arm up into the air and screamed, "YES" with a huge smile on my face. I looked up, thankful for all of the trials and triumphs that had gotten me to this point, knowing that there is a divine power ultimately guiding us. Shoulberg ran down the pool deck, receiving hugs, slaps on the back, and congratulations from many coaches and swimmers along the way. He got to my lane and hugged me. His glasses fell into the pool, and we both quickly grabbed them before they submerged.

All I could hear were the cheers throughout the natatorium. Reporters asked about my amazing kick on the last length. All the years of intense training had paid off in this one moment. I simply felt amazing, and I knew I had done my best.

After the award ceremony, my roommate Karen beamed as she congratulated me and asked, "Wow! How did you get that burst of energy to bring it home on that final length?"

"Belief," I said.

Almost anything is possible when you believe.

Chapter Two

Dream Big:
Embrace Your Inner Olympian

Reach high, for stars lie hidden in your soul.
Dream deep, for every dream precedes the goal.
— Pamela Vaull Starr

When we think about Olympians, we imagine power, confidence, ultimate success, and happiness. We might assume that "they" must be superhuman and that "I" am not as capable. Many people *believe* that Olympians are somehow different than they are, and live vicariously through these athletes while fearing their own dreams and abilities. We have been conditioned to view ourselves through the eyes of others, have often taken beliefs to heart that are not our own, or have created our own limits regarding what is possible.

You are as capable as any Olympian to own your power and achieve success. After all, we Olympians are human beings with our own dreams and fears, too. Being our true best does not require giving up family, friendship, and fun. We might, however, choose to reduce indecision, dawdling, and doubt. Miracles are possible for all of us; we just need to start changing the habits of how we think.

When I was young, I remember that I had put some Olympians on a pedestal. Most of us usually see them on TV in all of the glamour and excitement that fast-paced media brings. We watch these seemingly super-human athletes in their ultimate glory performing with millions watching—yet we must be careful to not forget who they really are.

On my first international trip at age fourteen, I learned that even Olympic Gold Medalists (against whom I was now competing) have their own desires and worries. I was not better or worse than they were; we were all there to push each other to achieve our personal best for ourselves and our countries, while having fun in the process.

Olympians are just like everyone else. We are all capable of maximizing our full potential and making our dreams come true—we just have to believe in our dreams (in ourselves and that anything is possible) and work hard. Olympic athletes have the courage and the will to commit to their goal even though the outcome is not guaranteed. Yes, Olympians have innate talent, and each has a body adaptable to a given sport, but their success ultimately depends on maintaining their vision and working hard to manifest their desired reality.

Everyone grows up with dreams, though some of us try to make them a reality, while others give up believing in them. Whatever we have chosen up until now is okay; there is no need to beat ourselves up for whatever choices we have already made. We were all doing the best we could with what we knew in any particular moment.

From this moment on, I hope that you will be empowered to live *your* life and will take a chance to allow yourself to fulfill your potential. When you pursue your heart's desire you're more likely to enjoy the process no matter how difficult the journey becomes.

I created my Olympic dream in third grade. Even though nobody around me told me to have this goal, and in fact some told me I was crazy, I still imagined it anyway. My vision rose from somewhere deep inside, a sort of artesian energy I didn't really understand but couldn't deny. I simply started organizing my world around doing what my dream required.

I encourage you to take this journey with me and allow yourself to also dream big! Start realizing that more is possible than you think. If others can do it, so can you. Dare to dream bigger than you ever thought possible. Your dreams might even come true!

When I was in sixth grade, I remember listening to my first audiocassette tape on relaxation and training my mind. I listened to it when I went to sleep at night, and I imagined exciting possibilities for myself. I envisioned standing on the podium at my local state championships that year and feeling happy inside. I imagined winning the high point award, and I saw myself being an Olympian on TV and tried to sense all the feelings I might have in that moment.

But now that I am an Olympian and have had many fabulous experiences in my life, I realize that, regardless of what we accomplish in sports, in our careers, or within our family life, we can all experience this feeling of bliss, calm, joy, and achievement. We get to have this more than once and we don't have to wait for a major event to feel this. We can feel blissful and happy multiple times. Some of my fondest memories are from swimming in practice, not just at the biggest meets. The key is to remember this feeling and know how to find it and have it more often. And in order to achieve our goals and reach this blissful state of mind, we must first believe that we are worthy and we have the power to make our dreams come true.

The Power of Beliefs

Beliefs are a powerful tool. We can either use them to our advantage or sabotage ourselves with them. In order to foster their power, we first must realize how we use beliefs to limit us. Then we can release the obstacles that keep us from reaching our goals. I was fortunate to grow up with parents who enjoyed testing what is possible within themselves and who helped me believe that whatever I set my mind to was attainable. Yet, many of us grow up being told that we can't achieve even if we try.

We tend to be our own worst enemies. As we get older, we may forget to dream in our daily lives. It is easy to get caught up in what is going on around us and live based on conditioned beliefs. From a young age, we take on beliefs from the people around us and make them our own. We get conditioned to view ourselves through the eyes of others. Then, we try to prove ourselves right and show that our beliefs are valid. But doing so limits our potential. When we live based on someone else's beliefs, we are denying who we really are or what we really want. We give up our spirited self and end up settling for something less than what our inner vision tells us to do. Many of us know a person who followed in a parent's footsteps, whether in a sport or career, even if it didn't fulfill them.

If we believe we have to do a certain thing to get what we want, we either choose to do it or prove to ourselves that we can't do it or don't deserve it. We might think that in order to succeed we must have had a "perfect" life up until now—an abundance of money, the best training facility or school, the right coaches or teachers, or infallible friends to create this perfect life. But these thoughts are fabricated in our own minds by limiting beliefs that we allow to define us.

What are some limiting beliefs that stand in your way? How do these beliefs and the resulting actions perpetuate this belief? Do you have to work eighty hours each week in a job you don't like to have enough money? If so, that becomes your reality. Do you fear speaking up and saying "no" because you believe you won't be liked (instead of sticking up for yourself to attain what you want and to feel good within)? If so, you might even manifest a voice or throat disorder as you give up your voice to be accepted—and you will certainly feel lousy inside. If you find that you continue to attract a certain negative person or type of harmful relationship, you need to review your beliefs. If someone hurt you, you might assume that "all" women or men will treat you that way. Realize that this is not true.

Allow yourself to have what you want and alter your limiting beliefs that get in the way. After all, it is valid to have concerns, but the question is: Are they serving you? To overcome limiting beliefs, question them. Are they true? Are you clear about what they are doing to or for you? Who would you be if you changed them? Be willing to transcend them.

When you allow other people's beliefs to supersede your own and/or continue to try to prove yourself right based on your own limiting beliefs, even if they are detrimental to you, you feel stress. Stress occurs when you are not being who you fully are. This is the bad kind of stress—distress. Living up to your dream can also be stressful, but in a good way—eustress. The endocrinologist and stress physiologist Hans Selye devised these terms to distinguish between healthy and unhealthy stress. *Eustress* is the healthy feeling of fulfillment that arises through achievement or simply exploring self-defined goals. *Distress* is the body's harmful, nonspecific, cortisol-pumping response to negative feelings and settings. This is the term that has evolved into what is called stress today.

Studies confirm that regular exposure to challenge is good for you. Like exercises that keep the body toned and more capable, mental tests help the mind retain its ability to react to whatever life throws at you. Everyone (even the wealthiest, prettiest, and smartest people) faces loss and change, the tumult of unforeseeable catastrophes, or the consequences of poorly chosen actions.

The key is to handle adversity and change with a willingness to try a new approach. Choose beliefs that allow you to be open to what is possible while leaving room for mistakes. As you sense that you are more capable than you thought, you'll encourage your spirited self to speak up and guide you.

Bring Out the Spirited Spark Within You

One goal of this book is for you to feel lighter and happier. The focus is to find your true self and love this person, *you*. This is difficult even with the best parenting, most enlightened schooling, a loving and supportive part-ner, and a fulfilling career. So how do you get back to being fully you, your true spirited self? How do you get back to dreaming if your childlike wonder has gotten lost, is hiding, or is waiting to be empowered again? How can you see the world through clear eyes, where everything is wondrous and new?

For me, I became most alive in the pool. It was in the water that I most easily expressed my joy and creativity, or even sadness and tears. It was the place where I felt most true to myself and could connect with my innermost desires. Where do you feel most alive? When you are playing music, drawing pictures, conducting science experiments, or flying to the moon in your mind?

When you realize your spirited child is still within you, and that you can allow this spark to come back out from hiding and play again, you can release the limiting beliefs that confine you. You can rediscover your inspi-ration, transform your life to be your best, and feel less tension and stress.

Take a moment right now and allow some image of yourself from your childhood to appear. What do you see, hear, feel? If nothing comes up, that is okay, too. Remember, if a voice is going on in your head right now, it might not be yours! It might be a parent's voice telling you that your dream is crazy. Do not believe this. Know you can reclaim your childhood desires and let go of the fears that other people placed on you.

If you can picture yourself, great! If not, imagine seeing a free-spirited young boy or girl who is purely in the moment, doing something that is fun. For example, when you go to a playground, most children seem happy. Up to age seven or so, most children still see the world innocently. To them, the sky is the limit; anything is possible. Sometimes they have such minimal fear that if you are a parent with a young child you worry about their safety since they are always so curious about trying everything. Children are content playing for hours in creative, imaginative play. This is their world of dreams, fantasies, and possibilities. They allow vivid scenes to be part of their reality in their hearts and minds.

How We Lose Touch With Our Spirited Selves

Oftentimes, through being criticized, judged, or even abused, we shut off this spirited part of ourselves. That is all we know how to do at the time. We might have gone through some events in life that were not perfect. We might have made a mistake or been upset with how we were treated by a parent or caregiver. By internalizing that pain, we then decided from that day on to squash our fun-loving little child inside. Fears came up as we didn't honor what we felt.

We began to follow the unspoken "rules" of what we had to do to be taken care of, fit in, and feel some sense of love (no matter how healthy or unhealthy it was). Regardless of how old we are, it is okay to allow ourselves to be a child again. It is okay to honor that we have made mistakes and be proud that we had amazing courage to handle painful events in life, too.

We Can Reclaim This Part of Ourselves

It's vital to stay connected to your true self within, your younger innocent self who wants to speak and be heard and often has great ideas to share. When you let yourself be validated, you no longer are caught up in trying to meet external needs such as gaining approval from others, needing to win or get a certain job title, or having specific items in order to look good and feel okay with yourself. You pursue goals that are genuinely yours as you satisfy your inner self. Stay focused on what it is that you are truly seeking.

If you are reading this and feel like you can't find your childlike self inside of you, let's get him or her back. He or she is still in there, but maybe is just hiding. Even if you were told (implicitly or explicitly) that he/she wasn't allowed to become what he or she wanted, remember that *you* get to decide. As you read this book, you will be empowered to continue to connect with your childlike self and the dreams that he or she had.

We will cover claiming our true self (versus living from limiting beliefs) and owning our power throughout the book. For now, let's focus on relaxing our mind to set the stage for the chapters ahead. In order to be our best, we first want to learn how to relax and let go. From this calmer place, we can find that child inside and get back to dreaming and creating what we want in our life.

Feeling Safe

In order to relax, it is best to feel safe. This helps us open up to the possibilities and adventurous journey in dreamland. Here are some questions to help remind you of when you feel most safe, to let yourself open up to receive inspiration.

Where and when do you feel most safe? What is one of your favorite places to be? What do you like about it? How do you feel when you are there? Where do you feel most "at home"? Does listening to music relax you? Where can you easily find *you*? For example, I felt at home at the pool. I felt safe as the water held me. It was as if it was speaking to me, telling me I was okay, and that everything around me would be okay, too. What does your special place say to you when you are in it? Can you imagine yourself there right now?

Now, go ahead and pretend that you are in your safe place, somewhere you go to feel protected and calm. It could be your bedroom, the beach, anywhere. Be willing to feel completely safe and be open to the unknown. It requires taking a risk and a leap of faith, but it is worth it. Once you start doing this, your mind will calm down, and you can begin to listen to the deeper yearnings within.

Dream And Imagine Like A Child Again

> *"Just because I'm old doesn't mean I don't have dreams."*
> – *John Glenn, Astronaut and former U.S. Senator*

Children have vivid imaginations. They don't worry about what other people think—they get immersed in their own creations. They believe in magic. As we get older, we try to protect our frail egos and don't think we are capable of achieving our childhood dreams. We allow ourselves to get stuck, to get bogged down in what we feel we "should" be doing. Yet, research shows that imagination enhances one's mood and performance—and, ultimately, life. Thus, it is vital to maintain our wonder and curiosity about this magnificent, mysterious world.

To begin, let's think for a moment about our breathing. When we are stressed, we feel heaviness and anxiety—we do not breathe fully and deeply. When I swim, if I am stressed, my body will show me since it tenses up and I have a harder time floating on top of the water. When we get stressed, our breathing might be concentrated in our neck area.

Our goal is to allow our lungs to receive the oxygen from the air and then release carbon dioxide, which helps to keep our body and mind functioning well. When we are stressed we do not exhale completely. We tend to hold onto worries and fears. We get comfortable with them and can actually be afraid to let go since we do not know what will replace them.

Breathing Exercise: Remember Yourself as a Child

Here is a simple breathing exercise to help release any stress, notice how you feel, and help you to be calm. We will cover breathing techniques in more depth later; right now, I just want to help you find a safe place so that you can become fully aware of your motivations and dreams.

Ideally, if you can, lie down. Let your body sink into the bed, floor, mat, grass, or whatever you are lying on. If you can't lie down, sit comfortably so you can relax. If sitting, place both feet on the floor. Then, go ahead and close your eyes. Place your hands on your abdomen. Breathe in through your nose as you keep your mouth closed. Hold it for a split second. Then, as you exhale, allow your mouth to open up fully, and your jaw to relax and hang down. As you breathe in, focus on your stomach rising as you inhale, then breathe out and focus on your stomach falling as you exhale. You do not need to force this; let it be easy.

As you do this consistently over time, you will notice that it will look like your ribs are also rising and falling, since your lungs underneath them are filling up with air and releasing. Go ahead and take ten deep breaths like this. When you exhale, open your mouth wider and let out a noise, a sigh, say, "Aahh." Go ahead—it is even okay to put a smile on your face and see where it leads you. Okay, good. How do you feel? I know this will come easily for some of you and be more challenging for others. Just keep practicing being aware of your breath and breathing more fully. (Added bonus: It is free, and you can breathe anytime and anywhere!)

Now that you are in this calm, safe place, imagine yourself as a young boy or girl. What wondrous experiences can you recall from your childhood? If you cannot recall yourself at that age, this is your time to make it up. What would you like to envision if you were that imaginative, happy, inspired kid? Just go for it. You might actually enjoy this!

As little kids, many of us dreamed of magical possibilities. My daughter reminds me of this innocence and ability to dream as she describes the world around her. She has a magic wand that was made by a "fairy." At night before she goes to sleep, she wishes upon the stars and asks them to bring her whatever her little heart desires. She smiles and feels wonderful inside, knowing the stars can do anything for her. She has an innate trust and belief that does not need any reason.

Your Magic Wand

Now that you have been breathing more deeply, you have either remembered yourself as a child or at least considered the idea. You have started feeling more in touch with your actual self instead of focusing on other stressors (such as role playing) that affect your daily life. From here, you'll create specific dreams about how you want to be, what you want to do, and what you want to have in your life.

If you were a child again and were given a magic wand that granted your every wish, what would you ask for? If you had no fear and were allowed to *be* whoever you wanted to be, could *do* anything you wanted and could accomplish amazing things, and you could *have* everything possible and more, what would you really want? If you allowed yourself to imagine beyond what you thought was possible, what would happen easily for you? If you could not fail or do it wrong, what would you give yourself permission to be, do, or have? Would you want to travel to a certain place, create a non-profit to help others, spend more time with family, make up from the argument you had with someone, jump out of an airplane, be an astronaut, find a cure for cancer, get a puppy, or maybe even be an Olympic champion?

Try to keep your conscious mind out of this. Let all ideas surface, no matter how silly or crazy they seem to you in this moment. Let all ideas be heard. Allow yourself to pretend you have your own magic wand in your hand—when you wave it around, these wishes become true right now! Just allow yourself to imagine. You have a creative imagination. Be willing to foster it and bring it forth. That is the first step.

Two-Minute Writing Exercise

Grab a pen and some paper. After you read the following directions, go ahead and write for two minutes straight. Keep the pen on the paper, writing the whole time, even when you are not sure what will be written next. If you wish, you can even write from your non-dominant hand, as that triggers the little child inside you to speak more. What will happen is that your subconscious ideas will come through more fully. Possibly, your child inside of you will start speaking to you (if he/she has been hiding) or will come up with so many ideas (since kids love to share ideas, and to be heard and validated) that you won't be able to write them down fast enough.

Remember, for the purposes of this exercise, anything is fair game, and you get to give yourself permission to be, do, and have it all. Nobody can stop you. Allow yourself to imagine you are truly granted every wish. Act as if they have already come true. Write in the present tense, imagining that you are experiencing this as you write. As you get more excited, allow more ideas to keep flowing onto the paper for you.

Great! Now, that you have done this, hopefully you feel a sense of "I had forgotten about that desire of mine," or "Yes, I would like to still go after this dream I had when I was younger," or maybe you'd like to alter a dream you had as a child. Honor all of these feelings. Now, go back and read everything you wrote down, and pick three to five items that mean the most to you. Do not overanalyze this. There are no rights or wrongs. Just notice what you are drawn to. Then, pick one item to work on.

Okay, now, imagine yourself *being* this person, *having* that something, or *doing* that activity. How do you feel inside? I have done this exercise with thousands of people. Many experience excitement and joy from this, but it's also common to feel some tension inside.

Letting Go of Tension and Judgment

How can you let go of tension? There is part of you that might not be sure that your wish can *really* be granted. Or, if you actually get it, you might feel more pressure from actually having what you wanted. We all get attached to wanting certain things to occur in our lives, but we have fears of them actually happening, too!

This brings up stress. If you were the first to do something successful in your family, it might stir up resentful feelings in other family members who subconsciously try to keep you from reaching your dream. Because of their reaction, you might worry that they will not support you or that they might even stop loving you. But realize that their worries and fears are *theirs*, not *yours*.

When I was younger, I remember a group of people teasing me, "All you do is swim." I felt tested, because I wanted them to like me. Yet, I knew I could not like myself if I gave up my joys to be accepted by them. Similarly, we all carry judgment at times, some more than others. How others judge us is how they judge themselves. If we know someone whose approval we are seeking, and we never get it, it probably is because they cannot give approval to themselves. They are so hard on themselves that they do not take time to appreciate and like themselves for everything that they are. We will have a hard time getting approval from someone like that. If we are not careful, we will feel controlled by them, too, since we are waiting to feel a certain way based on how they react to us!

Stress-Releasing Exercise

Allow yourself to feel okay with yourself. You deserve it, and nobody can take that away from you. When you start to feel tense about your wishes, just breathe in and exhale out any stress. Ask yourself, "Am I willing to let go of the tension?" There might be a part of you that is afraid to let it go—it's easy to get used to suffering. Be willing to say "yes" and imagine the tension going away. There are different ways to do this. Picture a vacuum cleaner sucking the tension out, a waterfall gushing down and taking away the stress, being at the ocean and having the waves take your worries away, or a balloon floating up to the sky and popping—and poof, the tension is gone.

Use your creativity to help you imagine how to release your tension as you exhale. Most important, though, is to notice when you feel tense, acknowledge the tension, and then know you can let it go (and deserve to!). In doing so, you'll help yourself relax and be less attached to your wish. Ironically, this will help you achieve it more easily!

Achieving Your Dreams

Now that you have decided on a dream to focus on, and have released any tension associated about your wish being granted, you have gotten started on your new journey. You have created an *outcome-oriented goal* about something you want to be, do, or have. It could be related to anything, such as getting a certain material item, traveling somewhere, or reaching a career milestone. For sports, you might want to achieve a certain time, or score so many goals. In politics, you might want to become the President of your country. If you have a chronic illness, you might want to be healthy (illness free). Other outcome goals might include one for school (get an A in history), your social life (have a boyfriend), family life (feel connected to each other), or work (become the CEO).

You can set various kinds of goals. The most important thing is to have your big dream, a long-term goal, be something that excites and motivates you. Then, set short- term goals. By completing simple goals along the way, you'll be encouraged to stay on your path. You can create tasks based on your outcome goal or on a process-oriented goal, to guide you.

With a *process-oriented goal*, you focus on the action steps themselves while in the process of reaching your outcome goal. I focused on steps to enhance my swim races. I did specific strength and flexibility work and relaxation techniques daily. If you're in school, study reading material or lecture notes. If you're sick, get more sleep, heal emotional wounds, and eat alkaline foods. In relationships, practice telling someone each day one thing you appreciate about them. In work, be on time, or practice sharing thoughts with colleagues so you can then express a great idea to your boss.

Finally, think about the *details of the actual performance or process*. How do you want to feel, what do you want to eat, to whom do you want to talk, what kind of music will you listen to, do you have a place to relax and breathe if you need it? When I raced in swimming, I often wrote up my race strategy and knew what and when I would do for the hours before and after the race.

The more I detailed what I would do before, during, and after the race, and about every step of the race (such as visualizing each length, tempo, and number of strokes per length in a race), the more likely it would come true.

In reference to your goal, envision what you want personally, socially, professionally, or health-wise (spiritually, mentally, emotionally, physically) that will enhance your life. How will your life be different once you have achieved your goal?

Check in with yourself to assess your progress along the way. In school, homework and quizzes can help you with this. In sports, you can do test sets or mid-season competitions. Ask for feedback from your coach or mentor. In the workforce, you can do a progress review with a colleague or boss.

S· M· A· R ·T Goals

As you formulate your action steps, apply the acronym S· M· A· R ·T, used by many therapists and coaches. Each goal or action step should be **s**pecific, **m**easurable, **a**chievable (realistic and yet challenging), **r**elevant to your goal, and be **t**imed (have a deadline).

Say you want "to lose weight." Make it S· M· A· R ·T by adding specifics for each essential element:

1. **Make it Specific.** "To lose weight" is direct, but vague. What *exactly* do you want to accomplish? What does achieving that look like? To be specific, say (for example), "My college jeans will fit again." Picture that. If you have a photograph of yourself in those jeans, post it on the refrigerator.

2. **Make it Measurable.** Dedicate a notebook to keeping track of your progress. Create definable steps you will follow: stretch five minutes, walk five minutes, eat eight servings of vegetables, sleep eight hours a night, do twenty push-ups, lift weights three times a week at the gym. Keep track of how your body fat decreases by taking a body fat test and note the results in your journal. When you fit into smaller clothes in your closet, write that down. Keeping track of specific, measurable goals will help give you a sense of accomplishment each step of the way.

3.   **Make it Achievable.** Don't zip over to fantasyland. Be realistic. Set a marker that is within your power. If those college jeans are more than a few pounds away, how willing are you to eat differently, exercise more, and release stress? Be honest with yourself. Often people set too many goals at once or don't plan enough small steps to get them from where they are currently to where they want to go. Don't get so stressed and overwhelmed that you give up. Instead, keep your steps simple, and follow through. Your goal is to be empowered.

4.   **Make it Relevant.** Your goal must fit within, alongside, or on top of the responsibilities and priorities of your life. Do something that pertains to your overall goal. Eat well if you are exercising. Let your body recover with rest. Throw out junk food and purchase what will give your body fuel. Of course, if you have bad habits, rethink whether they are working for you. Maybe you'll still choose to go out with friends on Friday night, but sit on your hands when the dessert arrives. Just keep good humor about yourself and those around you. No preaching; just doing, for yourself, with commitment.

5.   **Make it Timed.** What's a reasonable date for achieving your goal? Again, be realistic. Don't set the bar set the bar so low that your achievement will be uninspiring, or too high that you get overwhelmed. To feel like you have really accomplished something, the marker needs to be a little further out than it has been before. Decide how much time you will commit each day. You're going for progress, for personal bests, with each step. For example, "I will do this daily for five minutes." You can do this for your work, family, sports, music, whatever you desire!

Consider what resources you need to optimize your chances to succeed. For my dream, I needed my parents' emotional and logistical support. Enlist the support of family and friends—even bosses and co-workers if appropriate. Buy the supplies that you need. If you're going to lose weight, you might want to invest in a good pair of all-weather outdoor walking shoes. Log on and find a website aligned with your goal. Schedule the extra movement. Is it a run around the neighborhood, a new membership at a local gym, the first half-hour of the day with an aerobic exercise program? The world is full of choices. Make appropriate ones, and you will march your way through the milestones and achieve your goal.

Dreams-to-Action Process

Now, let's figure out which choices are right for you. Have your paper and pen handy so you can write down how to get what you want. Studies show that writing down your wishes helps you make them a reality. Once you have a list of goals, you'll start taking simple action steps daily.

First, imagine the timeframe in which this wish occurs for you. Does this dream become reality today, next month, in a year, in ten or twenty years? Let's say you see it happening in five years—where do you want to be in one year so that it is a reality by five years? How about in six months? One month? One week? And starting today? What are you willing to start doing today to take small action steps to reach your big dream? What action steps do you envision at one week, a month, six months and so on?

Here is an example. Let's say I want to become a psychologist:

1. What is your long-term dream/goal? *To become a psychologist and positively impact people's lives.*

2a. What is your one-year goal in order to reach your dream goal? *Be in graduate school for psychology.*

2b. What are at least three specific process-oriented tasks you will do to reach your one-year goal? *Decide which school to attend. Pack up my belongings and move there before school starts. Create a financial plan to pay for graduate school.*

3a. What is your goal for six months from now that will help you achieve your one-year goal? *Get accepted into the school of my dreams.*

3b. What are at least three specific tasks that will help you reach your six-month goal? *Research schools to attend, fill out applications, and save money to pay for applications and school.*

4a. What is your one-month goal? *Continue to get at least an A- or A in my courses during my last few months in college.*

4b. What are at least three specific tasks that will help you achieve this goal? *Spend three hours minimum daily on homework. Ask profes-*

sors for help when I get stuck. Make a list of priorities to take care of myself and my relationships to be my best (such as stretching for fifteen minutes, deep breathing for five minutes, and exercising for twenty minutes. Tell friends no if I am too tired to go out.).

5. What is your goal for one week from now? *Meet with a psychologist to ask him/her questions.*

5b. What are at least three specific tasks you will do this week to reach this goal? *Contact a few psychologists and ask to interview them. Set up a time within the week to meet. Make a list of questions I want to ask.*

6. What can you do today and every day starting now to have your dreams come true? *Research (in the library or online) what kind of psychologist I want to be. Ask teachers questions.*

Remember to keep your steps simple, so that you follow through on them. This will build your confidence and give you energy to keep going and reach bigger goals.

Staying Motivated

Now that you have created your wish list, envisioned your wildest dreams, and completed your dreams-to-action plan, ask yourself the following questions: What motivates and drives me? What makes me happy? Who or what am I doing this for? Focus on the bigger vision that's driving your goals. Where do you want to go? What will give you what you are looking for? This overarching vision needs to be big enough so that on those days when you doubt yourself and wonder if your goals are worth the effort, you will decide to stay focused and committed to the process to see what is possible.

For example, two years before I swam in the Olympics, I had mononucleosis and had to briefly suspend my training to get well. I still wanted to make the Olympic Team, but in moments of doubt I wondered if I'd get healthy enough to train hard again, and if all the effort was worth it. Yet I committed anyway. Even if I did everything perfectly, there was no guarantee I would make the team, but I had to give myself the chance.

Making Your Dream A Reality

As you focus on making your dream a reality, prioritize what is important to you. Set goals that harness your motivation, help you avoid procrastination, and prevent self-sabotage. Stay simple and realistic when you begin. By coming up with small steps and completing them, you will feel empowered and build your confidence. Praise or reward yourself for doing these action steps. As your investment in yourself grows, you'll begin to believe that your dreams are achievable.

When you are adept at handling the changes involved with attaining this goal, you can take on another. The biggest step is to show up and get started. It is like climbing to a mountaintop: You start with small steps and then, as long as you keep going consistently, you realize you are well on your path to the top, and very possibly exceeding your wildest dreams.

Dare to dream big, let go of limiting beliefs, and take action to realize your dreams. Celebrate the little successes along the way. Remember the spirited child inside you, and let your vision guide you to achieve everything you are capable of.

Chapter Three

Living My Dream: Enjoying Adventures and Testing My Limits

One can become whatever one wants to be
[if one constantly contemplates on the object of desire with faith].
– Bhagavad Gita

After the Olympics, many people thought I had it all. Popular, fit, and successful in both athletics and academics, I came back for my senior year at the prestigious prep school Germantown Academy near Philadelphia.

I had competed on September 25, 1988, and by the time the Closing Ceremonies were over and I arrived back at the Academy, I had missed the first month of school. On my first day back, I walked to the cafeteria to get a snack before my next class. I wore a new outfit and jewelry that I had bought in Itaewon, a shopping area near Seoul, Korea, where my Olympic Games had been held. I had been wearing USA clothing daily for the past eight weeks, and as much as I always treasured my USA goodies, it was nice to be in regular clothing again and hopefully blend in.

I was so wrong. As I walked into the cafeteria, I thought, "Wow, it is packed." I heard a big cheer. It was for me! I was in a daze, as my past few months had already been such a journey. Even though I had been respected and admired by many in my school due to my previous accomplishments, I was shocked, thinking, "The whole school must be in here!" Tony Garvin, my cross-country coach and history teacher, had helped to organize this special event. I felt so much love from my fellow classmates, and from K–12 students I didn't even know! I realized I was a role model for many of my schoolmates, especially the younger ones. Everyone gathered for an assembly, and I shared many of my Olympic stories with the crowd.

The next few months were a blur of fun activities and adventures, which I loved. I celebrated being an Olympian in many different ways. I signed autographs and spoke to teams, clubs, corporations, TV and radio stations, and non-profits. I was considered a hero. Rarely in those days did swimmers make the Olympics while in high school, and people believed the best for my career was yet to come. I enjoyed a nice social life, good grades, and a life filled with exciting travel, including a trip to the White House where I met President Ronald Reagan. I have a great picture with him, and with his security surrounding him. (Ironically, track star Edwin Moses took the photo for me, and I never got a photo with him!)

During this time, I also took several recruiting trips. Since I had been a world-class swimmer for several years, I was recruited by all of the top schools. I knew I could choose wherever I wanted to go, but I focused on just a few options. My decision to go to the University of California, Berkeley (aka Cal Berkeley), was an easy one. I went for the Big Game weekend, where Cal football, water polo, and other sports competed against Stanford. I felt right at home wearing my blue and gold, and cheering on the Golden Bears.

The head coach, Karen Moe Thornton, was not only a female (rare in those days), but she also had been an Olympic swimmer, in the 200-meter butterfly. One of my idols, Mary T. Meagher, a 200-meter butterfly world record holder and Olympic Gold Medalist, had also swum at Cal Berkeley in the mid-1980s. I felt good knowing that not only was I going to one of the top college programs, with the potential to win the NCAA title, but I had a coach who understood me as a female athlete. Karen focused on the importance of healthy body image. Her background in exercise physiology helped her choose training methods that were ahead of her time—she focused on intensity through quality and on the balance of training and recovery. The academics at Cal were also excellent, and the opportunity to interact with many international students was another blessing.

From a young age, I had dreamed of competing in the Olympics and going to a great college. I had specific goals, and I had achieved many of them. Yet, what I most enjoyed was the journey itself, seeing what was possible, what I was capable of doing. That was what motivated me. I also enjoyed the friendships I formed, the fun adventures I had, and the lessons I learned along the way.

From Childhood Idols to Lifelong Friends

In the summer of 1985, I was fourteen and on the bus with my USA teammates. I was making my first international trip to Tokyo, Japan, to compete in the biggest international competition of the year, the Pan Pacific Games. I felt excited to be a part of this elite group. As I got onto the bus for the airport, Mary T. Meagher, my idol and an Olympic Gold Medalist from the 1984 Olympics, sat down next to me. My heart pounded, and I wasn't sure whether I should look at her or out the window. I calmed down immediately as Mary T. introduced herself. Although I was still in awe of her, talking with Mary T. and getting to know her better made me realize that she was human, too, with her own fears and foibles.

The more I talked with other athletes, even those competing at the highest level, the more I realized that we all are more similar than different. Although the specifics of our drive and motivation might differ, we are all focused on the ultimate goal of winning and doing our personal best. And we are all capable of winning and being our best today, no matter what our past record says. When we focus on what is happening right now, we see that we are no better or worse than the next person. (This is a good lesson for life in general, too!)

I had another sweet surprise when Team USA got to Japan: I reunited with my Australian coach, Graeme Brown. Only four years after training with him in Australia, we were both here at the Pan Pacific Games. He was coaching for his country, and I was swimming for mine. I beamed with excitement as I hugged him, knowing he had been instrumental in me getting here; he had inspired me to focus on making my dreams a reality.

By the time I arrived home, I had a new "family" and friendships that continue today. During all of our trips together, we swimmers brought out the best in one another. Although we were in competition, we learned from and supported each other, whether we broke a record or had an off day. Through the experiences of travel and competition, we forged strong bonds that will last for a lifetime.

Getting in Gear

On the trip to Japan I received my first USA gear, including USA luggage, a USA parka, USA sweat suits, USA swim gear, and many other sponsored goodies. I was ecstatic. I had dreamed of the day when I could represent my country and wear USA proudly for all to see. That day was now.

Years later, when I made the Olympic team, we were outfitted with our Team USA gear at a hotel in Los Angeles. The Olympic Trials had been in Texas, and we had stayed there for two weeks before going to LA for the weekend to get outfitted before heading to Hawaii and then to Seoul, South Korea. The second floor of the hotel was devoted to getting outfitted. We wore swimsuits as we pushed around grocery carts, trying on clothing and loading our carts with the athletic gear.

We were so proud and excited to receive the goodies (swimsuits, jackets, shirts, pants, and shoes) that would become our USA uniforms for the next several weeks. Even after several years of travelling and representing my country, the thrill of getting outfitted never went away. Receiving my USA gear and clothing always made me feel like a little kid, with eyes open wide in a candy shop, thinking, "Wow, I get to represent my country and be part of this amazing group of people, making memories together that will last a lifetime."

My Favorite Olympic Memories

Although the 1988 Olympic competition itself was certainly memorable, some of my favorite memories are from the Opening and Closing Ceremonies.

Before the Opening Ceremonies, standing outside the big Olympic Stadium, the swimmers waited to march in with all of the other athletes from Team USA, and from countries all over the world. Images from throughout my life flashed by me in a split second. So many events had led up to this moment—and now here I was, getting ready to walk into the Olympic Stadium.

Testing Our Limits. We all had tested our limits to get to this world stage, to represent our countries. As the Olympic motto states: "Citius, Altius, Fortius" ("Faster, Higher, Stronger"). All of us there had continually sought what was possible within ourselves and done what motivated us to be our own personal best. When we had fears and doubts, we utilized our support systems. Many people had helped us along the way, including families, coaches, friends, and competitors. They reminded us to believe in ourselves, even in our darkest moments. Ironically, it is in those moments that we appreciate the sweetness of life. We experience how resilient we really are, and—even though there are no guarantees—we continue to commit to our dreams, to see what life has in store for us.

Connection of Humanity. It was a warm and sunny day. Anticipation and excitement were buzzing in the air. The Olympic competition was about to begin. A couple of friends and I went around to people from various countries and different sports. Even though we might not have spoken the same language, we connected nonverbally, exchanged pins or other memorabilia, smiled at and hugged each other, and got our pictures taken together. We felt a connection with every person, even though we had just met, as we all had something in common. Each of us had followed our own personal journey to get to this stage, to this moment of waiting to walk into the Olympic Stadium and participate in the Olympic Games. Whether from large cities or small villages, climates that were cold or hot, families with money or those who scraped by just to keep their dream a reality, we were all here together now, sharing a common goal and enjoying this amazing experience as Olympians.

In these moments, I felt a deep understanding of the Olympic Creed: "The most important thing in the Olympic Games is not to win but to take part, just as the most important thing in life is not the triumph but the struggle. The essential thing is not to have conquered but to have fought well."

Today, as I get together with my friends who competed globally for various sports whether at the Olympic Games, World Championships, or other international events, we fondly remember the fun times and memories created with one another. There is a feeling of connection and understanding beyond what a medal can give us. We remember testing each other in practice, and being challenged to the point where we didn't know if we would survive. In those times when we wanted to give up, somehow we found another reserve tank within us, and more energy would burst through. Relying on each other in both good times and bad forged a deep and meaningful bond between us—no other relationship quite compares.

The true meaning of the Olympics. Before walking into the stadium, we Americans anxiously awaited our turn. Since the United States team was near the back of the pack alphabetically, we had watched thousands of athletes representing dozens of countries already walk in. Just like me, everyone else there had also struggled, survived, and thrived. We had our dreams and had spent years training and committing to our goal of becoming an Olympian.

As I walked into the huge stadium full of color and noise and people, I sensed the power and beauty of humanity. We each have our own story, struggles, and joys. No matter where we're from or what we do, we are all connected by our shared human emotions and experiences. As I looked around, I felt connected to all the other athletes and coaches, and even the musicians, artists, producers, and audience who were gathered for this global celebration. In that moment, it felt as though peace was prevailing throughout the world.

Similarly, at the Closing Ceremonies of the Olympic Games, we dressed in our USA uniforms and ran out onto the field, full of energy as we celebrated the final stage, the closing of our Olympic Games. A bunch of us lay on the ground and created the five Olympic rings, which represent the five continents of athletes who participate in this global athletic event. The rings on the Olympic flag are interlinked, just as the Games bring all people together as one. The five colors represent at least one color in every country's flag.

All countries come together in peace, allowing the athletes to strive for their own personal best as they compete against the top athletes from other countries around the world. This is the magical symbolism of what our world is supposed to be—all people respected and allowed to dream and pursue what they love while finding ultimate happiness and inner peace through their shared and individual experiences. No matter what our skin color, sex, or country of origin, the Olympics celebrate the opportunity for each person to reach their full potential. For me, this defined the meaning of the Olympics.

Commitment to Living The Dream

Of course competing in the Olympics will always be a highlight of my life. But there were many other challenges and opportunities that stand out in my mind, too. Throughout my years of competitive swimming, I felt lucky and blessed to be doing something I loved so much. But although it might have looked to others like my life was "perfect," I had my share of tests, too.

Pushing Myself to the Limit

Over our Christmas break in 1986, two years before I made it to the Olympics, Coach Shoulberg decided to test me and one other swimmer, Greg Indrisano, with a 16,000-meter butterfly. Since Foxcatcher Farms, where we trained in owner John Dupont's fifty-meter pool, was a twenty-minute drive from Germantown Academy, we often carpooled together from the high school. Although I was excited about this challenge, I was also nervous.

For those unfamiliar with swimming, most coaches would never require more than a 400- or even 1,000-meter butterfly. If you equate running to swimming, 1K in swimming is like 4K in running; thus, 16K in swimming is 64k in running. A marathon is 26.2 miles or 40K. What I would be attempting to do was one-and-a-half times that of a marathon. And doing the butterfly rather than swimming freestyle is the equivalent of skipping versus running, or running while jumping rope (because your center of gravity moves up and down with each stroke, requiring more energy output).

Yes, my coach, whom I called "Shoulberg" was different than most. There were people who argued that he overtrained his athletes, but in his mind he was making us mentally tougher as he pushed us to do more sets, go for longer lengths, and swim at faster speeds. For the athletes who trained under Shoulberg, we had to decide what *really* motivated us, what kept us going when we felt like we couldn't push ourselves any harder. If you were not clear about that, you would not last.

"Hero" (Greg's nickname) and I swam the 16,000-meter butterfly as a race. He would be ahead for a while, and then I would catch up. We maintained our stroke (never used just one arm, which would have allowed us to rest our back and shoulders), and we touched each wall legally, with two hands, instead of just one. As my upper body got tired, I relied more on my legs, on having better streamlines and kicks off of the wall. No matter what it took, I was determined to make it.

As I swam every "100," which is two lengths in the fifty-meter pool, I would look at the pace clock to see how fast I was going. I tried to maintain the same pace as long as I could. Greg and I started out fast, and over the hours our pace waned, but we still were swimming well. We persevered even as our bodies grew tired.

It took me three hours and fifty-six minutes to swim the 16,000-meter butterfly. So I didn't just survive the challenge, I did it well. If you compare my time to a marathon pace, it would be like running a marathon-and-a-half while jumping rope at a marathon pace of under three hours. My holding average was slightly under a minute and thirty seconds per 100 meters.

I had surpassed what I thought was possible. I had kept going, gotten into the zone, and stayed present with each stroke. I lived for these tests, to see what I was made of. When I finished, I was tired in a good way, and thrilled. I knew if I could do this, I could do anything.

Since this 16K had gone so well, Shoulberg thought it would be great to have me do it *again*. On Thanksgiving Day 1987, the top eighty or so American swimmers went on a training trip to Hawaii. US Swimming often does this the year before the Olympics to help people see that they have a chance to be an Olympian and encourage them to train with the best coaches in the country. These training trips were always lots of fun. We spent time playing on the beach and in the sunshine and then racing each other in the pool.

In addition to physical training, there was a mental aspect at training camps, too. For some, it could be a boost to race their main competitor in practice and win. Shoulberg thought that if I repeated my performance of the 16K, people would take notice for the upcoming Olympic year. He had requested that Dave Wharton, my club teammate and an Olympian, do a 14,000-meter fly along with me at training camp. Most coaches thought Shoulberg was crazy, as something like this hurts a swimmer's technique, but we did it anyway.

Shoulberg's goal—and mine—was for me to beat my pace of the previous year's 16,000-meter fly. Mark Shubert, an Olympic and USA Coach for many years, and Frank Keefe, a Yale Swim Coach and USA Manager, timed me the whole way, up and down each length of the pool. I didn't break stroke, and it took three hours and twelve minutes—a faster pace than I'd done before. I loved tests like this, things that were a bit different, where I had to make a decision in the midst of it, whether I would keep going or stop. I had to feel enough internal drive and know why I was doing this. I knew that if I could do this, I could easily do a 200-meter butterfly. And less than one year later, I was an Olympian doing the 200-meter butterfly. If this challenging test was only a confidence boost, it was worth it.

Breaking A Record

Often, I felt great about myself when I had an amazing training session or achieved a certain time in a meet. Doing the long butterfly sets had certainly challenged me. I had gone through the whole range of emotions in the beginning of these intense challenges and then my mind had gone quiet, as I slipped into the zone.

Similarly, in November 1990 at Cal Berkeley, we had a double-distance dual meet against Stanford. We swam double the typical distance raced. I had told myself that if I could break Olympian and world-record holder Mary T. Meagher's record in this event that I was on my way to other great accomplishments. Mary T. held the world record in the actual Olympic event, the 200-meter butterfly, for over twenty years, and I wanted to go faster.

This meet was a step in getting closer to my ultimate goal of breaking her 200-meter butterfly world record. I swam the 400-yard butterfly and won with a time of four minutes and eight seconds, beating Mary T.'s Cal Berkeley record of four minutes and eleven seconds. In my first 200 of the 400, I had gone out in two minutes one second, beating the then-current NCAA time standard and achieving a time that would have scored well at NCAA's for the 200-meter butterfly. I was ecstatic. I wrote in my journal:

> *I really wanted this record as a steppingstone and I did it! I'm amazed I went out that fast, especially since it is only November (early in the race season). I focused on the race being 150, 100, 75, 50, 25, instead of a 400. This helped me focus on each length instead of the pain, and it worked. YES!*

My college coach, Karen, wrote in my logbook, "Congratulations on your awesome 400 fly! Your first of Mary T.'s records!"

From the Pan Pacific Games to the Olympics to my time at Cal Berkeley, in many ways I really was "living the dream." But in real life, dreams don't just happen. They require focused discipline and a lot of hard work. The trick is to find the balance in life between work and rest, between immersing yourself in the process and not losing yourself to distraction, to staying attentive but also being flexible to necessary changes in your plan. When you commit to this, you can achieve your dream.

Chapter Four

Live Your Dream: Commit to Your Plan

As long as you can start, you are all right.
- Ernest Hemingway

Hemingway may have been referring to the ups and downs of the writing life, but his advice applies to practically every endeavor requiring effort and progress. We have discussed dreams, beliefs, and action steps—now let's commit to following through with our plan.

The Power of Decisions

You are the director and main actor in your movie, called *My Life*. You get to choose to live your fullest life possible. Focus on your dreams, and take action on your plan, which will bring positive changes into your life. By completing these steps, you build your confidence and get into a productive, positive cycle. As this cycle continues, you get closer to your dreams and will likely achieve—or even surpass—them.

You get to decide who you are, how you want to live, and what you want to focus on. Tell yourself, "Life is an opportunity—my time is here, right now, and I am ready." In the movie of your life, you decide what scenes are in your movie, how you act and respond, and with whom you interact. Who is your character, and what would you like him/her to do? If you are shy and want to be more extroverted, play that out; try it on for a day in real life. Wear a purple hat and hot pink sunglasses, and dance around town if you want. Always wanted to be a doctor? You can; even people in their seventies go back to school and change careers. If you want to wear many different hats and like to perform, become an actor. You'll be fulfilled doing the thing you most love to do, and maybe you'll even become the next Brad Pitt or Meryl Streep! If your dream is to be an Olympic athlete, commit to your training. Find a coach you admire, focus on a goal, and set up action steps to get you there.

Some of you might be thinking, "I don't even know what I want." Review Chapter Two on dreams, and then allow this book to provide you with more tools as you continue on. Decisions do have consequences. Knowing this causes indecision, feeling stuck, and having fear. It is like saying, "I am not." *I am not worthy. I am not here. I am not allowed.* We are afraid of making the wrong decisions, or having to be responsible for the choices we make. When you are in charge, you are responsible. As Tony Robbins said, "It is in your moments of decision that your destiny is shaped." Affirm yourself by saying, "This is what I want, and here is how I will get it." It is like saying "I am." *I am worthy. I am here. I am allowed.*

If you are worried about not making the right decision, know that the only bad decision you can make is no decision. Take any step that feels like it will take you in the direction that you want to go. This will affirm you and give you energy to keep going. It could be as simple as meeting with someone you admire in your field, doing research online, or reading a book to get inspired. With every step you take, you become clearer and make better decisions. Your perspective shifts on what is possible and opens you up to create the life you want.

You do not need to worry. Life doesn't want to hurt you. Life wants to help you. It might teach you a few things along the way, but it loves you. Also, if you do not like a certain path, you can either choose to live with it or change it if it is not working for you. You have many options; be open to the possibilities that life presents you.

You vs. Circumstances

Many of us fall victim to circumstances around us. We blame others for our shame, our mistakes, our position at work, or our lack of will to be who we really are. It is easy to be reactive to the environment and people around us, to be miserable doing something we don't like as we strive to obtain material desires, a feeling of being great, or to fit in according to other people's standards. When we look outside of ourselves to validate our internal world, we are letting circumstances control us.

The critical difference between distress and eustress is choice: Did you choose the challenge, or do you feel victimized or bullied by someone or some circumstance? When doing your best to reach a self-defined goal, you may feel incredibly challenged at times, but not distressed, even in failure. On the other hand, distress storms in any time we abandon ownership of our dreams, our authentic selves, and are not being fully who we are. Honor your choices, and take responsibility for them.

We decide, not someone else, how important it is to reach our goals. Once we decide to commit, then we need to take action each day. If our goal is to be the best athlete we can be, we must be willing to train and rest our body and give it optimal nutrition and mental "food" so we can perform at our best.

We decide what affects us. If we let circumstances control us, it will be hard to stay focused and committed to the task at hand; we can easily fall prey to distractions. If we do not react to things like bad weather or people not supporting us in our goals, we will be able to stay committed to the daily tasks that will help get us where we want to go.

Be willing to be bigger than the circumstances around you, to see that you are in charge of your own destiny. If it is raining outside, you can go on with your day. I live in Minnesota, and I am always impressed with how many people do just that, even when it is below zero degrees, windy, and snowing. It is merely a decision. Once you decide to take responsibility for your life and can take care of yourself, you see that it no longer serves you to blame your parents, the weather, or the latest global leaders for current circumstances in your life. Commit to what you want to create for yourself even when obstacles get in the way.

Achieving your goals is like setting up a business plan—you can plan all you want, but when some random event occurs, you need to be prepared to adapt. This is the case with anything in life. You can be playing golf when the wind picks up right before you hit, and you have to adjust. It doesn't mean that you have to give up. You just might need to alter your course.

If you are easily distracted by circumstances, focus your mind and commit to a certain action plan for a specific amount of time. If you want to exercise regularly, decide that you will do it daily for the next week, regardless of the weather, your kids, your job, or how tired you might feel. Focus on what you can do, create a plan, and then stick to it.

To realize your power within, remember that you are the director and actor in your movie, not the victim or an "extra." Take the risk to start, rather than worrying what "might" happen if you step outside of your comfort zone. Ninety-nine percent of those worries won't happen anyway. Yes, there will be some bumps in the road, and big obstacles, too. But as you focus on your dreams and live your life to the fullest, you will learn to go around or avoid them altogether as you choose an entirely different path.

Be proactive. I have tended to walk my own path even if others didn't believe in me, or my dreams. I always knew I wanted to swim. In my hometown of Morris, Minnesota, we had a beautiful eight-lane, twenty-five-yard pool with a separate diving well. The pool even had underwater windows so you could observe the swimmers and their strokes. We often did not have a main coach when I was first swimming, since many of our coaches were either parents or high school or college students. When we did not have scheduled practice, I walked to the pool and swam anyway. I just wanted to be in the water. I had decided what I wanted to do, and I trusted my decision.

I knew in my heart that I was meant to be a competitive swimmer, and I would need to find a team that could help me reach a certain level. Nobody decided this for me. I chose this path. Thankfully, people around me, particularly my parents, supported me in my dream.

Make a daily decision to *thrive* instead of just *survive* in your life.

Old Patterns and Bad Habits

Like circumstances, old patterns can also get in the way. Notice when you stop doing what you said you would do. Many people get comfortable feeling down on themselves for not following through on their plans. When you notice an old pattern that no longer serves you, stop. You get to change your ineffective habits.

How do you feel when you break an old, unhealthy habit? In doing so, you build new beliefs in your abilities. As you follow through, you see that you can trust yourself since you do what you say. If you say you will win, you will believe it since you have demonstrated your ability to complete steps along the way. And yes, this does make you feel good, too. Remember your underlying motivation, as it will empower you to stay focused on your dream and remain committed even through change.

There are always obstacles in life; some are little pebbles, and some are big holes in the road. In the midst of change, we are forced to confront aspects of ourselves that we may not like. And we must be careful not to replace old bad habits with new ones. For instance, I had to learn the importance of balancing rest with training. I thought I could "will" my way through any obstacle, whatever the cost to my physical or emotional health. Rather than flowing down a river and going around a metaphorical rock, I wanted to lift up the rock and throw it out of my way. I was so focused on my ultimate achievements that I didn't always take care of myself throughout the process. While you are on the path to achieving your goals, be sure to check in with yourself—you want to maintain your health and joy along with your focus.

Be Willing to Commit to Your Dreams

Commitment comes down to your desire, determination, attitude, motivation, and your belief in yourself. Being fully committed to start and to keep going is the main difference between someone who reaches their goals and someone who does not. You are as capable as any Olympian or top performer to be your best.

Just by deciding to commit, your life will change. You validate yourself by believing in your dreams and making a plan to achieve your goals. Follow through even with the ups and downs of the daily routine. To stay motivated, love what you do, have a passion for it, and desire to see what you are capable of doing. Pushing yourself to live your fullest life will pay off in ways you may not have even expected!

Commit to Your Plan

Simple steps along the way will stoke the fire to empower you as you make your dream a reality. Be realistic, and commit to what you are willing to do. What is your commitment level for each step of reaching your goal? If you know you are only willing to commit to three days of practicing the piano each week, then your goals should match that. Be honest with yourself about this.

Looking back, I'm immensely grateful that I took hold of a big dream early. I was a better student and healthier kid because I organized my attention and energy toward whatever helped facilitate my dream. I designed my life as best I could with my goals in mind. Even if I was physically or mentally exhausted, I was committed and happy. I had a plan, followed the steps toward achieving my dream, and understood that my interior motivation was my driving force.

Commit to simple, realistic steps as you get started on a new goal. It is better to be eager to keep going rather than to get burnt out after a short time. If you start by consistently achieving steps toward your goal, no matter how small, you will feel empowered to continue. Let's say you tend to be stressed out, and you want to be more relaxed. Commit to one minute per day of taking ten slow deep breaths. Then, when you have done this for three days in a row, start doing it twice per day. It is a conscious decision to go from stressed, shallow breathing to full, deep breathing. You go from not breathing past your neck to relaxing enough so that your lungs fill up from the bottom to the top as you breathe. Ideally, you should breathe in through your nose and out through your mouth. This helps to calm you. However, there is no right or wrong way to do this; just make sure you inhale and exhale fully. Set yourself up to succeed—building on your achievements will help you reach your goal, no matter how long it takes.

Once you do a new action for three weeks, it becomes a habit. So take steps toward your goal for three weeks. This will help you stay committed. If you've mastered the first steps of your plan at that point, then continue on.

As described in Chapter Two, in order to achieve your dreams you must first create a plan and then stick to it. Be aware that any change, however small, will take some effort. There are days when you'll feel distracted or tired and won't want to do what needs to be done. It's important to be aware of your underlying motivation, your bigger vision, so you can rely on that when you're tempted to give up. Take a moment and write down what motivates you. Feeling a certain way? Proving something? Feeling important? Being afraid to fail and be a "nobody" (which makes you then keep going)? Making somebody happy? Helping another person? Doing something you didn't know you could do? Reflect on a time when you achieved a goal. What motivated you? What helped you see it through to the end?

Commit to something that tests you, helps you find your bliss, and ultimately is a source of comfort to you. There will be a time when you must decide whether to go for it or give up. That is a fork in the road. When you choose to go into the unknown even though a part of you is unsure, you allow for new possibilities. As you forge ahead and become more aware of your capabilities, you have more energy and build confidence in yourself and what you can do. You feel a sense of "yes," knowing you have proven to yourself over and over that you do as you say. By following through on your action plan, you handle obstacles that come your way and build trust within yourself. By taking small steps each day, you start to have more faith in yourself and your abilities, which will help you achieve your big aspirations.

Stay committed to your plan, even if it feels like work at first. Initially, commitment requires you to focus on what you want to achieve. It is like learning a new skill, such as riding a bike. If you train yourself to attend to what you want, and do not get distracted, you will find that, even though you fall a few times, you keep getting back up and moving closer to your goals. Although distractions might seem tempting, you gain more energy by staying attentive to your tasks. Distractions require more energy than staying focused (more about this in Chapters Six and Thirteen). As you focus and follow your plan, you will become increasingly inspired and energized to reach your goal.

Of course, things will come up that are beyond your control. Acknowledge them, but avoid wasting energy on them. Stay focused on what you want. Most top performers, no matter what their field, know how to commit and pay attention. They are disciplined about consistently working on skills in their field of interest. They know what motivates them and how to create the best possible energy within so they can spend time on what excites them. Since they have a big enough vision, they can keep coming back even after a bad performance, be it in a boardroom, an athletic arena, on stage, or at home. They know how to adapt to stressors and distractions, such as the media, travel, competitors, success, and failure. They follow a plan, evaluate it regularly, and adjust based on what they learn.

The Courage to Change

"There is nothing constant in the universe. All ebb and flow, and every shape that's born, bears in its womb the seeds of change."
– Ovid, Metamorphoses

Change can be scary. We might be unaware of being stuck in bad habits, or unwilling to change them yet, even if they are unsatisfying or unhealthy. We might blame someone else for our poor behavior as we pretend that our problem or obstacle does not exist, hoping it is a problem "out there" somewhere, not within or about ourselves. Fear of change might stop us from committing.

At first, making a change might seem like a sacrifice rather than an inspirational new way of living. You might ask yourself, "How can I let go of the fear and allow the change to occur?" or "Do I have to believe all of my fears and excuses?" Realize that negative thoughts have only been created to keep you from being true to yourself and your real desires.

As you become attentive to getting stuck, as if you fell into a hole and don't know how to get out, you start preparing to alter your course. The first step is recognizing what feels right within (and what does not). Then, as you become aware of how you feel, you can choose to take a certain direction, even while you are stuck in the hole.

You might think that being comfortable, even if stuck, is easier than taking the risk to explore other avenues. Ask yourself, "What am I afraid of? Is this fear justified?" When you are afraid, what happens to you? You might say, "I stop breathing," or "I feel tension in my stomach." What does this tension represent? Perhaps, "I feel rejected," or "People might think less of me." What follows from there? Maybe, "I feel alone. Nobody likes me. I feel worthless, like a 'nobody.'" Just by honoring your fear, and facing it, it will have less power over you. Be kind to yourself, recognize your fear, and believe that it does not control you.

Growth occurs most easily when you allow for mistakes. Through challenges, you find out what you are capable of. From mistakes, you learn what works and what doesn't. Focus on the art of learning, rather than getting bogged down in the details. Trust yourself and your instincts.

For now, tell yourself: I am ready to accept these necessary changes in my life. I am willing to let go of my fears and take a risk. I am ready to go for it.

Take the leap into the unknown. Until you try a new way, you won't know if it works. It may take a few attempts to find what works best for you, but have the courage to go into that unexplored realm. Once you do, you will wonder why you waited so long. Be willing to take that initial step. It is worth it. Your perspective will shift as you see that you are more capable than you thought.

Once you are willing to take a risk, you can take the new path and dare to live. You feel your spark; you feel free. Your willingness to change could prove to be revolutionary—not just for yourself, but for others, too. My friend and training partner, David Berkoff, illustrated this in the swimming world: He tried new ways to be faster, and in doing so, he was the first person to kick thirty-five meters underwater (versus five meters) before coming to the surface to swim. Now most swimmers, including young ones, are taught the importance of speed underwater and are developing their underwater kicking ability! David's willingness to try something new revolutionized swimming.

Inspired Change

> *"Where one door shuts, another opens."*
> – Spanish Proverb

Limiting beliefs can keep you from pursuing what you want. Where did these beliefs come from? Did you develop them on your own? Can you change them? Are you willing to change them? Say yes. Look at yourself differently. Change the filtered lens over your eyes that keeps your perspective limited. If your old belief is not serving you, see with fresh eyes as you reframe the way you think. Instead of, "I am not good enough to win," say, "I am committed to doing my steps to see what is possible." Or rather than, "I'm fat and hate to exercise," tell yourself, "I'm happy I am healthy, and I can take that first simple step to get in better shape." Then, take action.

It is easy to get comfortable staying where you are, even if you are not happy there. What would you like to let go of, clean out, or forgive in your life? By doing so, you will have room for a new opportunity or shift in your life to occur—allowing you to feel good!

You might feel nervous about opening a new door and having change take place. Allow a new experience to emerge by willingly receiving it and appreciating that "it" (whatever you wanted) has arrived for you. When you take that step, trust in yourself, and let go of old habits, new experiences will come more easily. What is available for you through the new door? Trust in the unknown. It is worth it.

Also, realize that just because you handled a scenario one way in your past does not mean you have to continue acting or believing that way. It is okay to change your beliefs, and to shift your focus, as long as it brings you toward what ultimately makes you feel happy and fulfilled. Luckily, every day you have the opportunity to change how you live and interact with yourself and with others. The choice is always up to you.

Your Support System

In order to continue believing in your dream, especially during moments of doubt, it helps to have a good support system. In choosing a mentor/support system, find someone you can trust and who inspires you. Some of us might have a parent we feel totally supported by. Others will need to look elsewhere to get their needs heard and addressed, perhaps to a coach, teacher, friend, professional therapist, meditation group, acupuncturist, doctor, colleague, or sibling. Even books can be a great source of inspiration. And if we have become adept at training our minds to stay focused, we can be our own source of support. However, it's always helpful to have mentors assist in guiding us along our paths.

When you pick a mentor, choose someone you feel safe with, can rely on, and whom you trust. Know that what you share with them remains confidential with them. Honor their wisdom, and be willing to learn from them and try out suggestions that they give you.

Wise, conscious mentors are someone who can listen to you, love you, tell you how to take better care of yourself, and gently nudge you when you lose your way or choose not to pay attention. Mentors might test you and challenge you. Know that they want to guide you to be your best. Great mentors see your potential, your abilities, and your power. They will help you become aware of it, too.

When I was in the sixth grade, I started listening to visualization tapes. In the 1980s I did Tony Robbins' live fire-walking seminar, and I listened to Louise Hay's affirmation tapes. I studied everything I could on peak potential. Coach Shoulberg paid attention to my needs in training and reminded me to stay focused on my dream. In the 1990s, I sought out my therapist and acupuncturist, and I learned a lot about my life that helped me take care of myself in relation to others. I studied self-help books, psychology, and religion to help me understand and to feel supported in my life journey.

Focus on people and sources of inspiration that enhance your energy. When you pay attention to how you feel, you will know when you have found them.

Who Inspires You?

Another way to feel inspired and happy is to imagine you are someone whom you admire. Notice that you most likely are attracted to people who have characteristics that you want.

Who is somebody you admire or would like to know? What is it about this person that you admire? What characteristics and values do they have? Now realize that you have these characteristics, too. Yes, it can be scary to compare yourself to someone you admire, and your mind might be trying to convince you it is crazy to believe you have this power within you, too. But guess what? You do!

Let's take this a step further. Describe characteristics of champions and their peak performances. What resonates within you? What values inspire you, and which ones would you like more of? Now, imagine watching the person who inspires you. How do they move? Imitate them right now. Pretend you are that person, and act out the qualities you admire in them. The qualities of the people who inspire you are within you, too! You just need to trust that they are there, bring them out, and say hello!

Building Your Confidence

When you make decisions about what you want to create in your life, commit to consistently following through with your purposeful action steps, have mentors to guide you, and celebrate your little and big successes along the way, your confidence will grow and you will have more trust in yourself.

Your mental toughness and determination will help keep you going no matter what circumstances arise. You can learn to have this strength of mind, no matter where you are mentally and emotionally at this point. Being mentally tough helps you build confidence in what is possible for your life.

When you believe in and trust yourself, you allow your ego to get out of the way and let your inner self guide you. When you trust the body's "genius mind," you can surrender to its ability to innately know what to do. When you listen to it, *you* also will know what to do.

Along the way, remember to be kind to yourself. We tend to be our own worst critics. Give yourself credit for where you are and how you are doing. Each day, find something you are doing well and that you feel good about, no matter how small it might seem to you.

Here are a couple of journal exercises for you:

- When do you feel most confident? How do you know that you feel confident? Does it have to do with what you "do," or do you feel great about yourself by just "being"? When do you feel most stressed? Typically, you will notice this is when you are not present in the moment with what is going on around you.

- How do you build confidence? When you feel like it goes away, how do you rebuild it within yourself? What do you associate with confidence? How is this connected to your personal belief systems? Can you change it? Are you willing to change?

What makes up a confident person? Confident people are mentally tough, and they believe they are capable of learning and successfully achieving a desired outcome. When things don't go according to plan, they don't get down on themselves—they are willing to adjust and grow. They might not be good at a particular task, but they still feel good about themselves and are willing to try it anyway. They know that "failure" does not define them personally, and they are willing to accept all possibilities in a situation, whether they are good or bad. Someone who is confident focuses more on the task at hand than on worrying about what others will think, and whether or not they will fail.

I used to be told I was very optimistic. I believed that anything was possible, and I wanted to test every avenue to see what I was capable of. Even when I became quite sick, I still believed my mind could overcome any odds. For me, this will was innate, but for others it might need to be learned. Keep going, and trust that you are capable of handling whatever life throws your way.

Friendly Advice

Continue to be honest about yourself, your decisions, and your actions. Recognize how your thoughts and actions can limit you—or help you attain your dreams. Remember that in every situation, and for every decision to be made, there are two options: Be open to new possibilities and build self-confidence, or have limiting beliefs and drag your confidence down. You get to choose. Are you following your plan based on the life you designed for yourself? Are you being honest with yourself?

Make excellence a habit in your life. Embrace it as you live your dreams. Focus on what makes you happy. Be your own biggest fan. Take time to celebrate the steps you are taking toward your goals. Regardless of circumstances, create healthy habits and commit to following through consistently. As you deal with obstacles and change, surround yourself with inspiring mentors to help you along the way. Have the desire and willingness to experience changes. As you shift your energy, you will shine your light and beam your radiant confidence. Others will be inspired by your uplifting energy, too.

As Norman Vincent Peale, author of *The Power of Positive Thinking*, advised, "If you want a quality, act as if you already have it. If you want to be courageous, act as if you were — and as you act and persevere in acting, so you tend to become."

PART TWO
MANAGING OBSTACLES

Chapter Five

Overtrained:
Afraid to Stop and Be a Nobody

Some of us think holding on makes us strong; but sometimes it is letting go.
– Herman Hesse

While swimming internationally for the United States, I looked like I was on top of the world, but beneath the surface I became very sick. Since age fifteen, I had been battling immune-system issues, which showed up initially as mononucleosis. This would continue to sap all my reserves. I wanted to believe that I was fine, and I tried to prove myself right. I fooled myself to a degree and was still able to compete for the United States on the international stage for seven more years. But eventually my health issues became too serious to ignore.

I loved being in the water even if I was sick; yet, I also had moments where I didn't know how I could possibly continue. My mind had been trained that anything was possible, and I ignored the truth of my illness as I kept pushing and testing this razor's edge. My aspiration had become my addiction. At the time, I didn't value the concept of balance. All I focused on was achieving my goals, breaking records, and pushing myself to the limit. I got a "rush" from competing that felt so good, I wanted it more and more. I refused to listen to my body when it told me to slow down; the illness felt like a distraction to me, and I thought that I could simply will myself through it. A big part of my identity was wrapped up in being a swimmer—if I quit or slowed down, what would that mean? Who would I be?

I constantly had flulike symptoms and other health problems as my suppressed immune system caused my body and mind to stop functioning properly. But I kept going as long as I could, believing that this irritating obstacle would just go away. It reminded me of when I was in high school and my car needed maintenance. Instead of acknowledging the issue, I turned up the radio to pretend the rattling noise was not there. I didn't want to have to attend to the problem, since I always had somewhere I needed to get to. Similarly, when I got sick, I was in a place in my career where the best was yet to come. I didn't want to stop.

I was comfortably numb, afraid to stop swimming for fear of having "nothing" and being a "nobody." I didn't want my friends to know what was going on with me because I thought they might not accept me anymore or understand my condition. I believed that it would be "weak" if I complained, had pain, or couldn't finish the tough intervals in practice. I rationalized my thinking by telling myself I was getting tougher and thus more able to win. I denied my feelings so I could pretend that I was fine and keep swimming.

Why couldn't I simply admit the truth and ask for help? Many people thought I was one of the next rising stars. I was unstoppable. I didn't overanalyze or worry that I wasn't good enough. I just raced and gave it my best. Yet, as I continued, I could not give up my motivation to want more. I had worked so hard and come so far, and I knew great things were yet to come. So I ignored the warning signs and distracted myself from the truth, as I rationalized how strong I was for not wavering from my plan.

Swimming With Shoulberg

In the summer of 1985, when I was fourteen, I made my first international trip for the United States, swimming at the Pan Pacific Games in Japan. Coach Shoulberg was one of the USA coaches on the trip, and my friends and teammates Jeff Prior and Erika Hansen were also swimming in the competition. We enjoyed this time together as we swam in the meet and toured Japan. I remember Shoulberg and I going up to some athletes from other countries and communicating nonverbally (since we didn't speak each other's language) about swapping national gear. We laughed as we traded goodies from our respective countries with each other. I also recall Shoulberg watching out for me, making sure I didn't stay out too late, or party like some other national team members. At this time in my life, I appreciated his care and concern for me. I felt important.

When I came back from Japan, Shoulberg was thrilled with my performance. But then the flipside—his fear and insecurity—kicked in. He became nervous about my successes: "You're gonna get a big head," he told me. I was caught off guard and wasn't even sure what he meant. I had been a confident swimmer and good student, and I just wanted to continue to thrive, to be myself. Yet, Shoulberg's concerns started to take a toll on me. I loved my coach and had fun training with him as he always kept things interesting, never dull. Yet, I needed to be told how successful I was. I wanted to be praised. Instead, Shoulberg tried to make me mentally tougher by putting me down, and I slowly started to lose my confidence.

Shoulberg seemed to think that by taking this approach he would somehow make me care more and work harder. It was like I had to pretend I wasn't swimming well, that I had no talent, and that the only way to succeed in the sport was to train, train, train. Then, when I was exhausted, we would see if I could do some more. I innately knew that I didn't totally believe in his ways, but another part of me thrived on seeing what was possible, so I was willing to go along with him.

He had developed many great athletes. And through his charismatic, fun personality, he knew how to keep us motivated, even in long training sessions. He and I loved playing games with each other. He could be like a little kid. Yet, we did not always agree on what it took to be fast. We bantered back and forth, and I'd eventually give in. He was an authority figure to me who helped me with life, not just in the pool. I trusted him.

Shoulberg wasn't the only tough coach. During my high school years in the mid-1980s, many coaches believed in overtraining. They wanted female athletes to look more like men, with very low body fat. Many athletes, especially in gymnastics, often did not get their menstrual cycles due to this mindset. In the United States, female swimmers were taught to be like the Eastern Europeans. The East Germans were on steroids, and the well-studied Russian athletes were part of the famed Soviet Regime's Athletic Sport Program. Similarly, in the business world at this time, women had to wear business suits and be more masculine in their appearance to be respected and fit in.

Swim-team training during the school year consisted of practices in the morning, Monday through Friday, from 6:30 to 7:50 a.m. The implicit rule was that those who wanted to be great would arrive at 6:00 a.m. to do their own "dry land" exercises (strength and flexibility work) for thirty minutes. (A few others and I did this.) After school the team trained from 3:00 until 6:00 p.m., and on Saturdays we trained from 7:00 a.m. until noon. This was, and still is, part of the mentality at Germantown Academy: experimenting on your own…and seeing what is possible.

Carrying Our Weight

Shoulberg's system of training had worked for some people, so he believed it must work for everyone. However, different people and different body types benefit from other kinds of training. We had been told that the East Germans were cheating by using steroids. Yet, we were told by all of the top coaches to pretend that they weren't, that they were still beatable, and to focus on training that much more. I began to ignore my pain as I kept pushing.

Every night at 6:00 p.m., after a full day of school and two swim practices, I had to weigh in for Shoulberg. I became increasingly stressed about my body weight and body image. I was told to lose weight so I could look more like a male. To get my body fat under sixteen percent, my body would have to cannibalize itself for fuel.

Studies show that two ninety-minute practices are more productive than one three-hour training session. After ninety minutes, we have used up our glycogen stores and, unless we refuel during training, our bodies start eating away at our muscle and fat, and our organs begin to strain. Once we have used up our glycogen, we get so depleted that it is hard to recover. To combat this, we need to monitor how we fuel the body during training so we can optimize its ability to recover and thrive, rather than become broken down to point where it cannot perform at its best.

Until this point, I had never focused on my looks. I liked my body, and I enjoyed what it could do, especially in the pool. In the sixth and seventh grades, I weighed 119 pounds, which was a lot for a young girl. But muscle weighs more than fat, and I was muscular and wiry, like a natural sprinter.

Eventually we had someone come in and determine our body fat a couple times each year. There are two main ways to calculate body fat. A simple way is to use calipers to pinch certain areas on the body, including fat on the upper back, upper leg, stomach, and by the triceps muscle. As with any science experiment, there is a certain level of error that can occur. But if the same person did the test each time, the reading would become more accurate. The other way to measure body fat is with an underwater test, which is more accurate. I remember going to the deepest part of the pool to get "dunked." There was a chair under the surface of the water. I would sit in the chair, blow out all of my air, and stick my head underwater. After I came back to the surface, I would get out of the water for them to do a lung test to determine the capacity of my lungs and the amount of oxygen in my body. The testers then did some math to determine my percentages of muscle and fat.

Most American world-class female swimmers averaged sixteen percent body fat; this is also what I averaged during my career. When my body fat was too low, at fourteen-and-a-half percent, I did not perform as well. But I was okay up to eighteen percent. Sprinters would be as low as fourteen percent, and distance swimmers, who tend to float better, might average closer to nineteen or twenty percent. United States Swimming and the Olympic Committee had a great science program that researched and studied many of these things over the years.

It was much more accurate to get our body composition determined than to weigh in on a scale. Yet, to do the underwater testing was expensive. The calipers were good as long as the person testing the athlete knew precisely how to only get the fat and not the muscle. Thus, weigh-ins were the standard way to check our bodies on a regular basis. I don't remember doing this my first couple years swimming with Shoulberg, but from the time I was fifteen until I went to college, I had to weigh in regularly.

I still can remember the daily routine: It was 6:00 at night. Practice had just ended. Several of us ran from the locker room to the bathroom to pee out any remaining fluid so we could get that "magic" number on the scale. Then, since there were football and lacrosse players and other athletes in the hallways, we put towels around ourselves, over our swimsuits, and walked to the infirmary where the scale was. Often the assistant coach, Diane McClain, was the lucky one to weigh us in. The energy in the room always felt so heavy, as if we were dutiful soldiers ready to be criticized. Nobody liked this. There was a lot of judgment if you did not weigh in at the "right" number. I often weighed around 135–140 pounds at this point.

What the coaches and athletes never discussed is that each person has a natural body weight, and to ask someone to veer drastically from that can be harmful. Top female athletes can weigh up to 160 pounds or more, and small-boned people who have a hard time putting on muscle might only weigh 100 pounds. But the coaches got specific numbers in their heads for us, with no scientific foundation. I thought to myself, "By whose standards should I weigh less than 130 pounds? I am never going to look like someone who can't put on muscle like my body can."

Also, if the body is chronically stressed it gets bloated, as the hormones and organs stop functioning effectively. It is not always because you haven't taken care of yourself (through proper eating, rest, and training). This occurs in people when they have food allergies, are overly tired, don't express their feelings, are not feeling safe, or when the body can no longer function optimally. It is your body's way of saying something is wrong. When you pay attention and listen to your body's natural feedback, you know what is best to do.

An additional challenge for young athletes is hitting puberty: hormones kick in, bodies develop and get larger, and girls begin their menstrual cycle. You can still swim fast and perform well, even when you gain weight and your body composition changes. The key is to maintain strength. But it is normal to weigh more as you get stronger and bigger. And we need some fat on our bodies to function well. In fact, if we are training intensely it is best to have reserve fat so that our bodies don't have to eat muscles for fuel.

I intuitively knew that this weigh-in deal had gotten out of hand. The day after the 1986 World Championships Trials when I did not make the team, Shoulberg gave the team a lecture about how what we eat determines how fast we swim. He singled me out and said that when we were at the Trials and he saw me eat *six* meatballs instead of *four*, he knew I was not going to swim fast. To him, keeping weight under control was a key part of winning—perhaps to an extreme. The day after Shoulberg's lecture, I found out I had mononucleosis—I had a severely swollen throat and a fever over 103 degrees. I guess it wasn't the meatballs.

Even though Shoulberg was tough, we generally had a good joking relationship. But he eventually took it too far. Around this time, after tolerating more than I should have, I finally lost my patience with him. I was walking onto the pool deck and knew that Shoulberg was eyeing me as I got into the pool. He yelled, "Your ass is wider than a barn door!" Normally I could take his joking remarks, as they were meant to be funny. But this time, I had had enough. Normally I would yell back and we'd have some fun. This time, I said nothing, as I was furious inside. Nothing was ever good enough for him. Even if I did weigh what he wanted, he probably would still not be satisfied, or some new fear would kick in about why I couldn't or might not swim fast. I felt like it was never his fault. Always ours.

I decided I was going to prove Shoulberg wrong. I would show him that weighing a magic number on the scale did not serve me; in fact, it made me swim like crap. I did the standard training plus more of my own training to lose weight. Throughout the season I biked, benched on the cardio upper-body machine, or worked out on the old ski machine for thirty minutes or more, while drinking lots of water. I ate hardly any fat and no sugar. (However, I never threw up to lose weight.) I was often hungry, but I was determined to prove that reaching some magic number on the scale was not always the way to become a faster swimmer. I succeeded in looking good in Shoulberg's eyes. But that season I didn't swim fast.

Of course, I thought I was winning this issue with him. I ate less and worked out more, got to Shoulberg's magic number, and swam like crap. But in hindsight, even though I was "right," I am the one who suffered. I lost the chance to have a great season.

Shoulberg and I would go at it on various occasions, but we would always hug and make up. Both of us were stubborn and strong-willed. It was never personal; we both just liked to win. In this case, I knew that the weigh-in situation had gone too far. I requested that he get a professional to help us. I was happy that he finally got a regular body composition person in, and he also hired a nutritionist to monitor how we ate. I focused more on eating well and tried to worry less about the coaches' responses to the number on the scale.

When we are too focused on the end result (in an athlete's case, winning), it is easy to lose sight of what keeps us healthy. Training hard and eating a certain way almost becomes like an addiction. We have to remember to allow our bodies to rest and to heal themselves. Our bodies and minds need balance. If we push them too hard for too long, eventually they'll break down.

Shoulberg Cared

My relationship with Shoulberg was complicated. Though we sometimes butted heads, I also felt as though his heart was in the right place and he truly wanted what was best for his swimmers. It was just that his fears and stubborn beliefs sometimes got in the way. But even though he seemed harsh and unrelenting at times, he could also be very funny.

I stayed with my dad most weekends, and we often went to church on Sundays. One time at practice, Shoulberg decided to see if I actually had attended church the previous weekend. We were doing a set where we dove from the blocks. He sneaked up behind me and teasingly said, "I know you didn't go to church yesterday!" I turned around, ready for a little fun and exclaimed, "Bullshit, I went to church!" People around me cracked up laughing.

The next weekend, I was at my dad's house. Sometimes on Saturday nights I would sleep fourteen hours in a row. I had one day off, and I needed the rest. But this weekend, we went to church. Someone from the church office came up to me and said I had a phone call. My dad and I thought this was strange. We figured it must be my mom calling from Minnesota, and we hoped everything was okay. Wrong! It was Shoulberg! He was calling to see if I was at church! He tried to catch me, but it didn't work.

Shoulberg was funny, and he liked to create adventure, but he could also be controlling. What prompted his interest in my church attendance, I'm not quite sure, but I found it amusing at the time.

I did feel special to Shoulberg, and I needed the attention at that point in my life. My parents had separated and would eventually divorce. I was distraught and wondered if I had done something wrong. Obviously, it wasn't my fault, but I still felt like I wanted to fix things in my parents' relationship somehow. During this time, I was sad and confused, and a few times I came to practice crying. Shoulberg would listen to me and provide a shoulder to lean on.

For better or worse, Shoulberg expected a lot of me. While it was nice that he paid attention to me, I was also burdened with additional pressure. I remember around eighth or ninth grade, several swimmers went to a party where there was alcohol. There was a team rule that nobody was allowed to drink or do drugs. On Monday morning Shoulberg held a team meeting. He started by saying, "I know that several of you were at a drinking party, which is not okay. But what is even worse, is those of you who knew and didn't tell me." He named me, and a couple of others. I shook my head in disbelief. I hadn't even gone to the party, but I was *still* in trouble for not tattling.

As I have gotten older, I have come to appreciate Shoulberg more. He cared enough that he did not want people ruining their lives through alcohol, drugs, or other distractions, and he wanted us to be honest. Shoulberg created a great sense of belonging and family, even though several of us lived away from home. He gave many of us nicknames. He had an infectious, fun-loving side and often made us laugh. But he also pushed each one of us to the brink.

Training the Mind

The mentality with Shoulberg and the swim team was "What is possible?" We believed we would *be* better and *do* better if we pushed ourselves to the limit.

Shoulberg helped us learn discipline and mind control. We had hours each day to practice letting go of distracting thoughts, as we mentally trained to become more efficient, to survive those grueling workouts. Our bodies eventually found the most effective way to relax into the movements and achieve maximum speed. We learned to get rid of the mental chatter and become fully immersed in what we were doing. We also had to understand what motivated us. If we didn't, there was no way we would last.

We got to choose whether to focus or be distracted, and once I learned how to focus my mind, the clarity of my movement increased. Shoulberg had sets leaving on thirty-seven seconds versus on the forty-second mark. If we were not paying attention, we would miss our interval on the clock. We could not daydream. Also, it became a game in practice to see if I could maintain or go faster on the next 100 of the 500 or 1000 yards.

When I was younger, I was willing to try new things and do whatever it took to be my best, to see what was possible. It made me feel alive. By the time I was training with Shoulberg, I had gotten used to punishing myself and seeing how much I could take. Even as I got sick with mononucleosis, I became curious about how much my mind could overcome my physical illness. I loved walking the razor's edge, testing my human limits—and then seeing if I could surpass them. I enjoyed experimenting and seeing what worked. I was eager and earnest. I thrived on trying anything I could do to become a faster swimmer.

My entire focus revolved around swimming—that was what defined me. Even when I got sick, all I could think of was how to push through the illness and make myself the best swimmer I could be. But my times got worse, and my body got weaker. And then my confidence waned as my performances faltered. If I couldn't be a world-class swimmer, I assumed I would be nobody.

College at Cal Berkeley

When I went to Cal Berkeley, I was excited to find that the women's swim coach, Karen Moe Thornton, was ahead of her time. She not only ruffled feathers because of her gender, but also by her forward-thinking ideas. While most coaches believed in doing a lot of endurance training and not much race work, Karen encouraged us to have a balance of rest, intensity, aerobic recovery, and threshold training.

At the beginning of each week, she gave us a sheet laying out the week's plan for our workouts—she wanted to maximize our ability to recover while also bringing out the best in us by having us swim as close to race speed as possible. (Many of her ideas, once considered radical, are now commonplace.) Eager for a change from Shoulberg's methods when I arrived at Berkeley, I soaked up what Karen was dispensing and begged for more.

Yet, I couldn't get Shoulberg off my back. In my freshman year at Berkeley, the fall of 1989, I wrote in my journal:

> *Shoulberg called, and asked how I did in my meet. I told him it was okay, and that I made my 200 fly NCAA cut. He goes, "It sounds like you are overweight." I tensely raised my voice and said, "What? You haven't even seen me!" He said, "No Trina, I can tell by your splits. You must not be training enough."*

> *This just blows me away. I decide to say nothing. I am so furious inside. What if my body has just had enough? Is it still sick from mono? I haven't felt well for so long!*

He goes on to tell me that he ordered this new white Australian bike for me to use after practice (to train more and lose weight). "Let me know when you get it." Then, he asked, "Are you going out too much?" Goodness—all of his worries hitting me at once. Am I training enough? Am I eating well? I am sick of worrying about all of this.

According to him I am supposed to work out more, so I can have a certain weight based on what he thinks, while I swim with KMT (Karen) at CAL! This is crazy. I am curious and want to buy into her training philosophy; yet, I have him calling me way too much, at the wee hours of 3 a.m., thinking it is funny and I am trying to get my sleep! Then he wants to make sure I am doing enough.

Doesn't he know that constantly questioning me, and my abilities, shuts me down and makes me doubt myself? I need someone to believe in me, and remind me of how great I am as a human being, not just because I put in 20,000 meters today and did my "extra" beyond that!

He does not control me. I get to decide what is best for me. Yet, I feel pulled. Why does he still have so much power over my mind? He seems to not want his athletes to do well with another coach. He can't let go. LET GO, SHOULBERG. Your swimmers do grow up and move on!

I knew Shoulberg's heart was in the right place and that he would do anything for me if I asked. Yet, I also felt like I needed to let go and move on. I wanted to be inspired through empowerment, not fear. But some of his beliefs, especially about overtraining and weight, were wedged deep in my psyche.

Trying to Feel Alive

As my immune system stopped functioning properly and my body ballooned, I searched for ways to feel "up" again, to have the "high" that I used to get from swimming. I wasn't ready to rest. To me, resting was giving up. I believed that I was supposed to be tough and manage anything thrown my way. So, to prove to myself that I was superhuman and that I was healthy, a couple times I went dancing until the early morning hours in San Francisco with my friend Pippa. We would arrive at morning swim practice happy, still dancing on the pool deck, and ready to have a great practice. Karen would just roll her eyes. What could she do?

I also partied particularly hard for two years when I was in denial. I wanted to feel "high" and have adventurous experiences, not feel exhaustion and pain anymore. By altering my consciousness, I felt alive again, at least temporarily.

At Cal Berkeley, Karen kept trying to wake me up and snap me out of my state of numbness, but I wouldn't listen to her. I had become accustomed to just surviving my practices with Shoulberg. I lost my ability to race. My natural speed had been trained out of me. I couldn't use my talents to their fullest. My body's nervous system had been dulled to the point where I could only stay at one gear.

I had been a natural sprinter from early in my career, demonstrating my speed by breaking records. Yet, at the 1988 Olympic Trials in the 200-meter fly I was in eighth place at the 100-meter mark. I physically was unable to go any faster, as my body had lost its ability to use its speed. But I still believed I could push through and luckily I had enough will to become an Olympian anyway.

Swimming Again with Shoulberg

After a lot of deliberation, I decided to go back to Pennsylvania and train with Shoulberg for the 1992 Olympics. I knew I was very sick, and while I believed that Karen could get me to the Olympics, I didn't know if I could be so sick, train, and go to school all at the same time. I figured I could sleep more to recover from the training if I took a year off from school. I had agonized about this decision. But I knew Shoulberg could get me physically and mentally ready for a meet, even it meant some overtraining.

Shoulberg, at this point, knew he tended to overdo, and he wanted to learn what he could do to help us work at our optimum level. He asked US Swimming for their support to monitor our workload. So they came to our pool about once a month and drew blood from each of us. They measured our cortisol (a stress marker), hemoglobin, hematocrit, white blood count, red blood cell count, cholesterol, and glucose. Many of my numbers were way out of whack. We knew I was sick, but we didn't know what my normal healthy numbers should be. For a couple months my cortisol levels increased immensely, and we attempted to back off from my full-force training regimen. To give us a break and let us have some fun, Shoulberg sent me and a few other swimmers to the World Cup competitions in Europe. The trip was a blast, and it renewed my confidence in my ability to race.

Exercise physiology studies show that, at a certain point, overtraining elite athletes for a brief time actually stimulates the body's ability to adapt and therefore get stronger. But chronic stress on the body, without the opportunity to recover, wears it down to the point where it cannot bounce back, even to its initial levels before training.

'92 Olympic Trials and Lessons Learned

Although the World Cup meets were great for me, what I really needed was a month of rest and relaxation. That would have given my body a chance to recover. But instead, I kept training, pushing myself as hard as I could before the 1992 Olympic Trials.

I didn't make the 1992 team. Ironically, a big part of me was relieved. My pride was hurt, and I knew that a few years earlier I could have excelled at this Olympics. But I was very sick and had spent a year in constant pain. I was actually confused, because I wasn't that upset. But in my heart, I had enjoyed training with some great people and with a coach who cared about us. My Cal coach, Karen, said to me, "Well, I know it is too bad that you didn't swim in the Olympics in Spain, but every time I talked with you on the phone, you sounded happy, even though you were so sick."

Even though that year of training didn't produce the desired outcome, I really treasured that time. I had lived on John Dupont's Foxcatcher Farm with the Schultz family, where many athletes from different sports came to live and train. It was like our own mini Olympic training center. I got to watch (and be inspired by) other awesome athletes as they excelled in sports they had trained for their whole lives: triathlon, modern pentathlon, shooting, wrestling, cycling, or swimming. I had immersed myself in learning, training, and focusing. I loved the training facilities, too: the fifty-meter pool had big glass sliding windows that could open up, allowing us to have fresh air, and the starting end had a big mural of the modern pentathlon's five sports. Even though I had not felt well, I thoroughly enjoyed myself that year, doing what I loved to do. I felt complete.

Am I A Nobody?

I was afraid to admit how sick I was, or that I needed to stop swimming. I had always felt most comfortable and alive in the pool. What if I couldn't do anything else? What if I never succeeded again and everyone forgot about me? Without swimming, would I be a nobody?

One way I initially dealt with my fears was by finding new, non-swimming-related adventures to immerse myself in. I wanted to know I would be okay, that I could still thrive and feel alive without swimming. When I did something that was scary, and I had to act on instinct since I did not have time to reason, I found myself being fully in the moment. And, if a situation meant life or death, I would be on hyper alert, believing that I would be fine but enjoying the thrilling "rush" of the unknown.

I did some daring things—most of which I wouldn't do again today. In the summer of 1992, after not making the Olympic team, I lived in Russia as part of a group that helped to start the second radio station in Moscow. One afternoon, a bunch of us took a bus to a field about forty-five minutes outside of Moscow so we could go skydiving. It was a beautiful, sunny day. One member of our group had skydived many times, and he explained a bunch of things to us in English. We had been told we could pay our money and someone would take us up in a plane to jump out. But after watching other skydivers and getting excited to get instruction and take our turns, we were told they weren't taking any more people up that day. As things were back then, when the Russians didn't feel like doing something, they would just say, "Closed." So, we watched some more and got ready to leave, thinking it wasn't happening that day.

All of a sudden, a man came over to us and spoke in Russian, "Okay we are ready to take you." One of us said in Russian, "But we haven't had any instruction yet." He said, "Okay" and then proceeded to give us about fifteen minutes of instruction in Russian. Luckily, I was quite fluent at the time, but I was still very nervous.

We got in the plane. It looked like a tiny 1930s warplane. We sat in a row, and one by one, someone jumped out from about 8,000 feet. I wasn't sure I still wanted to do this. *What if my parachute doesn't open?* I thought to myself. But suddenly it was my turn. I stood up and looked out at the sky and at the spec of land down below. I didn't take time to think—I just jumped. Luckily, I was on static line, and it worked. My parachute went up quickly. I had my camera with me, and took a picture of myself floating in the sky. My heart was pounding, and I could hear myself exhale loudly from the adrenaline. For a while, I floated as the wind carried me. It was beautiful. I felt alive. Then I gradually figured out how to steer myself since I was headed toward the woods, and I knew I didn't want to get stuck in *there*! I hadn't quite figured out the landing procedure from the brief instructions, so I decided to just touch the ground with my feet as I bent my knees and bounced back up a bit. Then, my feet touched again, and I rolled. Phew! I was safe!

A couple years later, back at Berkeley, when I had to stop swimming for what I hoped would only be a short amount of time, I was still looking for ways to distract myself from my frustration of not feeling well. I only knew how to feel good by getting an adrenaline rush. I ended up climbing the Golden Gate Bridge up to the top. I loved the "high" so much that I went back and did it a few more times with different friends. Each time was scary and yet exhilarating. We would celebrate at the top as we looked at the majestic city around us.

I was willing to do anything to feel alive, anything to know I was okay, to let my bruised pride deal with the fact that I didn't know what was going on with my health. I hated the thought of giving swimming up forever. I'd cry inside, *Please don't take this away from me! I'll show you that I am fine.*

Mentally, I knew I had to wake up and accept the fact that my swimming career was over. Was I ready?

Chapter Six

Stress and Distractions: Ways We Get Off Track

Tension is who you think you should be. Relaxation is who you are.
– Chinese Proverb

We all go through times when we want to keep living a certain way even if it no longer serves us. Change is scary. When we pretend that we are fine so that we can keep ignoring our deeper fears, we experience pain and stress. When we ruminate over our past, or when we worry about the unknown in our future, we are not living right now. We feel tension when we notice the difference between where we are and where we want to be.

Stress is an indicator that we are somehow not satisfied. We are trying to handle conflicting voices inside of us that have different needs and wants. When they do not match up, we feel anxiety. We can set goals in too many areas, get pulled in various directions, and then get overwhelmed trying to be perfect in all of them. Expectations—others' or our own—create a burden, too. In athletics, a lack of total recovery from heavy training leads to more burden (physically and emotionally). The same issue of burnout occurs in the workforce and in family life.

It is good to have goals and reach them, but it is also important to appreciate where we are *now* and know that the gap between what we crave and what we have does not need to trouble us. Once we know that getting what we want might not make us any happier, at least in the long run, we can enjoy giving our best effort without the worrying whether the outcome will define us or make us "whole."

Obstacles

Most people experience a calling to do something, whether through art, service, performing, or honorable sacrifice. In other words, we have a dream, a positive aspiration, or a vision of the higher self that we can be.

We might push to our absolute limits to achieve our goal. Yet, if we don't pay attention, we can get lost. Rather than managing obstacles along the way—including injury, illness, circumstances, attachments and aversions such as overtraining and being afraid to stop, denial, and distraction—we allow them to take over our lives. Too much of a good thing leads to wanting more, getting attached to needing it. Our aspirations become an addiction. Eventually, we feel stressed from trying so hard to have it. We then need a quick temporary high to release the tension created.

At the same time, others of us fear actually following through, as we don't want to face the pain of getting to where we want to really go, or we worry that we might commit and work hard but still not get what we want. Then we let distractions, our way of avoiding our true feelings, stir up questioning and doubt, throwing us off course on the way to realizing our dream.

Distractions

Resistance to achieving our goals appears in the form of fear, doubt, and self-sabotage. This causes distraction from our true desires and calling. And when distraction creeps in, we start to lose focus. If we are fearful and distracted, it is easy to rationalize why we are not pursuing our dreams. We might use distractions to avoid committing all of our energy to this one dream since there is no guarantee it will come true. If we fear success or failure, we might let our energy get pulled away from our vision. When we do this, we stop following our plan. We might even set ourselves up to prove that we're right—that we are only going to fail, so why even try. Life throws us tests to see how resilient, committed, and motivated we really are.

Distractions and obstacles are a part of life. We can get swayed into believing these temptations will soothe us and be best for us long term. Don't get deceived. Too much seduction gets us off track. It is crucial to maintain balance so our drive itself doesn't become the focus. Enjoy the journey, keep your eyes on the ultimate goal, but make sure you are staying healthy along the way.

My focus was so intense that I ignored my body and the warnings it tried to give me. I feared not doing what I loved, not knowing how to use my time if I didn't swim. I worried that I wouldn't know who I was anymore, or what truly satisfied me. I distracted myself through high-adrenaline activities and overtraining to pretend that I was healthy and fine. I rationalized that I could keep going by neglecting my body and my own needs. I didn't sabotage myself by drinking alcohol, eating poorly, or not going to practice.

My distraction was that I wanted to keep going so much I was afraid to stop. The gluttony of training became my norm; I needed the high (physically and emotionally) from it. I feared that taking a break would hurt me rather than help me. And my belief that I was weak if I didn't fight on also caused me to keep going.

We may distract ourselves through lies or rationalization. When this happens we become numb, restless, bored, or angry about nothing or everything. We are seeking something grand but are also confused. We don't know what to do or where to look. When we feel stuck, we get disoriented and experience a loss of self—we don't know who we are anymore or what we really want. We feel inauthentic and try to soothe ourselves by feeling connected—or numbed. We drink too much, have another romance, or repeat a bad habit over and over again. By doing so, distraction, and potentially addiction, replaces aspiration. If we're not careful, this quick fix can sabotage our dreams.

Because it's so uncomfortable to feel fear and shame, we obliterate them with a distraction. We take drugs or overindulge in non-drug stimulants: love, sex, work, feeling superior or inferior, television, computers, even parenting. Out of desperation to feel connected, we might have one all-consuming affair after another, which usually just leaves us feeling emptier. But we continue doing it to get that high of chasing, being chased, or feeling senselessly, passionately in love. We might be talented, gifted, and intelligent, but also addicted to wanting attention, approval, love, and connection.

As we get caught up in our distractions, we stray from the talents and bigger visions that could take us in a better direction. Yet when we are stuck, habituated, and comfortable being in a negative place, it is hard to stay focused on our vision. At that point the dream seems so far away, probably unattainable. We seek relief from the pain, the shame, or the difficulty of having to stay focused and committed. How do we get back and stay on track? How do we keep from sabotaging ourselves again?

We need to be attentive enough to listen to the inner voice that tells us when to stop and adjust. We need to build up our confidence so we feel good and don't want to sabotage ourselves. What outcome do we want from getting drunk or seeking more love? What is it that we are trying to feel in that moment that keeps us going back for more? How else can we attain that feeling while staying on our path? What do we want from being in that state? What does it give us?

When we slow down and take a step back to reflect, our focus will become clear again. A successful plan will include a balanced ratio of intelligent, purposeful work and well-designed and timed rest and recovery. When we're at rest, we get rejuvenated and we can look at ourselves, our desires, and our dreams with fresh eyes. When we stop trying to "force" things, we get inspired with new ideas or refresh our body and spirit so we are ready to go again. When we slow down and listen, we learn to hear our inner wisdom, intuition, and deeper intelligence. Then our true self can guide us.

Wanting More

It is not unusual to want things to be perfect—we'd like to have lots of friends, be a certain weight, look a specific way, get all A's in school, orgasm many times, win every race, make loads of money, and so on. You may have just created a successful product for your company and received a huge pay raise and bonus. Then you get used to having that amount of money so you can take out your friends and buy nice things that you couldn't afford before. Maybe you enjoy taking lavish trips. You want to be the big shot at work and not have anyone else be as successful as you. You want to make more money and keep getting promoted. In fact, you feel a certain sense of entitlement now.

This is just one example of how when we get what we want, we keep wanting more. Cravings for food, things, or people can become an addiction. We keep striving to get the moment of pleasure that occurs when we get the things we want. If we feed into our cravings, we tend to want more and more. We keep wanting that "high." Drug addicts increase the dosage as their body adapts—they need more and more to achieve the same effect. Whatever we're addicted to might not make us feel as good after a while, and then we get frustrated, and our focus becomes, "How do I get that feeling again?" That can be an all-consuming sensation, as we struggle just to feel good again, let alone have that "high."

Winning a medal, getting a raise, or going out with someone we've been pursuing is fun and satisfying, yet it can also leave us feeling like we need more unless it has a deeper meaning. We might wonder, "What if I can't do it again? I have to keep pushing to achieve more success. If I don't get it, does that mean I failed, that I'm no good, that I'm nobody special?" We try to top ourselves, to do even better than we did the last time. We feel the need to keep chasing. Many people who achieve their goals say they miss the "hunt," the "chase," the striving. When we are rewarded—especially if it happens without much effort—it is easy for our ego to want to sabotage us or say we didn't set the bar high enough! Now that we have gotten what we wanted, we might start wondering if we really deserved it.

Winning is fleeting; it only lasts for a moment. It is easy to get attached to the next event and outcome (to win, get a certain title, make money, feel euphoric) to have this "high" again. Then, fear comes back quickly ("What if I can't do it again?") if we do not take time to appreciate where we are in the moment. When we follow our crafted plan, through both fun and challenging times, we feel deep satisfaction from the process itself; any concerns about the future outcome are no longer as unsettling.

Attachment to a specific outcome causes our fears to surface (often unconscious things that we have not understood or been aware of). When we shove the pain down, we forget what it feels like because we have become so used to numbing ourselves. We want to avoid unwanted feelings. We might have shame from not getting the love we wanted, especially from parents who could not be emotionally or physically available. When we deny our needs or our feelings, we deny our child inside. Then, we try to make up for it by finding a way to feel good. We strive for approval from others in order to make up for feeling useless or worthless inside. As we do this, we get further from our true desires and self. Our real need is to give up the motivation for wanting more.

Denial

Human beings are very adaptable. Even when we are in a bad place, we eventually get comfortable there. The unknown can feel unnerving. Our primitive brain wants to feel comfort and safety instead of potential danger. So, we numb ourselves. But when we suppress difficult feelings, we create layers of armor, which causes imbalances in our body. We justify the position we are in—to ourselves, and others (we will discuss releasing armor in Chapter Ten).

During my period of overtraining, I became so good at mentally challenging myself that I could keep myself from feeling pain. I got accustomed to producing enough "feel good" chemicals in my body that I could forget I was sick. I believed I could be well, so I tried many things to prove myself right. Similarly, people who use drugs, spend too much money, or sleep around can deny that overuse of something is causing them harm.

In training, I had moments where I felt God work through me. For an instant, I felt a sense of pure love—I felt free. It was though my body was just an illusion. I experienced no "I," just space; I did not know where my body ended and the surroundings began. I would feel well in my mind even though my body said otherwise. I experienced miracles in these moments. I had amazing practices and meets like this; ones that I could not comprehend, given that I might have just been lying in bed an hour earlier. My body was solidly sick, aching beyond just being tired or sore from training—yet, I could enjoy moments of feeling free and alert, distanced from my physical pain.

I was curious how this occurred. After moments of feeling great, I thought I should be "well," but then I would sink back into my body. When I stopped training and the endorphins died down, I would be hit with immense pain. It was as though my body was reminding me it was unhappy.

Similarly, we might feel good for a while when we deny how we are feeling, but whatever we repressed will rear its ugly head in other ways to remind us that it is still there, even as we try to shove it down again. If we have a lot of unresolved anger, which is really a mask for grief (a normal and healthy feeling), it can present itself as rage. We might be startled and judge ourselves, believing, "I must be a bad person to have this feeling." We might even act on it, or think, "The only way to be good enough is to always smile and pretend that I am happy and nice." This creates fear and moves us further away from our true self. We worry about making mistakes, and we feel tension as we try to stay perfect. Then, eventually we blow up again. Similarly, some of us believe we have to handle our own problems. If we can't, we might lose respect for ourselves, thinking, "If I can't do this on my own, I am weak." We get upset that we are not perfect, put ourselves down, and feel stress.

Perfection Cycle

Children often feel the pressure to be perfect, too. They just want to be loved and feel appreciated and important. Unfortunately, many children don't develop their true sense of self, because they feel pressure to succeed, make their parents happy, help take care of younger siblings or even their parents, or feel torn between divorced parents. Many of us believe that, in order to be loved and accepted, we must do impossible things—get straight A's, win every track meet, become Student Council President. This feeling follows us into adulthood and then gets passed onto the next generation. But not everyone is going to win that medal or get the lead in the school play, and children need to know that they are still loved for who they are, no matter what. Praise the effort, not the achievement.

When we strive to reach a goal, we can get caught up in trying to be perfect. Let's say I want to lose weight, or be the next greatest athlete in a sport. I decide that I will stop eating "junk" food and only drink water, or if I am an athlete, I will train an extra hour even though my schedule is already booked. I rigidly commit for a few days, and then I can't sustain it anymore. I want some relief. I really want a cookie. In sports, I want that day off to rest instead of train. My mind wrestles with this a bit and then gives in. I binge: I eat not only one cookie, but ten. And I not only take one day off from training, but three. I initially feel better as I indulge instead of striving to be perfect. Then, I feel bad: guilty, shameful. I think, "I'm never good enough. I can't do this. I'll never succeed. I am worthless." Then, I decide to do better, to be good all over again. I might punish myself by eating less than before or working out twice as long the next few days. It is as if I need to make up for lost time or punish myself for what I did, thereby fueling stress instead of alleviating it.

These patterns distract us from our chosen path. Temptations show up. We need to be prepared so that we can deal with them, rather than allow them to throw us off track again and again. Where do we get stuck? How do we get unstuck? First, we need to be attentive to the sensations that we feel. Our body holds the answers if we pay attention. When feelings arise and evolve, we can either choose to cling to a certain experience, sensation, or thought, or we can simply notice the feeling and let it emerge and eventually dissolve.

Using principles from gestalt therapy, let's think about the process of eating. Initially, we have a *sensation*, such as "my stomach is grumbling." I then become *aware* that I am hungry. I *mobilize my energy*, as I consider getting something to eat. My body begins to warm up, ready to move. Then I *take action* by eating something, becoming engaged and connected with this object. My body takes it in and feels good (or not). The food and I are now one. Then I experience *withdrawal,* the relaxation of having completed the connection and feeling the release of energy after the contact.

The voices in our heads tell us different things at these various stages, which cause us to get stuck. The goal is to notice the places where we get stuck and then learn how to get unstuck. Some of us are not aware of the sensations in our body, since we have gotten so far away from ourselves through distraction or addiction. Others might be aware of a sensation but don't know what it means or are afraid to consider taking action. Some of us know we are hungry and want to eat, but we have blocks that stop us from actually eating. We might procrastinate ("Let me just finish this project first," or "I'll just wait and eat dinner with the family rather than having something on my own now"). After all, our ego likes to suffer, but our "being" self loves feeling connected and one with everything.

On a more extreme end, an anorexic has thoughts and emotions about needing to control herself, and look a certain way, which blocks her from easily eating. A bulimic attempts to avoid contact with food and then gives in by binging, though she still tries to avoid feeling anything while she is eating. She is merely trying to deal with emotions of being in control and out of control. Others of us get stuck wanting to hold on to the connection we get from taking action; we are attached to feeling good. To keep flowing, we need to let the natural evolution of these stages unfold and not get too attached or stuck at or between any stage.

Advertising and Attachment

Advertising feeds on our need to be perfect or get what we want by making us think we will be okay if we buy a certain product, achieve a certain level of success, or have a relationship with a certain kind of person. We can get fooled into repeating old patterns as we use the product to find relief, rather than contentment. We buy that car because we associate it with getting a beautiful woman, which we believe will make us feel special, loved, or attractive. A beer commercial might get us excited knowing we can escape responsibility as we party in an unhealthy way. We use these "wants" to avoid how we really feel. These quick fixes can lead to a temporary "high." But as with any high, eventually we crash.

Because of this attachment to getting, having, or doing a certain thing, we often feel suffering. Buddhist and other religious texts discuss this at length. The goal of advertising is to create a desire in us for the product being advertised. That's good in some ways, because the desire stirs us out of apathy. At the same time, it can trap us into thinking that achieving that item will be the ultimate source of pleasure. We often find, though, that whatever joy we achieve from this purchase doesn't last. Soon enough, it's gone and we're right back where we started, looking for the next temporary high to make us feel good.

Of course we want to pretend this unpleasant pain of feeling unfulfilled and dissatisfied doesn't exist. Sometimes we think that being numb is easier. That is what the drug companies count on to profit and make all of their shareholders happy. We have created a society where it's easy for people to dull their suffering. We might take pills or get an unnecessary surgery rather than deal with the source of an issue. We want to keep going at a fast pace, rather than taking the time to slow down and feel what is going on within us.

Some people escape through TV, video games, texting, videos, or the internet. Drugs, overworking, material possessions, sex, alcohol, and food can also numb our pain. Getting too caught up in these things can inhibit our ability to foster a desire for learning, relationships, imagination, empathy, and the wonder of life's magical mysteries. There are no quick fixes; no bandage can hide the symptoms. We need to get to the root of the problem. Nothing outside ourselves can give us everlasting peace or happiness. I can win an event right now and enjoy the success of that accomplishment. But soon I will be thinking about the next event and wondering if I can do better. And what if I can't? Similarly, I might feel good because I am popular. But what if the people whose opinions I based my self worth on suddenly change their minds, and I am not popular anymore? If I only feel good because I am popular, I will experience suffering if I lose that level of status. We must go to the vast depths of our true self to feel content.

For me, the sweet satisfaction of making the Olympic Team was more about staying true to myself and committing to the goal, even through the challenges in my path. The brief high of winning a medal, beating a record, or feeling special—even superior—is fleeting. Long-lasting fulfillment and true contentment come from envisioning a dream, crafting out a well-designed plan, and carrying out that plan faithfully, even in the face of fear, doubt and obstacles. A medal or title can be taken away, but nobody can take away your journey and experiences.

The Pain of Being Overly Attached

Why do we hold on to what we think will bring us happiness, even as it makes us miserable? Why do we strive to be (or at least appear) perfect? Why do we tend to focus on the one thing that did not go well or is not working, rather than on all of the things that have gone right? We fear loss and change, which can paralyze us and keep us from moving forward. When fear dominates, we lose our desire to explore the world and take chances.

Loss and Change

One form of stress is confronting loss, our own humanity, or an aging or ailing physical form. If we have a chronic illness, it is easy to get depressed because we no longer feel like we are in control. Then we struggle, trying to figure out how to get back to being healthy, or worse, we have to acknowledge that we're going to remain sick. When we fight an illness instead of acknowledging it, we actually spend more energy carrying the burden of denial. How can we learn to let go of our attachments to things, beliefs, or outdated ideas, and to what they represent to us? Can we still feel content and know we will be okay, regardless? Lessons come from changes and loss; when we stop stagnating, we can grow.

Expectations

Suffering can occur when others project their own unfulfilled desires onto us, or when we place unrealistic expectations on ourselves. Getting credit for achievements is fleeting—it becomes addictive to need the attention and rewards that others give us. But if we lose or do not measure up or are concerned about not being adored by the fans, we feel terrible when we are alone, and we end up living in a state of anxiety and stress. We have all experienced this in one way or another. We wear a mask over our imperfect selves, and fear, "What if somebody finds out the 'real' me and doesn't like me?"

It is stressful trying to measure up to expectations. People might not like us if we can't comply with their unrealistic demands. For example, it is common in sports to expect a top athlete to pull through for the win, and if they don't, people/corporations/schools blame this person. When we put somebody up on a pedestal they are bound to fall at some point. This happens in all fields. It is scary for most of us to admit to our own fears, and thus we try to repress them and pretend they don't exist. It's easier to project our expectations onto others and judge people around us who are expressing the emotions we can't or won't express.

Have you ever noticed that people will turn their back on a losing team they used to cheer for, and focus instead on a team that is winning? Someone who likes you today might not be there tomorrow. It is easy to have fans that love you when you are doing well. It makes them feel like they accomplished the wins with you, and thus they feel good. But if you are suffering, they might get uncomfortable with their own pain and then avoid you.

When Things Happen Easily

Even when things are going well, we can feel stress. Sometimes, we worry that if we actually feel satisfied, we won't continue to work hard, that we will become less motivated. We get attached to trying to feel some level of pain. If we're not striving to be the best, we might worry about being a failure. Actually, when we allow ourselves to feel good about our achievements, we build our confidence and enhance our energy, which allows us to try new things. We approach life from a place of pleasure rather than punishment, acting out of hope and curiosity rather than fear.

Judgment and Need For Approval

Everyone has worried about how others perceive them. We might have assumed that other people notice our every fault or flaw or imperfection and judge us accordingly. But it's usually not true. Everyone is so caught up in themselves and how they're being perceived, they're rarely paying much attention to anyone else. When we worry less about what other people think, we begin to let go of the judgments we place on ourselves. And gradually, we realize that we are okay just as we are.

The Roles We Play

We tend to view life through a filtered lens, which limits our perception, causing its own version of stress. One way we have cloudy vision is by merely seeing ourselves through the roles that we play. If we have defined ourselves as someone who feels important in our job, sport, or family, and then we lose that role (perhaps from layoffs, retirement, divorce, injury, or illness), we might have a hard time knowing who we are. We may have spent the majority of our life working to be a manager, CEO, lawyer, doctor, teacher, coach, astronaut, painter, mother, or athlete. When we lose that title, that defining role, or if we face another life-altering change such as a chronic illness, it feels like a mini death. We might feel like a "nobody" when this happens. We might have overachieved to please others and conformed to be loved. And now there is an emptiness left from the void of that outside approval.

Suffering also occurs when we pretend to be somebody we're not in order to be loved, to fit in, or to appear better than others. If we listen to how we feel and know that acting a certain way doesn't feel right, we can change what we are doing and start trying to live a more authentic life. But if we ignore it, we might act out our frustration in other ways, or look for a quick fix to alleviate our suffering. We might take out our anger on a family member, or become withdrawn and sullen. We would rather be numb, or fight to hold onto a false persona that makes us feel accepted by others, than admit what we're doing and strive to be true to ourselves.

Roles represent different things that we do and how we express ourselves, but they can never fully define *us*. So how can we look to our truest, deepest self and discover the path that will lead to deep, fulfilling contentment?

It is when we let go that we can finally heal, feel lighter, and be happier. I knew I needed to stop swimming, but I was afraid of the alternative, so I tried to keep going even as my body shut down. If we hold on to habits that no longer work, we suffer. If we can take the leap, let go, and pursue what really makes us happy inside, we can flourish.

You Can Relieve Stress

In Chapters Nine and Ten, you will learn how to become less attached, suffer less, and be more than the roles that define you. As you release external definitions and expectations, they will shed their stronghold on you. By acknowledging and facing the deepest, most repressed parts of yourself and bringing them up to the light, their dark power dissipates. You find compassion for the repressed parts of yourself that you created at some point in your life to help you survive. Honor your mistakes and learn from them.

When you learn to listen within, shed unnecessary stress, and use your own "toolbox" of affirmations and exercises, you begin to trust yourself and feel good, while maximizing your potential. You can accept yourself, feel calm, and trust in an innate wisdom that guides you to accomplish miraculous things.

Awareness Tools and Exercises

The following tools will help you become more aware, and decrease the stress in your life. When you feel internal or external pressure that creates feelings of conflict, anxiety, or fear, you no longer function effectively. Stress is often caused by change or loss. But it can have a beneficial effect when you are paying attention, by enhancing your ability to persevere and believe in yourself. You can learn more about your motivations, and recognize when something is not working.

Stress can be as simple as: I am not perfect. I have no money. I made a mistake. I hit someone. I am worried about my kid's behavior. I have too many commitments. Here are some strategies to deal with stress: Talk about it. Take care of yourself through treatments such as acupuncture or massage, martial arts, meditation, exercise, breathing, and emotional healing. Formulate strategies to be your best, and prioritize what you want in life. (The book will continue to cover this.)

Get out your notebook/journal and delve into the following statements and questions. The first step toward change is to be aware. Identify what is bothering you, such as too little time, not balancing work and family, dealing with health concerns, or facing money issues. What is your body telling you? Do you have any physical symptoms, such as a tight neck and shoulders or an upset stomach? What are your emotions about this situation? Anger, sadness, fear? How are you handling stress? Overeating? Smoking? Drinking too much?

What happened? Did someone get mad at you? How did you react? What feelings came up? What is within your power to change? (Remember to not let circumstances stop you.) What can you do to manage the stress? Keep it in perspective. Talk to yourself, or seek help. Exercise, relax, do something fun. Communicate. Manage your time. Set limits so you have balance.

What can you learn from this? Be guided from your inner wisdom. Set simple goals to manage your energy. Reward yourself when you do something to take care of yourself. Rely on a support system. Delegate to help you get things done. Have a proper balance of fun time and work time. Ask yourself if you have enough time for what is important to you. If not, reprioritize your time.

Do a reality check: What is the worst that could happen, and what is the best that could happen? How does it feel to say it out loud/write it down? Be willing to adjust; bend like a tree branch in the wind. If you don't, you will break. Remain open to change. Let yourself get energized again. Be willing. Feel lighter and free by doing something you love.

Chapter Seven

Bedridden: Existing in the Unknown

We are all faced with a series of great opportunities disguised as unsolvable problems.

– John Gardner

Screaming surrounded me, and yet I could not hear it. My body screamed, not my voice: *Stop! I can't take any more pain!* Even though I knew I was not feeling well, I was afraid to take the plunge and change what I was doing. I denied the truth and kept pushing.

In my personal journey, I feared listening to my body. I chose some unhealthy options to keep my illusion of good health going. I was afraid to stop and listen. I did not want to know the truth. I was too scared.

Freezing cold while sweating, I lay down on the examining table in yet another doctor's office, similar to the dozen or more I had seen since my first mononucleosis outbreak seven years earlier. A fully bearded, twinkly-eyed man walked into the room, wearing a white physician's coat. As much as I hoped that he would be the one to understand how I was feeling, I knew the odds were against me. General physicians, endocrinologists, blood specialists, optometrists, infectious disease doctors, and neurologists had all acted as if, out of their own frustration, it was best to give me curt responses such as "just quit swimming" or "take this pill." The standard response was to put me on more antibiotics, even though I did not have a bacterial infection, causing my already weakened immune system to plummet even further.

I prayed that this time would be different. As I lay there, the day after the 1993 NCAA Division I College National Championships, I hoped that this doctor might be able to give me some new test that had not been performed yet, that there would be a simple explanation for all of these crazy symptoms, and that I would miraculously get well. Unfortunately, that was not the case.

"What are you going to do with yourself now that you can't be physically active?" Dr. Coomes asked.

His words ripped through my heart.

I cried inside, still clinging to the hope that my solidly tough mind could get my health back.

At the end of my visit, Dr. Coomes (who practiced in Minnesota) referred me to Dr. Helms, a physician in Berkeley who was a pioneer in acupuncture. When I arrived at Dr. Helms's cozy office I immediately felt at home. The walls were full of colorful murals, the ceiling was painted like a sky, and the bathroom wall was plastered with papers sharing stories and humorous facts. Each decorated room had a distinct personality.

Although Dr. Helms looked like a conservative doctor with his white coat on, I would soon learn that he was much more than that. His office was not a standard sterile doctor's office, and he was no ordinary doctor. When I told Dr. Helms what the other doctors had said, he laughed. He had created the American Academy for Medical Acupuncture and had started teaching acupuncture to physicians who came to take his courses from around the world. Mine was not the first case in which a patient had not received the proper help (or even a correct diagnosis) due to a traditional physician's inability to understand and treat their issues.

Dr. Helms methodically asked about my health history and what symptoms I was experiencing. He checked my pulses on my wrists and looked at my tongue to determine what was going on with me internally. After ruling out many other possibilities, he finally diagnosed me with Chronic Fatigue Immune Dysfunction Syndrome (CFIDS), also known as Chronic Fatigue Syndrome (CFS).

The symptoms of CFIDS are varied and debilitating, and there is no known cure. My crazy array of symptoms had affected my whole self. For the past few years, I had felt like a different person, like I was living a nightmare. As I felt more out of control, I began to lose confidence in myself. I regularly experienced incapacitating fatigue, flulike symptoms (fever, nausea, sore throat, swollen head/eyes), severe pain in my joints and muscles, headaches, dizziness, dry flaking skin, thinning hair, aching teeth (including a couple that fell out), loss of feeling in my arms, an inability to think clearly or remember basic facts, and insomnia. My body bloated as my organs shut down.

Even though Dr. Helms admitted there was no known cure for CFIDS, he said he would do his best to take care of me. He was the first physician who made me believe that I could get well. I felt a huge burden lifted off my shoulders, just knowing that someone understood me. I was not crazy, and I didn't have to handle this alone.

Even though I now knew I had CFIDS, there were still many unknowns. I did not know when I might feel good for a few moments in a day. Sometimes I was unable to move or do anything that I had been used to doing. When would I get well, or could I? Exactly what caused me to feel this way? Sometimes I would drive myself crazy trying to figure it out—was it what I ate, my emotions, or was my health beyond my control? It killed me to not know. I wanted to reach for something to numb myself but I didn't even have the energy to distract myself anymore.

My life was coming apart in every possible way. For the past two years I had been living with little control. I had tried to prove to myself that I was fine and not let anyone else (including myself) know that I really wasn't. As I started to finally acknowledge that I was not okay, that I had serious health issues to deal with, a new reality set in and a deeper despair hit on all levels. I was no longer fighting to stay afloat. I felt like I was drowning.

That spring, I spent days and weeks just lying in bed. Swimming had been my life, but I couldn't imagine racing, or even training anymore. It was hard enough to simply get out of bed. Right before I saw Dr. Coomes, I had just finished the 1993 college season, during which I would have to sleep the two days before a meet in order to have a chance of performing. I would muster up enough strength to barely survive through the unbearable pain, even though I had always been known as someone with an incredibly high pain threshold. After the competition, I would be back in bed for days. Amazingly, I could still race, but not up to my typical standards. I knew something was seriously wrong.

During these mentally foggy days in my final Cal Berkeley swim season, I kept reflecting on how I had attempted to fake some energy over the past year as I tried to motivate the team and, therefore, myself.

*****

It was the fall of 1992 and that time of day for me to head to the pool for our mid-afternoon workout. I said to myself, "Come on, Trina, let's get the team excited." This became my daily routine, starting the practice with the girls on the pool deck, stretching, and getting psyched up.

I'd ride my blue Nishiki mountain bike to the pool and park it at the bike rack. Then I'd walk into the aquatics area, seeing the beautiful, clean blue water in the pool. In the hallway to our locker room, Teri McKeever, our new college coach, had created a great bulletin board of press articles and team pictures, celebrating our fun times (My former Cal coach, Karen, had retired due to personal reasons.). I loved how Teri focused on team bonding, and I felt responsible for helping to enhance this team energy.

I'd take a deep breath and say to myself, "Okay, time to be 'on' for the team." I'd walk into the brightly lit, blue-carpeted locker room; go to my locker to get changed; grab my goggles, Cal cap, and swim gear; and head out to the pool deck.

This became my routine.

"Hey everyone, how was your day so far?" I would ask with a big smile on my face. "Are you ready for some fun?!" I loved to rally the team and get everyone's energy moving. "Let's start with this stretch," I'd say as I demonstrated it. Then I'd ask someone to lead us with another stretch. I'd do this for about five minutes before each practice. Sometimes I started a cheer to help motivate everyone to rise to the occasion on that day. By getting the other swimmers excited to be at practice, I also felt more ready, as I received the positive energy generated within the team.

After practice, when I was back in my own room in my apartment, I'd let my guard down, collapse into bed, and wonder when this pain would end.

*****

Although I kept pretending that I was fine with my teammates, I finally told a couple of my closest friends how I felt. They told me it was important that I talk to Teri and tell her how I was *really* feeling. I knew she cared about me and the team and that she wanted what was best for all of us. Yet, I was scared. I knew her transition to a new coaching job had been tough for her. I did not want to hurt her, and I also wished I could train as I had in the past, but my body screamed "no."

I had already done things that I never imagined I would do. I copped out of many dry-land sessions and runs. I took caffeine pills to stay awake, and I numbed myself with ibuprofen in order to get through a race. But I couldn't do it anymore. How was Teri going to respond?

It was mid-January in 1993, and we were on our training trip. I talked myself through each arm stroke and each length in the pool, not knowing how many more I could take. Teri pulled me out of the pool and asked if I was okay.

"I'm not sure," I said.

Teri knew I had not been well the past fall, but she still gasped a quick breath. "Are you going to quit?"

Part of me wanted to swim, but I had been suffering intolerable pain for too long. "You know I haven't been able to properly train these past few months. I keep trying different ways to gear myself up for practices, but I don't know if I can make it through another two months. Something has to change," I said.

"Do you think you can get through the meet season?"

"I want to. I just don't know if I can."

We talked further, and we agreed that I would do one practice during the week and then rest until I raced at the dual meets, Conference Pac-10s, and NCAA Championships on their respective weekends. But a couple months later, I was finished. I had been seeing Dr. Helms twice a week, trying to get healthy. I also had been told, and knew, that CFIDS was not something that disappears overnight. I had to tell my teammates and Teri that I couldn't swim anymore. I'd been team captain as a junior, and the underclassmen looked up to me. I had been a major shoulder for Teri to lean on. At the time, she was a new, nervous coach at a top NCAA school. I knew she relied heavily on me, not only for my swimming performances, but also as someone to confide in. I had tried my best to empower her confidence in her coaching abilities. But now I needed to focus on myself.

Instead of motivating everyone around me, I was the one who needed help. I felt guilty not being able to do my part, and I felt responsible to others, yet I knew that I could not be there for the team and the coach anymore. I had already given beyond what I could, and it was time to attend to my own needs for a while.

In my journal from around this time, I wrote:

> *I feel tension between Teri and me, which is disconcerting. I feel like I gave so much to the team for three years and now I am lost. Swimming was my life and now it is all uncertain, and it's uncomfortable for me to be around the team. I feel like, since I am sick, I do not belong on the team. I am nervous about what is going to happen next year. What if I lose my scholarship over this?*

> *I am frustrated. I can't swim. I can't participate in many things. I have lost my health and the life I had, and I don't know how I'll feel in a year. I am scared that if I try again, I will relapse. I can't go through all of this again.*

I didn't swim that spring, but Teri and I spoke on several occasions. Sometimes we met for lunch. She would share how the team was doing and how she was trying out new things. She listened as I talked about my journey of seeing health professionals. And eventually she asked me about swimming and being captain the next year. "The team really misses you, and we need you," she said. There was a slight pause as I shifted in my chair. She continued, "You look healthy. Do you think you will be able to swim by next fall? Do you want to be captain again?" As she told me how much I was needed and that I looked healthier, I felt a heavy burden. I knew Teri was more compassionate and understanding than most coaches, but I still had a hard time expressing my needs to her. I felt like she didn't want to admit how sick I had been this past year. Now she wanted me to swim again. I didn't know if I *could*.

During this time, I went to the pool to watch the swimmers train a few times. Even though the sun was shining and it was about seventy-five degrees outside, I bundled up in a sweatshirt and sweatpants to stay warm. And even though I ate more than before, I went from being overweight to rapidly emaciated, as my wounded body cannibalized itself trying to heal. In a daze, I watched my old teammates train. I associated that with another life. I was no longer in that place, but not in a new one yet, either.

I felt alone and isolated, with so many unknowns. Besides my body fighting to get well, my mind was also fuzzy. In school, I went to the Learning Disability Center. Over the past two years, it had been hard for me to focus, read, listen, and study. I experienced severe headaches and flulike symptoms constantly, and I was extremely exhausted. When I tried to study in the Cal Berkeley libraries, I felt nauseous and could not stay focused on what I was reading. The lights made everything appear to move. As I stood up to move around, I felt off balance, sometimes even bumping into walls.

I had to accept the fact that I could no longer think and reason like before. I took some tests to determine my abilities, and based on the results I had literally become mentally disabled. My immune system was so shot that it took all my energy to try to focus for even a brief amount of time. I was now given extra time to take tests, so I could complete my classes. Even though I was embarrassed and sad about my situation, I was relieved and proud of myself for taking this big step of asking for help. I had been trying to get by on my own, and now I was finally willing to try every option that might help me function.

I pulled away from the typical fun life of a college gal in many respects. I no longer socialized, because I didn't have the energy, and I realized that it no longer served me to fake it. I moved out of my apartment, where I had lived with two other swimmers and a diver, into a place in the Berkeley hills, where it was easier to rest. My mother and brother Earl came out to help me move because I could hardly do anything myself. When they arrived, they couldn't believe that I had not begun to pack. I was simply unable to. They packed my things, and we managed to get my belongings into a U-Haul and up the winding road that led to my new home.

I was lucky enough to rent a room in a house owned by the men's assistant swimming coach. My new roommates were nice, quiet grad students. From my bedroom, I had a view of the Golden Gate Bridge, and out our backdoor were peaceful running trails that meandered through the woods. This became my new sanctuary, as I began to focus on getting better.

After a few weeks in my new surroundings, summer arrived. I spent a couple weeks at my father's home in Iowa, where he had lived since I graduated high school. I loved being among the cornfields and the quietness of farm country. I also enjoyed being with my dad, even though I was so sick.

During this time in Iowa, I remember getting the most painful menstrual cycle that I had ever experienced, multiplied by all of the other symptoms. I just wanted to leave my body. *I don't know if I can take this anymore,* I thought.

I had been known for handling extreme levels of pain in athletics, but I would have taken *any* physical challenge that I had endured over *this*. I perspired profusely, and I cried and screamed at the same time. Luckily, my father was at work. I didn't want anyone to know how much pain I was in. I barely acknowledged it myself.

I doubled over as the arthritic pain in my hips, knees, and lower back intensified. My arms were numb. I had severe abdominal and rectal pain, and I couldn't imagine ever wanting to be sexual again. My head throbbed and felt like a big bowling ball. I tried to move, then stay still, just trying to do something to decrease my pain. I went to the toilet to see if I could release, to alleviate the intensity. When that didn't work, I laid down in bed, first flat on my back, then on my side, and then finally in a fetal position as I prayed for the pain to subside.

After hours of severe pain, I wondered why this was happening to me. Maybe I deserved to be punished. I cried, wondering why I believed such a thought. I tried to visualize being well…but that didn't work, either. I tried to let go of the control. It was as if I were crying for my life—making up for all the times I had pretended that I was fine when I wasn't. I tried to recall what I did the last time I had felt this much pain. Did I take a certain herb to alleviate it and, if so, when was the best time to take it? Should I take a shower, write in my journal, or move a certain way? It might not work, but I felt desperate to try anything.

I cried because I truly missed swimming. I missed being in the calm waves of the water, and I was sad that I couldn't swim even a few simple laps. I wanted to dive in and have that amazing feeling of being connected with the water and racing at top speed. I loved anything that involved moving my body—swimming, running, pumping iron. Exercise had been my life, and now it was gone, just like that.

In the midst of all these emotions, I also had moments of revelation. All the pain and crying over the past year seemed like a rebirth, a new beginning. It was during this time that I learned that nothing lasts forever. This, too, would pass. I would be okay. In fact, I learned that I *was* okay, even as I experienced some of the worst pain of my life.

My dad had hoped that while I was visiting him in Iowa, I could accompany him on a trip to Russia. He was going there for work, and he wanted me to be his translator, since I spoke fluent Russian. As much as I wanted to go, I just knew there was no way I'd have the energy.

When my dad came home from work one day, I gave him a letter I had written.

"What's this?" he asked.

"I need to talk to you about going to Russia, and I don't know how to express it, so I decided to write it down."

He sat down at the dining room table and read the letter. I waited quietly on the living room couch for his response. I felt like a little girl, wondering what my daddy was going to say.

Finally, after what seemed like an eternity, he finished. He came over to me with tears in his eyes, as if he had hurt *me*. I could tell that he was concerned about what I had written, which included many things about how I had been feeling. He had no idea how sick I had been.

My eyes welled up with tears as I said, "Dad, I am so sorry I can't go with you to Russia. I dreamed of being able to do something like this for you, and I feel like I have let you down."

"Trina, I know." He paused with a sigh. "I know you haven't been well, and you need to get healthy."

We talked more, and then he hugged me and told me he was proud of me and that he loved me. "I love you too, Dad," I said.

After visiting my dad, I returned to Cal and got into a regular routine. My weekly outings consisted of seeing Dr. Helms and maybe talking to a friend or two on the phone, or perhaps having a friend visit me. Before getting sick, I had loved to socialize and bring people together. Now, even talking took a lot out of me. I had to carefully manage my time with others and how I spent my energy.

I now doubled my already intense focus in an attempt to regain my health. I paid attention to what made me feel good. If I had strong emotions, I had to let them go. I could no longer just swim them off. I had to choose whether to deal with them, write about them, exhale them out of me, or let them exhaust me. With my immune system so shot, I often chose to accept my feelings rather than expend energy to repress them. Now I could let them go...and feel better.

Additionally, my eating changed. I had always focused on giving my body fuel, but now I discovered a new purpose for nutrition. I met with a nutritionist, who gave me information and options. The first thing I did was cut out dairy, sugar, wheat, coffee, and alcohol. Ironically, even though I was not training, I was eating more as my body desperately tried to heal. I learned from whole-food experts about the medicinal power of food. When my mind was able, I read everything possible, hoping to find out what could rejuvenate me.

I noticed that if I did not eat enough, or ate too much, I would be wiped out. Or if I mixed certain foods, I felt a certain way. Each morning, I swallowed five small Sun Chlorella green pills that lay on my bedside table. Fifteen minutes later, I summoned enough energy to get up, go to the bathroom, and make it to the kitchen, where I prepared weird concoctions to drink and took various nutritional supplements.

As I made changes to feel better, my curiosity got the better of me. Although I was committed to my new routine, I desperately wanted my old life back. Dr. Coomes's voice still echoed in my head. Could I ever be physically active again? I didn't know but I wanted to try. Could I do something, *anything*, and be okay? It became like a game for me. In my last few years of swimming, I justified that if I could perform well, then I must be okay. Similarly, as I immersed myself into getting well, I developed some silly beliefs. If I could swim a length of the pool and not get wiped out right away, then I must be 100% better, or at least getting close.

All these years, the pool had been my playground and the water, my playmate. I just wanted to get a small dose. I could tell how I felt when I swam, more than at any other time. I would get in and do one length, to feel my toes and feet loosen up as I propelled myself by kicking on top of the surface, or playing like a dolphin underneath.

But every time I did this, I ended up back in bed. It was hard for me to comprehend. How could one easy length of the pool incapacitate me for days? I had been used to training thirty or more hours per week. The pool had been my source of peace and joy, where I could constantly be on the move; but now it seemed lifeless, as did I.

Every time I pretended I was healthy, I got a clear message to the contrary. Up until then, I believed that anything was possible, or if it wasn't, that I could make it possible. I had yet to learn that I was human, and that even though years of testing my abilities had its merit, I also had to learn to respect my rapidly encroaching limits.

During this late spring and summer of 1993, I tried to apply my mental focus to regain my health. I decided, "I will fully immerse myself in being healthy. Then, in two or three months, I'll be back to normal."

But that time came and went, and I realized that the power of my mind wasn't working like it had before. I had hoped that by the end of the summer I would be well. Instead, I felt like nothing had changed. I was still lying in bed, unable to get up and unable to sleep, and my aching body did not want to move. I did not know what tricks life was playing on me or how long they were going to last. I wasn't sure if these feelings would end, or if I would be like this forever.

By early fall, I was not any better. Even though I had lessened my courses to half a normal load, and I hadn't been swimming for months, I didn't know if I could stay in school. I couldn't concentrate in class. In fact, just getting there took a lot out of me.

I wrote in my journal:

> *It is 7 p.m., I am exhausted, have a fever, and my throat is swollen shut and hurts. I am frustrated. I had to rest all day and didn't want to, and I don't feel any better. I feel like a wreck. I had to miss classes today, which I am upset about, but I must have health before I can do anything else. I just want a moment of feeling alert and alive. I can't worry about missing classes even though I never would have considered missing a class in my life! I get to ask for support and get notes from others. I can do this.*

Several months back, Dr. Helms had signed a form for me to take to the Department of Motor Vehicles so I could start using disabled parking. Was it time for me to heed his advice? I stared at the form, not sure if I wanted to go through with it. Yet, I'd had just about enough. I could not function in class anymore, and even though I drove my truck to get there, I still had to walk from the road to the buildings, and my fatigue was unbearable.

I went to the DMV in southern Berkeley. The woman at the counter took my application, looked at my driver's license, filled out another form, stamped it, then went and got a blue disabled placard. When she handed it to me, I thought, "Wow, that was easy."

Now, would I be willing to use it?

The first time was the hardest. At age twenty-two, I resorted to using disabled parking so I could stop staring at the four walls in my bedroom and get some fresh air. In my head, I thanked my physician and the DMV lady for making it easy for me. I was no longer chained to my bed, and I could move around, maybe not by using my body, but at least my car. Initially, I didn't want anyone who might know me to see me using a disabled spot. But over time I appreciated having the option and didn't care who saw me. I was able to drive right up to buildings and park, then walk into my classroom. Of course, my friends enjoyed getting a ride, too. Overall, it saved me a lot of heartache and energy.

Yet, I still had uncomfortable moments, too. One in particular stands out. I had parked my truck in a handicapped spot at Cal Berkeley. As I leaned over to the passenger seat to gather my belongings, I heard a knock on my window. Startled, I saw a street person pressing his head up against my window. My heart raced. I rationalized that he must want some change. I rolled down my window.

"Ma'am, do you know that you are parking in a disabled parking spot?" he asked.

Initially a wave of guilt came over me. After all, I didn't look disabled. I didn't have a wheelchair, or a broken leg, or a disease that defined my condition. I still looked like a strong world-class athlete.

I wanted to get out of the car and limp or walk funny so that my disability would seem more real. I wanted to have a cast on my leg or an ailment that was more obvious, or more explainable and treatable than CFIDS. Instead, I did what I had become accustomed to doing. I got out of the car, shook out my aching joints, and walked slowly to where I was going. I just smiled and waved to the man as I passed by.

As I started using my disabled parking permit on a regular basis, I realized that my swimming career was likely over for good. I focused on getting healthy enough to function like a normal person. I wasn't sure what that meant, but it sounded better than the way I was living now.

Existing in this empty, mysterious unknown was a challenge. I hoped that my new identity would emerge soon. After all, I had spent my life on the go and now I could barely walk. Forced to stop the life I once knew, I had to relearn who I was, what I wanted, and what I could do.

Could I ever accept this?

PART THREE
TAKING CARE OF YOURSELF

Chapter Eight

You Are Okay: Accept Your Life and Feel Good No Matter What

"It's only after we've lost everything that we're free to do anything."
– Brad Pitt, in the movie Fight Club

I had experienced triumphant glory and devastating loss by the age of 22. In one respect, when I got sick everything I knew was taken from me. Yet, I ultimately regained my true self. It was like a death and rebirth. I began to *know* that I was okay no matter how bad my health was. As I let go of my attachments to my former athletic life and learned to live with being sick, I understood, on a deeper level, how all expectations (other people's and my own) could not stop me from listening to my heart. By being naked, with no energy, and no more need to hide my true self, I was free. My young, spirited, innocent child inside was re-emerging, and I knew I was okay just as I was. I could be me again.

Even in the midst of struggle and hard times, it is crucial to stay centered and know what makes you feel happy. Appreciate what you have and who you are. Even if you have lost a job, a home, or a relationship, you are alive. Sometimes it's important to just focus on that. You can still be who you are meant to be.

It is easy to judge ourselves; we tend to be our own worst critics, and it is easy to feel alone and misunderstood. The best thing we can do to initiate change is to love and appreciate who we are now. We can begin by accepting where we have come from, regardless of the circumstances.

When I was bedridden with CFIDS, I learned humility and acceptance in a new way. Even though I was in bed, unable to do much, I slowly began to appreciate myself and accept where I was, to live in each moment. During this time, I was renting a room from the men's assistant swimming coach, who had a home in the Berkeley Hills. Out our backdoor were the Berkeley running trails, surrounded by beautiful woods. I could go for walks, enjoy the fresh air, and see a meandering creek that wandered down the hill. I often encountered deer and other animals. And from my bed I could see one of the most beautiful scenes in the world: the Golden Gate Bridge and San Francisco. As I witnessed a glorious sunset one evening, I wrote in my journal:

> *Even though my body feels broken, my spirit feels so alive. I just want to cry. I love feeling this way. As I write, I look out my bedroom window and marvel at God's creations. From my bed, I see the Golden Gate Bridge, the shimmering water, San Francisco, and the most amazing sunset. The sky is full of reds, oranges, purples, and yellow as the sun sets over the Golden Gate Bridge. Wow—words cannot describe this beauty that I see. Majestic! Then, there are the people who created this bridge and this city that people from all over the world come to see. Life is a miracle. Even when my body feels so dead, my spirit can still be free.*

I began to have a new kind of courage in handling adversity. I started to see my power and beauty, to appreciate my successes, and to realize how lucky I was. For once, I became immersed in taking care of *myself* rather than everyone else. I began to accept that I could live with my health issues, even if they lasted forever.

We are okay just as we are. We don't have to try harder, be better, or even be healthy to be okay. I realized that I could be in bed all day, sick, and still be worthy. We are complete *right now*. When we forgive our past mistakes, we can accept where we are in our life. If we feel stuck, it is merely a sign that we need to make some positive changes. Change starts when we can accept ourselves within. By taking responsibility for our past and who we are now, we become empowered. There is so much to be thankful for when we realize how resilient and strong we have been in our lives. In these times of illness or transition, we realize these moments of crisis give us opportunities.

When we can come to peace with whatever is going on around us and within us, we begin a powerful healing process. By surrendering, I spent less energy trying to fix myself, or get myself well. It doesn't mean that I was weak. Instead, by surrendering, I tapped into my deepest source of power.

How do we do this? We let go of control, we trust, we see humor in our mistakes along the way. We have compassion for every part of ourselves—our mean side, the part of us that constantly wants, the one who judges, the part that sometimes feels selfish and unsatisfied. It is okay to not be perfect. Recognizing that is a huge step in releasing stress.

I had to learn to accept that I was sick and that it might be a long time, if ever, before I felt healthy again. When we go through a big transition, we might feel nervous because we do not know what our new role might be. But should the role be what we are looking for? It is most important to get back in touch with ourselves, to explore what truly makes us happy.

Go to Your Happy Place

The more you can relax into your "happy place," the more you can attract what you want into your life. How does this work? There is an electromagnetic energy field that surrounds your physical body. This energy vibrates at various frequencies and gives off different colors, and it affects you and others around you. You can use this energy to attract experiences and things into your life. You literally can alter the energy field, which has a frequency around your body. In doing so, you attract the frequencies related to your desires. Studies have demonstrated that when you train yourself to feel good on a regular basis, you are more optimistic, have higher confidence, and cope with stress better. By altering your mood, you can influence your genetic expression, too!

A variety of studies have demonstrated these ideas, including Dr. Masaru Emoto's research on water, and ones done on plants. In Dr. Emoto's water crystal experiments, he exposed water to different words, pictures, and music to study the change in the crystals, using microscopic photography. Similar studies have been done on other living organisms.

Thoughts and feelings affect physical reality. Water, like plants (and all living things), can be altered based on the energetic frequencies around it. When we say words or feel a certain way around a living organism (humans, plants, animals, and even water), the being responds to the frequencies given off from these words and emotions. Let's take three plants as an example. One is given a lot of love and positive attention. It is talked to every day and showered with praise. This plant will thrive. The second one is given a lot of negative attention, told that it is not doing well, that it is not liked. This plant will struggle. The third one is ignored, and it withers.

This is exactly the same in households, schools, and work. A child would rather act out and get into trouble, and at least get *some* attention—even if it's negative—rather than not be noticed at all. Similarly, many institutions, teams, schools, and families *believe* they have to treat people poorly, and put them into a state of fear, to get them to work or perform. This can get results, but not to the degree that receiving love can. And this only sets up our world to have more and more people who are not truly happy inside.

Children who grew up receiving a lot of critical, negative attention are often uncomfortable receiving praise and love and might not know how to respond to it, initially. They have to get used to being allowed to feel good, to know that they are worthy and deserving—not because of any achievement, but because they exist! Once they fully understand this, both emotionally and intellectually, they will open themselves up to receive love, and they will be motivated from a place of love rather than from fear or ignorance.

Be Present

So how do you get to your happy place? One simple way to start feeling happy is to be in the moment. Do you ever remember racing with a friend to the swing set, to see who could get there first? You might have been laughing along the way, enjoying the pursuit while having fun with your friend. In some ways, you didn't care who got to the swing first. You just enjoyed going for it and weren't thinking about anything else at the time.

This is our ultimate goal. The more we can live from this place—*this moment*—the more we will see amazing miracles show up for us. If we don't enjoy each moment, if we're always focused on the past or the future, we won't fully appreciate our blessings.

You can start "living in the moment" right now. What do you see, hear, feel, taste, smell, and touch/sense? Be fully aware of your senses and your surroundings. Practice doing this at various times throughout the day. Stop, be aware, and pay attention.

Say I am walking in the rain. I look up in the sky. I see a light-blue hue with white puffy clouds moving in the breeze, as I feel the lightness of a cool rain-drop on my skin. I walk through puddles, feeling the warmth of the summer air, followed by a nice cool breeze, as the rain trickles down on me.

When we begin to focus on the feelings and sensations we are feeling in the moment, we start to fully appreciate who we are, what we are doing, and the miracles of life. We feel more connected to the world around us, and we start seeing (and feeling) things in a new way. It's wonderful!

If it's hard to feel happy in your current circumstances, imagine a time in the past when you felt good, contented, joyful. Remember the situation and the sensations you were feeling. Imagine that moment as though it was hap-pening right now. By pretending that a past happy event is happening in the present, our body takes it in and feels it as though it is happening now. We can re-create those positive sensations and begin to move forward, rather than feeling stuck in a place of negativity, pain, and hopelessness. We don't have to hope that we will feel good some day. With practice, your mind and body will start to believe that positive experiences and feelings are happen-ing NOW—and they will be!

What Do You Want?

Focus on what makes you feel happy. It might be something tangible and obvious—a big purchase you made or something you earned. It is okay to want those things—you deserve them. Or you might feel happy when you think about your spouse, your children, or a good friend. What is *not* cur-rently in your life that would make you feel happy if you had it? A new car? More time? Nice clothes? A fulfilling relationship? Better health? By allow-ing yourself to feel happy *now*, you open yourself up to manifesting the very things you don't have yet. By changing your internal world, you will change your external world, too.

Know that you have the power and ability to heal yourself much more than you give yourself credit for. After all, you are much more than just your body. You are part of the world's mass consciousness, and you can tap into this higher level of energy. A problem, negative attitude, or illness has its own frequency. In order to heal or to solve a problem, it is best to do so from another frequency. The more you allow yourself to take on a new positive frequency, the more you will attract happiness and good health into your life.

Change Your Outside to Change Your Inside

When you smile, you get out of your head and move into your heart. You change your physiology, which alters your emotions. It's a quick way to change how you feel. You might notice resistance to wanting to feel good. Do it anyway.

One simple way to begin feeling better is to change how you sit, stand, or walk. In general, when you feel depressed or not so good about yourself, you tend to walk with slumped shoulders and downcast eyes. If you look at the ground, you are more likely to feel sad and uncertain than if you walk with confidence, looking upward, your body relaxed yet straight. If you are slouching and frowning, you do not generate much energy. How you walk can alter your mood. If you want to feel better, stand up tall, put a smile on your face, and relax your shoulders. It only takes about sixteen seconds to change your energy state, which can then last for hours.

Let's say you are nervous before giving a big presentation at a meeting. You might get caught up in future expectations of yourself or focus on a time in the past when you made a mistake—either way, you will feel stressed, and it will show in your body. Be aware of yourself, and then shift into a more confident position, even if you are not actually feeling confident. Think about how a confident person would feel, act, believe, and move. By changing your physical posture, you will start to embody the feelings associated with this, too. And this will bring you into the moment so you can perform at your best.

Smile High Exercise

Another way to get an "instant fix" is to do this Smile High exercise. By looking up to the sky and smiling, you change your physiology immediately. Firmly plant your feet on the ground. Stand up straight—get as tall as you can. Then, look up to the sky or ceiling, and put the biggest, silliest grin on your face that you can. Now exaggerate it even more! Yes, it is okay to laugh if that makes you feel good. You might have some emotions come up, or thoughts, like "I feel stupid doing this" or "What if someone is watching me?" Just allow yourself to take in the change in feeling. You should feel better already!

Appreciation and Joy

You might have resistance to feeling good, laughing, and coming out of your shell. This is normal and to be expected if your fun-loving self has been hiding for a while. In order to experience joy regularly, you must first have a *willingness* to stop suffering and to feel good. By doing so, you decrease stuck energy and allow it to flow right out of you. Your second step is to continue on even when you want to resist. One way to do this is to take time each day to appreciate what you have, what you have done, who you are, the people around you, your living space, your work, your school, and so on. Do this daily, even for just a minute. Let feelings of joy come over you as give thanks for people, events, and other blessings in your life. This will keep you open to receiving more joy.

Express gratitude for yourself and the people, teachers, mentors, and supporters who have inspired you. You will feel good doing this, especially if you share this with those who have positively impacted you. Gratitude soothes the soul. Scientific studies show that when you feel appreciation for yourself, others, and your life, you change how your cells operate. You're not just changing your thinking—you're also changing your DNA!

When you allow yourself to feel good, it is hard to also feel bad at the same time. By focusing on the present, you are not lost in the past or future, which is where most of your fears show up.

When you are kind to yourself, you feel free and light. This can be scary if you are not used to it. That is why it is important to practice feeling happy consistently, so it becomes a habit. Eventually, the fear-based voices in your head dissolve, and they can no longer consume your mind. Stress dissolves, and you will feel more positive energy.

What do you appreciate about *you* today? Are you willing to make today a brand-new day? A fresh start? Do you appreciate your life? Friends? Family? Pets? Children? Warm weather? Cool weather? Your work? The abundance of blessings all around you? When you appreciate these things, how do you feel?

When you approach life from this place of contentment and gratitude, you will feel less judgment, anger, and resentment toward your bosses, colleagues, family, friends, competitors, and your own conflicting voices within. You will have more compassion for them, and in turn they will respond differently to you. This allows more possibilities and opportunities to enter your life. You might find it easier now to start your own business, tackle that difficult homework that was giving you trouble, or challenge yourself to try something you have put off until now.

Self-Acceptance

When I was most sick, and doubted who I was, I learned to find peace by looking at a picture of myself as a young girl, radiant and confident in my youth. In doing so, I could remember and reclaim that part of me.

If you don't feel okay right now, you might spend moments, days, and even years trying to fix whatever's "wrong" with you. Yet, even if you do lose the weight, break the record, buy the house, or get the job that you thought would give you a feeling of self-worth, you become disillusioned because that exterior achievement doesn't provide you with a feeling of self-acceptance. So you keep searching for it. But it was always within you and available to you!

How can you become more accepting of yourself? First, you need to take it easy and not demand perfection. Remember, how you judge others is how you judge yourself—though you're usually your own worst critic. You get to realize that you are not crazy, bad, or unworthy, regardless of what others might have told you, or what you have believed in the past. As you learn to forgive yourself, you will find that you also forgive others more easily. In doing so, you will also have more positive energy to share.

Realize your own power and strength. Honor your fear, but take action anyway. With each change, no matter how small, you will begin to realize what you are capable of. Have compassion for yourself as you face life's obstacles. Trust that you are strong and resilient enough to handle all the challenges and adventures that will come your way.

Even as I suffered excruciating pain from CFIDS, I knew I would be okay. Even if the pain lasted forever, I found ultimate peace in this moment. I had to accept this, not knowing when (or if) I would feel good again. I realized my full strength and learned that I can handle much more than I had thought. **Change starts by accepting yourself!** The power is within. You can handle more than you think. When you decide what you want to manifest, and commit to it, you will be energized for the journey.

I have experienced "wanting" even in my healthy days of life. I have experienced peace even when I was most sick. These emotional states were not tied to the circumstances around me. You can let go and find peace in the moment. Tell yourself: I can find my personal best and be okay with me right now.

You are enough, just because you exist. Regardless of what you may have been taught to believe, you are great just the way you are now. You do not need to *do* or *own* something special to "be enough." If you feel unworthy before getting what you want (external validation), you still won't feel worthy after you have it. You will probably feel disappointed and then be upset with yourself for not feeling happier about getting what you wanted! But you were already okay—you just need to believe it. Your needs can be met by nourishing your inner self rather than looking outside for approval and acceptance.

Setbacks and Obstacles

We might think we want to avoid setback and obstacles, but they are what help us to grow. Life's ups and downs give us opportunities. We all make mistakes, but we carry on, and we get to appreciate this about ourselves, too. Humility and awareness help us tap into our true power instead of fooling ourselves (with narcissism and rationalization) by pretending to be "perfect," which is exhausting.

We all experience setbacks—illness, injury, job loss, breakups. How do we overcome them? Mainly, we do not let them define us! Know that you are still great even if you cannot do what you used to do. In sports, if you have been doing well and then have a bad meet, season, or year, you will tend to doubt your abilities, and this can affect your confidence. It is important to stay focused on who you are and what you can control.

When you have a bad day or give a poor performance, it is easy to be hard on yourself. Instead, try to focus on one thing you did well, and see what you can learn from this so you'll do better next time. If you keep your performance detached from your confidence, you will be able to still feel good about who you are, while learning from your mistakes. Remember: Your human value is not based on your performance.

Trust in your abilities. Talk nicely to yourself. Appreciate what is going well for you. If you are chronically ill, injured, or can no longer perform, know that you are still worthy of love. It is normal to go through various emotions, including denial and anger. You might feel depressed and lose hope. Or you might accept the situation. Typically we have a range of emotions, and the key is to know you are still worthy of love even if you cannot perform, regardless of what you are told.

Our performance outcome does not determine who we are. We are beings first, then we do things, then we achieve and have things. Society—and advertising—tries to convince us that if we buy the right product or do something amazing, we will be liked and accepted. But we want to focus on being content with who we are, regardless of what we have or what we do. By living in each moment and exploring what we are capable of, we will be more content and our true selves will shine through.

Self-Affirmations

One way to help you feel worthy is to tell yourself that you are. How you talk to yourself and who you believe you are affects how you play out your life. Don't believe everything you think! Be mindful of how you talk to yourself. Just as standing a certain way affects your mood, how you talk to yourself affects your state of mind.

When you have a negative thought, change it to a positive. Talk to yourself—say something that you are grateful for or something you feel good about. In some ways it helps to "fake it 'til you make it."

When we say something to ourselves, we experience it as if it is real. Get in the habit of saying positive things to yourself. Phrase it as if it already happened. State it in present tense. Here are a few examples: "I allow myself to laugh," "I deserve to experience joy," "I give myself permission to be happy." As you say each self-affirmation, feel it inside of you. Allow yourself to feel good from it. Post your own affirmations on a mirror and say them to your-self every morning.

One affirmation that I like to say, especially when I am getting hard on myself is "I love you" as I look into my own eyes in the mirror. I usually laugh and end up with a big grin on my face—it's hard to be too critical of myself at a time like that!

Love Your Body

You can do this with body parts, too, where you stand naked in front of a mirror. Look from your head to your feet, and notice the feelings that come up about different parts of yourself. What is each one saying to you? What parts of your body do you judge harshly or dislike? Tell each part that you love it. As tension comes up, exhale it out. Try to say to each body part, "I love you." Even if you think your tummy is chubby, love the chub. It is your body. Talk to your tummy. Have a compassionate conversation back and forth. Who knows, maybe you two will come to some agreement!

The more you practice feeling good, the more you *will* feel good. And when you feel good, it is easier to be confident, let go of distractions, and focus on the task at hand.

Muscle Testing

One way to determine the power of your affirmations is to do muscle test-ing. This is based on kinesiology, the study of human movement, and it can determine what is going on with you physically, spiritually, mentally, and emotionally. Many health care professionals use it.

Your body is an electrical system. Along with your muscles, this system determines if the surrounding and internal energy positively or negatively impacts you. With muscle testing, you can determine what is best for you, and find out whether you are enhancing your health or hindering it.

You can test yourself, or have a partner do it with you. One way to test is to ask a "yes/no" question—start with something simple like, "Is your name ___ (say the person's name)?" If testing with a partner, have the person who is being tested raise one arm out horizontally. The tester then places their hand on the outstretched arm and pushes down as the other partner tries to resist. The arm will remain strong if the answer is "yes" and go weak if the answer is "no." Try a variety of questions or statements, such as, "Is it good for me to do X?" or "Is X better for me than Y?" or "I am ready to do X." You can also hold a food product up to your heart and see if it is best for you to eat it in that given moment. You will know the answer based on whether your body reacts positively or negatively about the things you're asking or stating.

You can also test yourself. There are different ways to do this; one way is to place your third finger on top of your second finger. You ask the question and see if your fingers can remain firm showing a "yes," or if the finger easily falls, which indicates a "no" response.

My husband and I often use muscle testing. It is a way to test if we are strong when making a decision, eating a certain food, or feeling good enough to perform. If we talk negatively to ourselves or try to rationalize feeling a certain way, our body goes weak. But if we talk and feel positively to ourselves, or make a good decision, our body is strong.

Muscle testing shows how much our body and mind work together. They cannot be separated. The body doesn't lie as much as the conscious mind does. It can give answers that are hidden in the subconscious and won't alter them just because our rational mind wants a certain response. Our body gives us answers that our cognitive mind may not even grasp or know yet. Muscle testing illustrates our innate wisdom within, and shows that when listened to, it can guide our lives.

Brag Book

Since I was in the third grade, I have kept a journal of my daily activities. Sometimes, I have written extensively and other times it's been more of a sketch. I have learned that when I write what I appreciate about myself, events in my day, the people in my life, and life in general, I feel better. And when I feel better, I attract a different energy toward myself, compared to when I do not feel as good.

Get a notebook, and start keeping your own "brag book." Commit to writing at least one thing from your day that makes you feel good about yourself.

This might be challenging at first if you are self-critical, if it is hard for you to acknowledge your feelings, or if feeling good makes you uncomfortable. But do it anyway. The biggest obstacle is getting started.

Write down, in as much detail as possible, something that made you feel great. Use all five senses to describe it. For example, "I smelled the humid chlorinated air as I walked out onto the pool deck. I felt at home." You might say, I enjoyed feeling the rain on my back, playing with my cat or dog, I enjoyed the snow, I made my bed even though I normally don't, I ate a healthy breakfast, I brushed my teeth, I spoke up for myself, I got an A on a test, I cleaned out my closet, or I put on some music and enjoyed a bubble bath. It can be anything. There is no right or wrong here. Even the things you take for granted can be appreciated…yes, even your parents, spouse, or competitor!

As you start to do this exercise daily, you will compile a long list of things you appreciate and that make you feel good about yourself. After you write something, allow yourself to *feel* it. You might feel happy, proud, amazing, joyful, or content. Maybe you'll realize how much fun you had doing something. You might believe in yourself more and give yourself praise in a new way. This will allow you to feel more confident, and then you will trust yourself more.

Here are additional ideas for your brag book:

- Write down good things that happen each day—it can be something simple, such as "Someone let me go ahead of them in the grocery line," or "I gave it my best in practice today. I focused on a specific technique. By doing so, I felt _____."

- Relive your own successes so that positive emotions can occur over and over. When we feel good, and surround ourselves with people who support us, we tend to perform better. Who are the people in your life that make you feel good?

- Remember, you create your reality. Change your thoughts. Focus on the positive. Record five things you are thankful for today.

- Sometimes we tell ourselves that a performance will not go well or we are going to have a bad day. When you "know" this, surprise yourself—decide to change it. Write about an event that hasn't happened yet as though you have already done it successfully.

- If you made a mistake or didn't perform as well as you'd hoped to, remind yourself that each event is separate from the next. Just because one did not go as expected does not mean the next will be a failure. Turn a negative into a positive by thinking of it as a learning opportunity. Write down the lessons you learned so you can feel in control of the situation and do better next time.

- Read your brag book. Review what you have written when things have gone well and you felt great about yourself. This will build your confidence.

Magnificence

We often are more afraid of our own magnificence than of our inadequacies. When we allow ourselves to be enlightened and shine, we inspire others, too! We all are truly magnificent. When we honor this about ourselves, we can do amazing things with our gifts.

When I recognize how resilient I am, how I have overcome obstacles, and how I have gotten back on track, I feel vibrant and confident. Today, I encourage you to take a look at your own life—and focus on your magnificence!

Here are a few ways you can feel better about yourself right now:

1. Forgive yourself and others for past mistakes. Have compassion for your human limitations.

2. Write down ten things you love to do, and do one of those things today.

3. When that silly judgmental voice comes up and tells you that you can't be happy and succeed, first listen. Then, tell this voice that you appreciate its use to you in the past, as you may have needed it to survive at the time. But you are in a different place now and no longer need to beat yourself up. You can say good-bye to that voice, since you know that you are worthy and deserve to feel good.

4.   Allow yourself to feel beautiful and in your power. Dress up in clothes that help you feel this way. Walk around with confidence.

5.   Write down what you like to do for fun. Why do you enjoy each activity? What feeling do you get from it? Now go out and do something fun!

6.   If you have a performance (sports or otherwise) coming up, imagine yourself being at your best, feeling great, accomplishing your goals, and then celebrating. You might enjoy lying down, relaxing, and imagining it as if it is happening right now. By doing so, your body assumes it already has happened.

7.   What are you passionate about? What gives you that spark, gets you excited, makes you want to take action? What would happen if you went out and did those things?

8.   If you tend to get caught up in what others think of you, or you worry about competing against someone else in sports, remember to only compare yourself to you. Think about what you need, and focus on doing your best. This will help you live in the moment, which is the best place to perform from, too. You cannot control what others think or do, but you can control how you respond to events and people around you.

9.   APPRECIATE YOU! Write down three things that you appreciate from your day, and *feel* the great feelings that come along with that. When you allow yourself to experience a feeling for more than sixteen seconds, it literally changes your emotional state!

Love Yourself, and Do What You Love

We get to love ourselves even if we are fat, have been raped, were cheated on by someone, or if *we* hurt someone. When we learn to forgive ourselves, and others, we are set free. When we realize that we no longer need to hide our scars or life lessons, and can embrace all of ourselves, we see that we are okay just as we are. When we stop distracting ourselves (criticizing ourselves for something we did "wrong" or somehow staying away from our true self), the truth is revealed. Love is right here. We do not need to seek it elsewhere. We can love everything about ourselves.

When we do not love or accept ourselves, we tend to attract people who prove our beliefs that we are not worthy or capable of love. Or we seek out love in unhealthy ways since we are not giving it to ourselves. On the other hand, when we love ourselves, we attract people who are loving. We all want love, and once we start honoring the love we have within ourselves, we can give love to others. When we realize that there is an abundance for all, we feel good and attract more inspirational energy.

One of my favorite quotes is from Mahatma Gandhi: "Power is of two kinds. One is obtained by the **fear** of punishment and the other by acts of **love**. Power based on love is a thousand times more effective and permanent then the one derived from fear of punishment."

There are two main forces of power: love and fear. Which one do you choose? When you commit to being your best, you are willing to face fear, and to love yourself no matter what. When you choose love, your energy radiates out to others.

In addition to loving yourself, it is important to do what you love. When you follow your heart this way, you have abundant energy as life works with you to be successful, regardless of what obstacles you might encounter. When you realize that life is brief, you listen to your heart and focus on doing what you love.

Chapter Nine

Meditation: Listen and Be Aware

At the center of your being you have the answer;
You know who you are and you know what you want.
– Lao Tzu

Now that you are learning to accept yourself and to believe how much you can accomplish in your life, it is important to take a step back and listen. Are you truly following your deepest desires, or are they somebody else's? Are they dreams that are focused on making you look good, feel secure, be in control, or seem superior to others, at the expense of being happy in the process—or are they dreams that make you feel content inside? As you pursue your dreams, do you feel happy with yourself? Are you taking good care of yourself as you focus on being whom you want to be, doing what you love, and having what you always wanted? Or are you about to explode from the stress that it is all causing?

In order to answer these questions and take proper care of ourselves, it helps to train our minds so that we can attend to our deeper yearnings, intentions, and answers. As we listen, we engage our power within as we come from a place of love, not fear. We discipline ourselves to the process of being present. Then we can make ourselves available to whatever experience arises. The more we learn how to pay attention to ourselves, the more we get beyond the rational mind and awaken to whom we really are. In this place, we can be clear about what *really* motivates us.

Be Aware and Present

Our ultimate goal is to be present. Have you ever noticed that answers to your questions come when you are living in the moment and quiet within?

For example, I can be drying my hair or going for a walk when all of a sudden I have a flood of new ideas. All of us have creativity and clarity—we just have to tap into it. Awareness is the first step because we must notice what we are attached to and holding onto and where we feel tension, so that we can let go of outdated beliefs and others' expectations and free ourselves to be who we really are. From here, we can motivate ourselves on a deeper level. Our intentions for our life will shift to a more conscious place.

To get more aware, we first want to quiet our mind and listen to the voices inside us. Do not try to control them. Initially you will hear various parts of yourself within your mind. It is easy to get pulled in different directions and feel conflicted by diverse opinions and ideas. Just acknowledge each feeling or idea and have compassion for every experience or thought. As you begin to accept who you are, without judgment, your real self, your innermost being, will emerge to guide you. In this place there is nothing you have to do. There is emptiness and also a vastness. Just be conscious of each moment as it unfolds.

When we practice this consistently, we can merge this attentiveness into our daily lives. When we master the act of meditation, we experience bliss. It is a place of vastness beyond words—a place of peace, wonder, and joy.

Everything in life is interlinked and entwined. We are constantly changing and evolving and so is every living thing in the world around us; we are all interdependent. Although each piece of ourselves is important, our full being is greater than the sum of our many parts.

The body, mind, heart, and spirit, the environment, nature, people around us, and global events all alter how we live. When we value the complexity and mysteries of life (and ourselves), we can also appreciate their simplicity. When we start paying attention, we can focus on what is truly important and learn to let go of what is not. Then we can use our time and resources wisely, as we accomplish what we are meant to do.

In order to concentrate on what matters most, we start by quieting the mind and being present. In college at Cal Berkeley, a friend of mine, Brooke Hanley, gave me the story "The Precious Present" by Spencer Johnson about the best gift we can give ourselves, which is being present. What is the only moment in time that we have? Right now. When we start realizing the preciousness of this instant, we don't want to be anywhere else. There is nowhere else to go, as we have it all right here.

We can explore ourselves as if our life was a science lab by stepping back and being curious. What's really going on inside of us? As we learn to slow down, get quiet, and pay attention, we start to recognize patterns in our life. We understand our desires and motivation. We even start to see the world in a new way. From this place, we can let our true self guide us.

What Is Meditation?

"I have passed beyond all thoughts."

– Rumi

Meditation is a mind/body practice dating back to ancient spiritual traditions. Some believe that primitive hunter-gatherer societies learned to alter their state of consciousness as they sat around a fire, staring at the flames. But history considers Buddha to be the founding icon, from whom Buddhist, Hindu, and other meditation practices formed. Over thousands of years, Eastern countries, especially in Asia and India, practiced and developed different forms of meditation. Now, all over the world, meditation is considered a valid and powerful way to focus and enhance one's energy. We learn to slow down, manage our mind, decrease stress, and pay attention.

When we focus and listen, patterns of how we think and act emerge. We can acknowledge things about ourselves, accept them, change them, let them go, or choose to hang on. We begin to take responsibility for how we have lived up until now as we understand ourselves better. We let go of judgment and become freer—to be ourselves, to be less stressed, and to be our best.

As we learn to be more centered within, we can stop letting external pressures intrude in our internal world. We get to allow thoughts to come and go. There is nothing we have to do; the flow happens on its own. Rather than trying to fix a problem, we see that it will be taken care of when we are less attached. We relax into our awareness. From this deeper state of being, we observe the rising and dissolving of a thought, and the spaces in between. As we are open to what is, we can see our life emerging in each moment as we discover and live from our true nature, our Self.

We get to choose. We can either distract and numb ourselves or learn to be present and engaged, and then transcend the mind and experience bliss. When we notice ourselves tuning out, we can bring ourselves back to be present. If you find yourself worrying about an upcoming presentation or fretting about a conversation you had with a friend, STOP. This is your mind leading you somewhere that you don't need to go. It's wasting your energy. Focus on right now, breathing.

The more we are present and attentive to each moment—whether we are studying for school, training for a sport, or playing with our children—the more we will improve our awareness and, in turn, our performances, relationships, and our life in general.

Concentration and Focus

Typically when we are not aware, we are caught up in the past or the future, and have gotten away from ourselves. If we analyze what happened last night, or wonder about the outcome of a race or test, we lose focus. The first thing to do when we go off track is to refocus and get back into the moment. This helps us manage stress as we notice subtle feelings and sensations that can guide us. Also, we further develop our skills and execute them more precisely when we are focused on the task at hand.

In meditation and martial arts, we train our minds and bodies to be centered and focused. We learn to breathe fully and stand with our feet planted firmly on the ground, which helps shift our body to its center of gravity. Power in our abdomen area (or "core") directs the rest of our body and is vital to the process of being centered.

Try this exercise right now: Stand up and imagine that you are a tree. Raise your arms up to the sky and smile. Now breathe in, and as you exhale bring your arms down to your side, with the palms of your hands facing toward the earth. As you do this, feel as though you are rooted into the ground (picture energy going into the earth), yet stand tall and erect. Your core is firm and strong. Feel energy go down from your head to your abdomen to your feet and beyond, into the ground. It is as if you have roots that extend below your feet and center you strongly and securely. Then, feel the energy come from the earth into you. Allow nature's powerful source of energy to electrify your body. From this centered place, as the wind blows, your branches are flexible enough to bend and adapt; if they were rigid and tense, they could easily break. Now you are strengthened and know you can weather anything that comes your way.

What Happens as We Meditate?

As stated in Dr. Herbert Benson's book The Relaxation Response, and in scientific studies, it has been shown that meditation can alter our genetic expression. As we change how we live (our thoughts and actions), we change our DNA. We can rewire our brains by changing our beliefs and by manifesting clear intentions.

The Bhagavad Gita says, "Little by little, through patience and repeated effort, the mind will become stilled in the Self." In meditation/Eastern philosophy, it is commonly said that to allow your small self to die, we must allow our true self to be alive forever. The small self is our ego, our "small mind" that chatters away, has fears and needs. This small self also includes the roles we play. As we become less attached to them, we are willing to let various roles "die" and let go of fears that we have believed were important for so long. This is often called an "ego death." When we can allow our true self to emerge, we feel light and free. We realize that we really are one with everything, that there is no need to live from a place of fear and longing.

If we feel emptiness, we want to fill the void—with a role, job, tasks, thoughts, emotions. But as we relax into the quietness of our mind, we will be guided by a deeper voice. Focus on finding this place. Listen to your breath, merge into the emptiness between breaths, and stay present from moment to moment.

It is easy to get too attached to our thoughts. When we obsess over our thoughts, no matter how great they are, they can become tainted, and we feel less free. Part of the goal of meditation is to detach ourselves from these thoughts. They might still continue on, but we stop being bothered by them as we let them go. As the Bhagavad Gita states, "One who has control over the mind is tranquil in heat and cold, in pleasure and pain, and in honor and dishonor; and is ever steadfast with the Supreme Self." We feel our power and are free.

Just as we notice our thoughts and emotions when we sit quietly, we also notice sensations in our bodies. Initially we might sense tension in parts of our bodies that we had previously ignored. As we practice meditation and relaxation, this tension dissipates, and our body's energy opens up and flows more easily. During meditation, our breathing slows down and we feel relaxed. As we become more aware, we can feel energy flowing throughout, like a light buzz. Once in a deep meditative state, we don't feel just our body; we feel energy in and all around us.

What is the Goal of Meditation?

To listen, you must first be willing to hear. As you listen to the silence, you will come to know yourself. Listen and feel your inner body even as you are engaged in activity. Focus your attention inward, not just on the outside world. Feel quiet within while you are engaged. From a place of peace, open yourself to the flow of life. When you are able to connect your human body and mind with your spirit and to God within you, you are at your best. You do not need to seek by going and doing. By listening to and honoring your truest inner self, you can change your beliefs and see the world differently, which will then change how you act toward yourself and others.

Your goal is to live consciously and be divinely aware. When you listen, you hear your heart's desire, your inner voice, your intuition. This allows you to feel safe, and to trust. You notice, but don't need to be attached. When you are quiet inside, you can ask yourself questions and listen for answers that come from deep within.

Meditation also enhances your physical well-being. It strengthens the immune system as the body becomes more balanced and is allowed to function optimally. Meditation alters hormone, muscular, and cellular activity, thereby improving your mood, increasing your energy, and minimizing illnesses. As your body runs more smoothly, you feel more balanced, healthier, and happier.

How Do I Meditate?

There are various methods that you can use to meditate, and no way is right or wrong. If you prefer to move while meditating (while you are playing a sport, performing a task, even walking your dog), then do so. As I mentioned, my favorite place to be with my true self is in the water. Nowadays, I often start my meditation through Chi Kung (also known as Qigong) and then go into sitting meditation. If you like to sit still, then honor that. It is also okay to lie down; however, some meditation groups do not recommend this, as it is easy to fall asleep if you are not fully engaged.

If you are just beginning, pick one method and stick with it for a given period of time. It is more beneficial to dig one deeper well as opposed to many shallow wells. Wear comfortable clothing. You can sit in a chair with hands on your knees and feet firmly planted on the floor, or sit on a cushion, or zafu, cross-legged. Either way, make sure your back is straight, so energy can flow easily.

If, at first, it is hard to sit still, you can listen to soothing music that calms your mind. Ideally, you will get to a place where everything is quiet. Start by doing five minutes once a day. Over time, you might build up to thirty minutes or more, or to twice per day. Later in the chapter, you will be guided on different way to meditate. Also, a good introductory book is Meditation by Eknath Easwaran (Nilgiri Press).

It's best to meditate in a quiet, contemplative place where your wisdom can shine through. You might want to create a space in your home, perhaps a corner in a room that is dedicated to your meditation practice. You can even put flowers, a special picture, or a book there. Yet, really you can meditate anywhere. I remember eating at The Thai House in Berkeley and people would be meditating at their table before they ate.

Keep it simple. Be grateful and humble. Focus on your heart's desire. Let your other needs (attention and acceptance from others, needs to achieve, desire for material goods) quiet down. Can you really get these voices to stop? Yes, but what is most important is to realize that they can still be there and not have to run your life. You can be detached from the drama and emotions that they can carry.

When people first practice meditation, they often hold their breath, or have a hard time relaxing enough to exhale. Just relax, and do not try so hard. Let your breathing happen naturally. Breathe in, breathe out. Feel the space between your breaths. Don't make it more difficult than it needs to be. Begin to trust your inner wisdom and stop struggling.

Listen to and observe yourself. When you do this, you become more aware of how you think, your patterns, and your beliefs. When you get deeply quiet, all of the voices in your head are just chatter. The deep reservoir within you holds all of your answers—just get quiet enough to learn to let go of the layers hiding them. It is like cleaning out a closet—you can get overloaded with stuff you no longer need; you're just accustomed to having it there. The key is to be willing to observe and let go of your attachments, to be present to everything that goes on inside. By doing so, you change your "perception lens," which allows you to see differently, thus altering your life view.

How Do You Stay Focused?

Stay present with what you are doing. Allow yourself to get immersed in what you are experiencing. A simple way is to focus on your breath, the inhalation and exhalation. Then focus on the space between each breath. What do you feel, notice, experience? When you slow down, you can observe yourself and notice what you feel, say, and do. Even if you are in severe pain, or your thoughts are driving you crazy, recognize this as only a moment; it will not last forever. Sometimes, just by acknowledging something, it goes away.

We all have moments of doubt and fear. They even show up while we are meditating, and since we are quiet and focused, free from our usual distractions, our doubts and fears might become magnified. The key is to pay attention to your true voice inside and focus less on the other chatter. It is easy to get swayed into believing all of the thoughts—these might be things you have told yourself or heard from others for years. It is important to quiet those unruly voices and concentrate on what really matters to you and motivates you.

No matter what kind of meditation you do, there will be similar patterns as you struggle with focus and distractions. Just let your thoughts come and go, acknowledge them but do not judge, and go back to paying attention to yourself. As you practice this, you will eventually become less attached to your thoughts and distractions. You will concentrate more on your breath, an object, a mantra, or whatever you use to focus your mind and then go beyond that. When you learn to quiet your mind and get fully immersed in whatever you are doing, it will help you in all areas of life!

Focus And Meditation Exercises

There are many different ways to meditate. Here are a few examples:

Using an Object: Take an object (for instance, a pen, book, candle, or flowers), and stare at it for three minutes. What do you notice? Focus on everything you see in that object—the colors, textures, or unique marks. If your mind starts to wander, just calmly bring yourself back to the object. As you become more skilled at this, feel the energy between you and the object as you experience being "connected" to each other.

I remember first experimenting with this in sixth grade. My teacher drew a circle on the chalkboard and had us all focus on it for a few minutes. I remember the room being quiet, but then hearing the rattling of desk chairs as people lost their focus. I felt stiff and tense as I sat still that first time. I have since learned how to relax and enjoy the stillness. I often love to look at a candle burning, or focus on the rustling wind blowing through the trees.

Appreciation Meditation: Start by taking five slow deep breaths. As you inhale with your mouth closed, feel the air surround your nose as it goes in and your belly rises. As you exhale, open your mouth and relax your jaw as you feel the air and any tension leave you. Tell yourself three things that you appreciate about you, your partner, your children, parents, mentors, pets, job, home, or whatever you wish. Let your subconscious do the work. There is no need to control your answer, or try to censor it. Let your ideas surface and be heard. Sometimes our silliest thoughts lead to the most rewarding actions.

Acknowledging Our Inner Voices: For my first weeklong silent meditation retreat, I went to a Zen Buddhist retreat center. I wanted to understand the voices in my head, which had begun to appear at different times in my life. I named them as I became clearer about what they represented to me. I had a Judge, Supporter, Innocent Little Girl, Victim, and so on. As I allowed each voice to have its own personality, I no longer let them define me. I could appreciate each one for serving a purpose at a certain time in my life, but I said good-bye since I did not need them anymore. I rarely see those fragmented parts of myself anymore. They have all been integrated into my whole self.

By finding my center—the core of my being—I could hear all the parts of myself but not have to engage them. I didn't need to analyze why they were created, or for what reason. They had served their purpose, and now I could willingly let them go.

Mantra Meditation: I studied meditation and Eastern religions and philosophies extensively when I was sick with CFIDS. I wanted to understand how I could be content without striving. When I was in college at Cal Berkeley, I studied meditation with Professor Michael Nagler, who lived at an ashram with meditation teacher Eknath Easwaran, who I had the pleasure of meeting a few times. We focused on having a phrase or mantra to say to ourselves as we meditated. By giving the mind an uplifting message to focus on, we take the message into our subconscious. I used to recite Hindu and Buddhist mantras, and I also recited the Christian prayer of St. Francis of Assisi in my mind very slowly. I would breathe in, say one word, and then breathe out and say the next word. My higher consciousness processed the meaning of the prayer and how I could allow myself to live from its meaning. Learning to let go of other thoughts as they came up, and refocusing back onto my breath and the words of the prayer, I was able to become less attached and more present and aware.

Dzogchen Tibetan Buddhist Meditation: In the late 1990s and early 2000s, I went to several weeklong silent retreats focused on Dzogchen, with Lama Surya Das. Even though I am not a practicing Buddhist, I valued the silence and a new way of meditating for me. We meditated with our eyes open and mouth and jaws open and relaxed. There was no need to meditate on a phrase or focus on anything. We simply allowed ourselves to be a part of the openness and vastness of life as we listened within. This helped me focus in the external world, too, knowing I could keep meditating even as I did daily tasks.

"Who am I?" Exercise: Ask yourself, "Who Am I?" and focus your attention on whatever answers arise. Breathe deeply, and do not judge yourself. As you keep meditating and listening to your innermost self, answers will keep coming from a deeper place within. This will help you release limiting beliefs as you get to know and trust your truest self.

Walking Meditation: Any form of movement can be done while meditating. Many people like to walk very slowly as they repeat a mantra or focus on their breath. As you do so, concentrate on your body. Pay attention to the movement of your foot as it goes from the heel to the toes touching the ground, and feel how your arms sway back and forth. Think about your shoulders, your back, your neck. Be aware of yourself and the space around you.

Breathing Meditation: There are many forms of breath work that can be done. One exercise is to feel the energy go up the front side of your body as you inhale and then down your backside as you exhale. Then, rotate it to your sides, up one and down the other. Finish by having the energy go up your back and down your front. The energy of your breath will be coursing throughout your entire body.

Outcome Meditation: Once you get quiet and open yourself up to your subconscious, imagine a meaningful outcome you would like to have in your life (a healthy body, resolved issue with someone, winning a competition). Picture it happening right now. Feel it and enjoy the sensations. If tension arises, acknowledge it and let it go.

Counting One to Ten: Breathe deeply to calm your body. Then breathe in as you imagine writing the number "one." Exhale, and imagine writing the number "two." Do this all the way up to ten. If *any* other thoughts arise, go back to number one. Thoughts include: "Oh, I am at number seven this time!" or "What do I want this number to look like?" By having something to focus on, it helps us stay on task; yet, we realize that other thoughts try to distract us. With practice, this exercise will help you focus your mind—it's excellent in helping to prepare for a performance.

Sunshine Meditation: Envision a white or golden light all around you that protects you and makes you feel safe inside. Then imagine that you are the sun, full of radiant, powerful energy. Feel the energy of this light filling you up and flowing through you. Carry this energy with you for the rest of the day.

Closed-Mouth, Tongue-Up Breathing: Sit in a chair or cross-legged on a zafu (meditation cushion). Close your eyes, and breathe in and out through your nose, feeling the air go in your nose and then out your nose. Does it feel warm, cool, heavy, soft? Let the tongue rest on the roof of your mouth. Feel as though the tongue is reaching lightly toward the tip of your nose. As you feel this, it can calm your mind.

Water Meditation: When I float in the water, I love to take a big breath in, hold it, and let my full body dangle limply. If I need to breathe, I lift only my head and inhale, then place my head back in the water. I close my eyes and just float and breathe, listening to the sound of the water and quieting my mind. By allowing all my muscles to relax, I am held up by the water—I trust that I will float without trying. Try this exercise yourself the next time you're relaxing in a pool.

Meditation in Motion: If sitting on a cushion trying to meditate is difficult for you, honor that—you can meditate while you move. Whether you are doing martial arts, walking, running, or participating in a sport, focus on your movement, breath, or a mantra to center yourself. As you get adept at this, you will feel energy moving around you while noticing a shift inside as you allow yourself to be quiet within. Your sport/acting/music/field of interest becomes your meditation. Be present and acknowledge all emotions or thoughts (or the quiet) as you are doing that task.

Meditating Around Higher Energy: You can receive energy just from being around someone who is highly conscious. Their mere presence can heal you. I had the good fortune to be near His Holiness The Dalai Lama on a few occasions. When I first saw him, I felt like my heart had just been blasted open with love. I wasn't even sitting that close to him—about thirty yards away. I stared at him, seeing him as another human being. Then a rush of energy went through me and tears welled up in my eyes as I felt immense compassion for myself, and others. You can feel this by merely looking at a photo of someone who inspires you. Post a picture of a "guru" in your meditation space, then meditate on the energy that radiates from them. Also, meditating in a group of people, with the focused intention of clear energy, will also enhance your state.

Alone With Yourself

Meditation is about focusing on the moment. There is nothing else we need to do. It sounds simple, and we might wonder if that is enough. Yes, this is plenty.

Initially it might be hard to be alone with yourself, to listen and do nothing. When you first slow down, it can be difficult to hear yourself over all the mental chatter. In fact, it can be exhausting. We realize that this noise has been going on all along, and now we are aware of it. It has been wearing you out, and you didn't even notice. You might be afraid to stop the chatter, since you've grown accustomed to it. But the more you are willing to listen in this quiet, solitary place, the more answers and insights will come to you. The chatter will fade, or you will learn to let it go. With practice, you will start to like being alone—though, in fact, you are connected to so much more. Within all of us is a rich source of love that binds us to everyone and everything else in the universe. We are never truly alone.

Let Life Flow

In the past few years, I have studied Taoism, and practiced Chi Kung daily. The Tao is about taking the path of least resistance. It is like a river going downstream. Water finds an easy way to flow past obstacles in its way. Initially when we face a problem, we struggle and fight. Then, as we become more aware, we learn to change, avoid the obstacle, or take a new path entirely. In my most powerful training and racing moments, I went downstream and it was easy. I would finish a practice or a performance feeling confident and connected to a power greater than myself. It was almost though I hadn't done the race; I had just gone along for the ride.

At different times in my career, I believed that fear and struggle were necessary in order to succeed. Yes, we need to focus and commit, which requires discipline, yet once we train our minds, we need to let go of fear. We just need to trust. Champions and successful people find what makes them happy in life and spend a lot of time and energy mastering it. In mastery, detachment comes easily, because we know what the experience is like. When we are "in the flow," not worried about the outcome, we are attentive to what we are doing and lose ourselves in it. This is when we feel true bliss.

Living Life to the Fullest

When we commit to being aware regardless of how scary it is to pay attention, our lives will change. As we honor our inner voice, we become willing to make a conscious shift and act. Our goal is to connect with the deepest part of ourselves and to be real in our interactions with others. As we welcome our experiences, we connect to a new consciousness within.

Focusing on the present moment can be powerful. If you make only one change after reading this book, I hope it will be to do deep breathing and meditation exercises every day. All of the tools discussed in this book are useful for taking care of yourself mentally, physically, emotionally, and spiritually. But meditation will guide you most quickly to be your best self. Your stress level will decrease as you're able to handle problems more easily, and you will be calmer when faced with challenges and obstacles. You will feel more confident and clear about who you are and what you want.

We have the opportunity every day to be in awe of the world around us and to experience life to the fullest. When we do this, we appreciate who we are, what we are doing, and the miracles of life. By staying connected to each moment and exploring everything around us (rather than worrying about the past, future, or others), we see the world in a whole new way.

Your true power lies within! The simplest way to change your future and yourself is to bring your attention to the present. By being aware in this moment, everything is here for you to know.

Be here in this moment. This moment is all there is.

Chapter Ten

Your Road to Health: Taking Care of Your Physical Body

No one can listen to your body for you. To grow and heal, you have to take responsibility for listening to it yourself.

—Jon Kabat-Zinn

I was required to take my discipline to a whole new level when I focused on getting well. I sought out every possible resource. Through physical, emotional, and spiritual modalities, I started a process of deep healing, and I learned how to take care of myself in new ways. In the last two chapters, we discussed how to be more attentive and accepting of ourselves. In the next couple of chapters, we will focus on healing emotionally. In this chapter, I'll share what I learned and experienced on the road to physical recovery, so you can apply these lessons to your own life.

Listen to What Your Body is Telling You

One day after playing for a long time, my energetic four-year-old son emphatically said to me, "Mom, I don't like to nap, but my body makes me." I smiled at him, knowing that on some level he was listening to his body. Even though he wanted to keep playing, his body was telling him to rest. When we pay attention, our body tells us everything we need to know—what is happening emotionally, mentally, and spiritually. This is our guide.

Everything in our bodies is interlinked. Our kidneys are in charge of maintaining our health and vitality; they activate the functioning of all other organs. If the kidneys get off balance, other organs are affected, too. This affects our physical well-being, which also has an impact on our emotional and mental health. Similarly, our physical body stores and expresses what is going on in our mind and heart (how we feel, think, and act). It tells us how we are taking care of ourselves (or not). If we listen to what our body needs, we can address deficiencies and ailments with exercise, nutrition, and other healing techniques. Sometimes, what our body needs most is rest.

The Importance of Rest

"Take rest; a field that has rested gives a bountiful crop."
– Ovid

As I healed from CFIDS (Chronic Fatigue and Immune Dysfunction Syndrome), I began to fully appreciate the importance of rest. Many people push and do not know how to stop and relax. If you do not rest and sleep enough, you jeopardize your health. Symptoms of too little rest might include: difficulty thinking clearly, change in mood, feeling stressed, lack of muscle recovery, or indigestion. If you become chronically tired, serious illnesses can occur. This is your body's way of saying that you need to take a break.

How much rest is enough? This varies for each person. The average night's sleep is around eight hours, but some people need more and others need less. You might need more sleep or downtime if you have been burning the candle at both ends. Other times, one day or night of poor sleep will not affect you much. How you consistently take care of yourself (via food, drink, exercise, breathing, expressing emotions, and rest) determines your ability to feel good.

Make sleeping as pleasurable as possible, and give yourself the tools to fully relax, such as have darkening shades or comfortable sheets, comforter, or pajamas. Create a sleep routine and stick to it—maybe take a warm shower before bed or have some soothing tea. If you drink caffeine too late in the evening or get overly stimulated—perhaps by exercise, watching TV, playing video games, or spending time on the computer—it will be more difficult for you to sleep or rest well.

In addition to getting enough sleep, it is also important to take breaks when you need them. Step away from the computer, allow yourself quiet time to meditate, walk the dog, or take a nap. Listen to what your body needs in order to keep from burning out.

When you get enough rest, you help your organs work effectively, allowing your body to function optimally. With adequate rest, you actually lose weight, have a clearer mind, digest food more easily, and feel happier. You also rebuild your muscles, enhancing your ability to perform in sports. All parts of your body get rejuvenated, so they are ready to do their jobs again. It is vital to care for yourself by getting enough rest. Even if you begin by adding twenty minutes of meditation or deep breathing to your daily schedule, you will notice a difference in your energy.

Acupuncture

In college, when I had full-blown CFIDS, I began my regular visits to Dr. Helms, founder of The American Academy of Medical Acupuncture. I had seen a variety of other doctors and specialists who could not diagnose me, or who thought my illness was all in my head. They would just give me a pill and send me on my way. With Dr. Helms, I was relieved to finally be treated as a whole person, who was more than just a myriad of physical symptoms.

I had hoped Dr. Helms would be the one to facilitate my healing, and thankfully he was. My head was swollen; it felt bigger than what my body could coordinate or carry. My spatial orientation was off, and my eyes couldn't focus. My organs were inflamed. I could not digest food well. I couldn't think or sleep. I had dizziness, fevers, a sore throat, swollen glands, and feelings of arthritis in my joints. I felt cold even if I dressed warmly, and I had no energy. I knew my immune system was shot, and in order to heal I would need to care for not only my physical self, but the emotional part, too.

As I walked into the bright pink building on Milvia Street in Berkeley, I noticed an interesting aroma. If I didn't know better, I might have mistaken it for marijuana. I later learned that this smell was moxa, or mugwort herb. Moxa is an herb wrapped up into a stick that's the shape of a cigar. It is used to heat up the needles on the body during acupuncture. The herb helps to stimulate circulation via the points where the needles lie. This enhances blood flow and qi, life force or energy flow, throughout the body. Research shows that moxa acts as an agent that increases blood circulation and enhances the immune system.

I walked into the waiting room and saw a balding man about the size of my father, with vivacious eyes and an energetic gait. He approached me and introduced himself. I smiled at Dr. Helms, already feeling better. We went into one of the treatment rooms, one that became my favorite. On one of the light-blue walls hung a beautiful painting of a feminine-looking vivacious woman carrying a fruit basket as she walked from her garden (and I always imagined the ocean in the distance) into the courtyard by her home. Over the years, I'd look at this painting as I reconnected with my own radiant beauty.

Dr. Helms and I discussed my health history and then I lay face down on a massage table with a pillow under my stomach and my arms by my side. Soothing classical music played in the background. I had learned how important it was for me to trust. I felt very safe here and knew I would be well taken care of by Dr. Helms. My racing mind slowly started to calm down. Dr. Helms came in to start the acupuncture treatment. I drilled him with questions, wanting to know what everything meant and how my body was responding. After checking my tongue and my pulse, Dr. Helms said my pulses were hollow and weak, meaning that we needed to get energy flow moving again. By doing so, my body's organs would be rejuvenated and healed, thus enhancing my overall immune system and vitality.

Acupuncture accounts for the whole body and its varying interactions within. If one area is deficient, that affects another area. Acupuncture not only heals the physical realm, it also restores emotional balance and mental clarity. Imagine the body having highways or rivers running through it. These are called meridians—they are channels that allow the energy, *qi* (pronounced "chee"), to flow throughout the body.

When we are sick, stress manifests as physical symptoms. Imbalances cause our energy to get stuck and to not flow along these passages, causing disturbances physically, mentally, and emotionally. Blockages lead to unhealthy organ functioning, often causing them to become inflamed or blocked. This causes changes in physical appearance, mood, and action. Acupuncture locates the areas of disturbance, releases these blocks, and rebalances our body so energy can easily circulate through the meridian system and keep our organs healthy. Each treatment is based on what is needed at that time; sometimes the focus is to clean out toxins, to tonify or strengthen our body.

Dr. Helms put the needles in at specific points along the meridians. He would twist them, heat them with moxa, and/or stimulate them with electricity. This allowed more energy to go into rebalancing my body by moving qi, energy. This process rebuilds our reserves and strengthens our body—and therefore our mind, heart, and spirit. Once the circulation of energy is corrected, the body can heal itself. It can eliminate symptoms, diseases, and pain. After treatment, proper nutrition, rest, exercise, and a happy heart (inner calm) help keep the body in balance.

I felt a slight tingling sensation from the needles. Dr. Helms put two needles in my neck—the one on my right, in particular, really relaxed my body. As the electricity was turned on and the current ran into the needles, I could feel my tension dissipating. My whole body gradually relaxed. I let go and felt my body melt into the table.

My mind went into a meditative state. I enjoyed this blissful place as my mind slowed down, my body felt free of pain, and more energy flowed through me. The moxa man came in to heat up the needles. As he did so, a heated energy formed around the acupuncture point, which soothed my body even more.

Time flew by as I enjoyed my state of bliss. Dr. Helms came in to turn the electricity off. I felt energy shoot through my body, like a light "pitter patter" feeling. I felt relaxed, as if I had just woken up from a deep sleep.

Dr. Helms asked me to turn over onto my back. He put more needles around my face, head, and throat to relieve pain. He also put needles near my elbows, above my wrists, and near my ankles and knees, and then hooked up the electricity. Compared to being on my front, this seemed more invigorating, and I became more alert rather than feeling like I was floating. Yet I was still very relaxed and calm.

The current of electricity in my legs was creating a "pulse." I visualized light pink energy flowing from leg to leg. After about thirty minutes, Dr. Helms came in to check on me, and then he took the needles out. He gave me a shot with vitamin B12, and a homeopathic remedy. After the treatment, I sensed a light buzz throughout my body. I felt calmer, more alert, and focused.

Dr. Helms's office became like a second home for me. Initially, to heal from CFIDS, I saw Dr. Helms twice per week. As I got healthier, my visits decreased to once per week, and then eventually twice per month. I healed rapidly and went through drastic changes from the spring of 1993 until 1997.

Acupuncture does so much more than eliminate physical pain. It affects the whole person. In addition to helping with my CFIDS, acupuncture also affected my speech, which became strong, slow, and clear (not my norm). Emotionally, I felt more grounded. I was able to grieve more easily and let go of old emotions as my heart opened up. Additionally, I often had concentrated bundles of energy and could be productive, which was valuable when I was bedridden. Other times, I would go home and sleep, and wake up feeling much more refreshed.

Over time, I let go of unhealthy patterns that were embedded in my body and memory. I gradually stopped overdoing. Once you can rebalance your body, you have a better chance of also responding differently to other stressors in your life. For me, acupuncture was a saving grace. While other modalities helped, this was the foundation of my healing. Dr. Helms was not just my acupuncturist—he also became like a parent figure to me, and a mentor, therapist, and friend. I looked forward to seeing him every week. He knew more about my personal life than anyone else, and he helped me learn how to manage my energy output in all facets of my life.

Nutrition: You are What You Eat (Choose Wisely!)

With my compromised immune system, I became very aware of how my body reacted to food. Dr. Helms and I discussed nutrition, with an emphasis on how the body works overall. Sometimes he suggested that I eat red meat to rebuild; at other times, he urged me to eat more whole grains and vegetables, based on what parts of my body needed a break. I learned to listen to what my body wanted. During this time, I also saw a nutritionist to ensure that I ate foods to help me heal. I cut out all sugar, dairy, wheat, and was told to eliminate caffeine and alcohol, which I already didn't consume. I drank water to ensure a well-hydrated body. I studied nutrition on my own and spent a lot of time perusing the aisles at Whole Foods.

I became very sensitive to what I ate, when I ate, and how much or little I ate. It takes energy to digest food. If I ate something that used more energy to get absorbed than I actually received from it, I felt tired. Likewise, if I ate too much, combined the wrong foods, or ate too little in one sitting, I could be wiped out. Through learning about food combinations and how food can heal, I continued to maintain the energetic balance that I had gained from acupuncture.

I used to view food as a fuel for my performances. Now, I used food to heal my body. Food, like a drug, can alter your mood, energy level, and how your body functions. It can destroy your immune system or enhance it. Like medicine, when food is improperly mixed, there are side effects.

Similarly, what you eat can alter your pH balance (a measure of the acidity or alkaline nature of water). You can test the pH balance of the water in your body by urinating on a stick designed for this purpose. If your pH is lower than 7, it is considered acidic, and if above 7, it is alkaline. You want your pH to be alkaline. This is when your body can heal. Cancer and most diseases can only live when your pH is at 5 or less. Focus on eating foods that can create an alkaline pH, and cut out those that are acidic. A simple place to start is to eliminate sugar, dairy, caffeine, alcohol, and breads from your diet. Eat more whole foods that were planted in rich, organic soil and fewer processed foods.

Research shows that processed foods, chemicals, and sugar suppress your immune system for several hours after you eat them. Sugar and many stimulants are acidic and a known cancer food supply. Aspartame, an artificial sweetener, is even worse; it changes to formaldehyde at 84 degrees, and your body temperature averages 98.6! Your body then stores these nasty toxins. Some chemicals used to preserve products are also carcinogenic. Cancer loves acidity. It also feeds on mucus (which prevents absorption of nutrients), which is formed in the body by milk products. Many physicians, including Dr. Christiane Northrup and Dr. Benjamin, have stated that cow's milk and some other dairy products can cause a burden on the body's respiratory, digestive, and immune systems. If you reduce or cut out such products, you can potentially alleviate ear and sinus infections, allergies, and other more serious health issues.

Stimulants can also have a negative effect on the body—they cause increased heart rate, hypertension, anxiety, headaches, dehydration, and disturbed sleep. Some, such as caffeine, overstimulate the adrenals, liver, and kidney to provide a boost of immediate energy. However, you experience a "crash" soon after if you do not have more. To try to avoid the crash, people will have sugary doughnuts and then coffee or soda. Later, when they need to feel recharged, they have a cigarette. By consuming so many stimulants, they are chronically overusing their sympathetic nervous system, the "fight or flight" response, as their body tries to counteract this onslaught of "uppers."

The more we chronically stress our sympathetic nervous system, the less our body has a chance to rejuvenate and therefore work properly. Our organs stop functioning as they should, which shows up as indigestion, constipation, and more serious diseases. When we chronically overuse stimulants or acidic foods, we feel fatigue, stress, or burnout.

Have you ever been around someone who eats like this? Maybe yourself? If you eat like this (or you overeat, or don't eat enough), you can get quite moody and not know why. Your body has been off balance for so long that your blood has a continuous amount of toxins in it, which then go into your liver. An overtaxed liver makes you grouchy. Or your adrenal glands have been over-stimulated for too long, and since they no longer work effectively you are constantly tired. Remember, when you feel low energy or are depressed, your body is telling you that something is wrong.

Before I acknowledged that I was sick, I tried to create energy by eating "quick energy and crash" food. I ate more sugar and tried coffee, which I had never done before. Often, I didn't even get the initial quick "high," since my body was already so sick. I took note of the body-food connection and started paying attention to what I ate and how it affected me. If you are numb to why you eat, you might continue to feed your body more, rather than clean it out to feel better. If so, your body will start to show the effects through weight gain, pimples, hormonal imbalances, feelings of moodiness, organs not functioning properly, getting constipated, or a variety of illnesses.

Focus on What Works for You

You need to pay attention to what works for your body. Do you feel energized after eating certain foods? Some days, you will need more protein; other days, more fat. If you have eaten rich, heavy foods for a couple days, you might need a day of lighter fare. The key is to have balance and not to overuse.

Right before I get my menstrual cycle, my body wants more fat and protein. I have a yummy hamburger (good-quality grass-fed beef, not fast food) and will treat myself to homemade ice cream or an avocado. Honor what you need, and feel good about eating in moderation rather than trying to be perfect.

When you start feeling more balanced energetically, you won't crave sugar or stimulants. You will lose weight, be less stressed, sleep better, feel more rested, and have less anxiety or depression.

Initially as you take care of yourself, you might go through a period of detoxification, which is tough the first few days. It can be like a drug addict getting off heroin. But if you commit, once the toxins leave your blood stream you will feel much more clear and energized.

Many books out there tell you how to diet. But do not get stuck following someone else's rigid guidelines. Every body needs different things based on what is happening with you. Listen to what your body needs and wants. If your energy is balanced and functioning well, your body will correctly guide you. It has an amazing ability to heal itself, if you let it. Don't wait to get really sick to discover this. Listen to yourself now, and notice your energy soar!

Manage Your Energy Throughout the Day

How do you keep your energy balanced, your mind alert, and your emotions content? Listen to what your body is telling you. Have a healthy balance. Pay attention to your energy two hours after you eat. If you have a spike and then crash, that is often food or glucose related. A proper balance of nutrition, rest, and exercise helps you maintain a consistent energy level. Say no to diets, yes to eating for life. Design your eating plan.

My husband and I follow the 80/20 rule: 80% of the time we eat healthy, and 20% of the time we allow ourselves to eat whatever we want. Over time, you will not even want "bad" food. You will feel better by eating well.

Another way to feel consistent energy is to eat often and drink plenty of clean water. Never get hungry, never get full. The hypothalamus regulates your metabolism, which determines whether food is converted into energy or put into storage. When you have five meals a day, your metabolism keeps working compared to if you "diet" and only eat one meal per day, which slows your metabolism to a halt. When you don't eat, your body stores food as extra fat since it does not know when the body will get fed again. Then when you do eat, the metabolism is still slow and stores more food, until you start eating or exercising more regularly.

When I was sick, my body was out of balance. It did not function properly, and I gained weight. As I started to heal, I slept more, ate more, did no exercise, and yet still lost weight. My body was healing and needed good-quality food to get well; as my body started functioning better, weight just came off, even as I ate more.

Even if you are busy, you can still eat healthfully. My husband and I start our day with a smoothie, which gives us balanced energy that lasts. We use a blender to mix good oils, such as a blend of omega-3 and omega-6 fatty acids (which can be purchased in liquid form at a health-food store), one fruit (typically frozen blueberries), fresh greens, crushed nuts, and either juice or rice or almond milk. There are many cookbooks available to help you create delicious and nutritious smoothies and juices. This is just one way to get the healthy nutrients you need throughout the day.

Chemical Concerns

People with chronic illness, such as diabetes, heart disease, or depression, are particularly susceptible to the negative effects of what they ingest. Many chronically ill people develop depression due to a lack of serotonin in the brain. Serotonin is a neurotransmitter that is known to contribute to feeling good. The hypothalamus section of our brain regulates metabolic processes (including hunger and thirst), serotonin production, sleep (circadian rhythms), mood, pain, hormones, and stress.

To feel better you might want to take a drug to alleviate depression or other pain. But often, if your body is depleted, the drug cannot perform the way it should. Most anti-depressant medication, specifically SSRIs, use the chemicals you already have—they do not make more serotonin to help you feel good. If you have enough serotonin and need it to be redirected or better utilized, drugs can help, but they come with many side effects since they alter other organs' health. The more you can focus on staying away from drugs, stimulants, or processed foods for a quick fix (or to feel numb), the easier it will be to improve your overall health. You can produce more serotonin through food, exercise, and emotional healing. So eat well, and rest when needed. When you give your body the nutrients it needs, your organs can do their job, which provides you with energy.

You might be thinking, "But I crave sugar," or "I need caffeine to get through the day." When your body is not balanced, you very well might crave sugar or other stimulants. But this temporary stimulation results in long-term energy drain. It can become addictive and cause the loss of valuable nutrients in your body. When overly acidic, our body becomes inflamed. If chronic, you get diseases.

If you do not replenish yourself with rest and balancing foods (ones that enhance your pH and increase your energy long term), you stress important organs, including your adrenal glands, which hinders your health. A lot of food today is packaged and processed with ingredients to maintain their shelf life. Many of these preservatives cannot be processed in your body, which inhibits the health of your cells and organs. Even products that seem good for you because they are advertised as healthy and "fat free" are actually worse than having the whole food with fat. Whole foods always digest more easily. Additionally, many whole foods with good fat are needed to help your body heal and function properly.

Other products to be mindful of are foods that have minerals and vitamins added via processing. They have been sprayed on so companies can label their product this way, to state that they have a certain amount of FDA-approved ingredients. But often, the sprayed-on nutrients cannot be properly assimilated. The body goes through steps to utilize nutrients, and when they appear in the wrong form they often don't get used at all.

If we are not properly informed about nutrition, we will only hurt ourselves. Pay attention to what your body tells you, and take the time to learn how various food choices can either hinder or help you. There are many books and resources to help you make wise decisions. Another tip to help you eat well is to shop along the perimeter of most grocery stores, where the unprocessed food is located. By making wise food choices based on what your body needs, you will be taking a huge step toward improving your physical health.

Supplements

It can be difficult to get all the nutrients we need from food, especially if we are not eating well. To ensure a healthy body, take a good nutritional supplement, ideally in as close to its whole, original form as possible. Some of the supplements I take are green chlorophyll powder (rich source of nutrients), liquid complex vitamin B (a great powerhouse to help the body work properly and have energy), powdered Vitamin C, and ionic liquid minerals, especially magnesium, potassium, and calcium. These three minerals are the primary transporters of nutrients into your cells, but it's hard to get enough of them unless you are eating whole foods. If you have enough magnesium, potassium, and calcium, they will facilitate the easy absorption of other nutrients.

If you are constipated, it is a sign that your organs are inflamed and cannot function properly. You might be stuck emotionally or not eating enough live foods. Change what you are eating, and drink more water. Have more "good" fat. Magnesium helps, too. To eliminate constipation or upset stomach, you need to create a healthy balance in your gut. When I was sick and kept receiving antibiotics from physicians who didn't know how to treat me, all of my friendly bacteria were killed. So I started taking probiotics, such as acidophilus, to help my intestines function well again.

Some people worry about having fat in their diet. Trans and saturated fats are mainly found in processed foods and are not good for you. But polyunsaturated and monosaturated fats, also known as "good fats," are healthy and necessary (in moderation). Some saturated fat can also be good for you. Good fats help your body absorb necessary nutrients, have proper nerve activity, and allow for a healthy immune system and cells. Good fats can stimulate your metabolism, resulting in weight loss, and also reduce inflammation, lowering your risk of certain cancers. You can find good fats in salmon and other fish, avocadoes, nuts (especially walnuts, almonds, cashews, and natural peanut butter), sunflower and sesame seeds, and certain oils such as flax, fish, hemp, grape seed, flax, or olive oil.

These are just some general nutritional guidelines for you to follow. Research your options, talk to health-care professionals, and most of all, listen to what your body needs.

Exercise

As in all other facets of life, moderation is the key to healthy exercise. Do what you enjoy, do it regularly, and listen to what your body is telling you.

If you have eaten poorly, you might think that you need to punish yourself by exercising harder or longer. Or, if you have had a stressful day, you might be tempted to overexert your body to release stress. Be kind to yourself and mindful of what is best.

As I started to heal from CFIDS, I could not do any exercise. Gradually, I was able to do sitting meditation. Then I went to a yoga class at Berkeley, and the teacher just let me lay in the back of the room with my feet up against the wall, resting and breathing. With stretching and deep breathing, I was allowing energy to flow through my body. And being with others who were doing yoga and breath work, I absorbed their quiet, focused energy and felt a sense of connection. I could not do the moves, but I still left class feeling better.

I had always found my peaceful place through swimming—for me, it was like meditation in motion. To reach a similar state of mind, I tried Tai Chi, Chi Kung, and Dahn Yoga. They are all forms of martial arts that balance and enhance energy by circulating it through the meridian system. By enhancing energy flow, the whole body becomes healthier and more balanced.

Eventually, I started biking and even swimming again. To this day, no matter what I do, I feel best when I do some martial arts each day. I feel balanced and calm. Even stretching and deep breathing are powerful in terms of keeping the body healthy, and you can do these at any time (even while you are working). If you work at a desk all day, standing up and doing some stretches will give you a jolt of energy. One of the best quick exercises you can do to feel more alert is push-ups. Do twenty, even in your office. This will stimulate your body and help revive your mind.

Assuming you are healthy, it is ideal to physically move for at least twenty minutes per day. Research shows that twenty minutes of exercise stimulates your immune system. Go for a walk, stretch, run, swim, bike, lift weights, do calisthenics, practice martial arts, or do yoga. Mix it up; cross training is more fun and easier on your body than doing the same routine repeatedly.

Honor what you feel. If you are tired, keep your heart rate lower and move slowly. If feel like you want to blow off some steam, or you have a lot of energy, allow yourself to have a more intense workout. If you are a parent with young children or don't have much time, even a few minutes per day can alter your energy and health. Do breathing, stretching, walking, or a few strengthening exercises. Once you get used to a few minutes each day, do this twice per day. Soon, you will feel so good from this that you won't want to miss a workout, or these few precious minutes of movement.

As you progress in your exercise program, it is best to first increase the number of sessions per week, then increase the duration (minutes) of exercise in each session. Finally, change the intensity of effort. With any exercise program, it is a good idea to vary the duration and intensity of your workouts. If you build a strong foundation like this, you will easily maintain your fitness and health, and it will be harder to get out of shape.

If weight loss (fat) is your primary goal, increase your activity level a little bit each day. Your goal is to stimulate your metabolism, preferably in the morning before eating too much. An early workout stokes your body's furnace and sets the tone for an energetic day. Dance to your favorite music, skate, swim, bike, jog, or walk for twenty minutes. If you are currently more than a little overweight, choose an exercise that is easier on your joints such as yoga, biking, or swimming. As always, be sure to talk to your doctor before starting any exercise program.

Your main goal is to feel invigorated, not exhausted. Exercise is meant to calm your mind, invigorate your mood, and enhance your physical energy.

Bodywork

Sometimes, when you are extremely tired, it is wise to let someone else work on you for your "exercise." I did acupuncture, and I also felt better when I treated myself to a massage or some form of bodywork.

I have also benefitted greatly from regular visits to the chiropractor. When we have an accident, feel tension, or push ourselves too hard, it is easy for our body to get unbalanced. A chiropractor treats the body by adjusting the musculoskeletal system, especially the spine, which keeps the nervous system healthy and helps the organs and tissues in our body function optimally. After a chiropractic adjustment, I often feel more alert and energetic, especially when my neck and upper back have been tight.

Over the years, I also trained in and treated people with Reiki, a Japanese technique to reduce stress and promote healing. This is another way of working with a person's life force, and helping them to heal by moving their energy.

All living matter is made up of an energy field that carries frequencies. When we are blocked or imbalanced, we can heal ourselves by applying a balancing energy to alter the frequencies, thus regaining and optimizing our health. Disease can only function in a certain frequency, and so can health. There are many ways to treat overall energy in order to balance your energetic frequencies, including acupuncture, nutrition, chiropractic sessions, mind/body treatments, and exercise. In the next two chapters, we will discuss emotional healing; releasing blocked energy from emotional dysfunction enables us to feel better and contributes to overall health and well-being.

Body Image

In my teenage years, I struggled with how I looked even though I was a world-class athlete. Later in life, when I was pregnant, I loved my body as it grew big preparing for the birth of each of my two children. As I got more comfortable within, I learned to love myself and my body.

As you take care of yourself physically, and begin to feel stronger and healthier, you will learn to appreciate your body and what it can do. No matter what you look like, you can like your body when you take care of yourself and feel content within. Participate in activities you enjoy, and appreciate yourself. As your self-perception changes, your body image will, too.

In Conclusion

I have only touched on some basic recommendations to help you improve your physical health. Advice from others can educate you; yet, your most powerful coach is your own body—listen to what it tells you. If you have to take a day off from your plan to recover, do so. The key is for you to follow your health-and-wellness plan while also being flexible and making necessary adjustments along the way.

Be honest with yourself. By maintaining a healthy body, you foster a healthy mind and lifestyle. If you are being lazy about taking care of yourself, know that. If you need to exercise, start today. If you truly need rest, carve out time. Keep listening. Your body has answers for you.

Chapter Eleven

Shedding Armor: Drop the Baggage and Take Care of Yourself Emotionally

There came a time when the risk to remain tight in the bud
was more painful than the risk it took to blossom.
– Anaïs Nin

As I worked on healing myself physically, I realized that I also needed to confront emotions and events that I had not dealt with previously. I had always been excellent at hiding my fears of not feeling loved, safe, approved of, or good enough. It seemed easier to deny these feelings than to deal with them. But as I learned to listen to my body, I also started trusting what I experienced emotionally. Since my immune system was so weak, I quickly learned what required energy. Hiding my true self from the world took more out of me than simply being true to myself.

Seeing A Therapist

The major catalyst for understanding myself better while I was healing from CFIDS was my therapist, Anneke. I started seeing her in the spring of 1993 because I wanted to not only get well, but also to feel relaxed and content again. I knew I was mentally tough and I believed that, with proper focus, I could beat this chronic illness in three months. Maybe I was naïve, or overly optimistic. Either way, I had to learn to accept the truth of my situation and have humility. I began to surrender to a bigger plan, whatever that was, and realize there might be more for me to learn and gain from CFIDS than I had cared to admit.

After all of my years of training, I finally gave myself permission to rest, heal, and recuperate. I had visited another therapist for two sessions, but I hadn't felt fully comfortable opening up to her, so I decided to give Anneke a try. I walked up the few stairs to Anneke's office near the Berkeley campus and sat down in a comfy chair in the waiting room. Relaxing music played while flowing water peacefully gurgled in a nearby waterfall.

The door opened, and a middle-aged, gray-haired woman dressed in a colorful blouse and flowing pants walked in and smiled at me. I had shocked myself by crying in Dr. Coomes's office a couple months earlier, so I didn't know what I would experience with Anneke. But I knew I was ready to immerse myself in this adventure of healing.

Eagerly wanting to better understand myself and be healthy, I made sure my tape recorder had a new cassette tape and fresh batteries. I didn't want to miss a single word of our sessions. Over time, Anneke's office would become another place where I felt at home, a place I looked forward to visiting. I would review my tape at home and come in with questions. I sought out patterns that had gotten me stuck, trying to find my true self.

For years, I had focused more on taking care of others than myself. It was easier for me to help other people with their problems than to admit to and deal with my own. With my therapist I felt safe to be vulnerable, to share my doubts and fears. I learned that being open to all of my feelings gave me power.

Shed Your Armor

In my family of origin, feelings were rarely discussed or expressed, typical of German and English backgrounds. Even though I knew my parents loved me, and we had many happy moments, I also intuitively sensed that it was best to ignore my deeper feelings, especially painful ones. Often, even when parents did their best, children still end up feeling abandoned, smothered, unsure of their own security or whom to trust, confused about how to feel, or worried about someone else's judgment.

For me, the unspoken rule growing up was that we were capable, could do things on our own, and people who whined or needed help were weak. So I learned at an early age to go after my dreams independently and pretend that I was fine and didn't need help (as many of us do).

Yet, with full-blown CFIDS, these became some of my biggest lessons: to ask for help, to feel safe by surrounding myself with people whom I trusted, and to be honest about my feelings and experiences (and know that I would still be loved and supported). I also realized that I had to take care of myself first in order to be more available to help others.

As children, we often learn to ignore some of our feelings and needs. If we express ourselves in a way that people around us don't like, they might try to change us or our actions. Because we love our family and feel loyal to them, we do not want to say what we think or feel if that hurts or upsets them. We internalize this and believe that we must be doing or feeling something wrong; we have to change to meet someone else's needs rather than our own.

Parents go through similar feelings. Many have not had their own needs met, and they often are not even aware of this. As parents, we need a break, too. We need to take care of ourselves, and it is okay to do this. We just need to clearly state this to our children so they know they are loved and that our needs are not their responsibility.

If we denied our own feelings as children, we will probably continue to do so as we get older, and then we'll have a hard time accepting the feelings that our children express. But as adults, we can recognize that it is best to express ourselves and meet our own needs, and then we can help our children do the same. However, we do not want to use our children to meet our needs, and we must teach our children to be true to themselves. Although it is important to reach out and ask others for help, we each hold ultimate responsibility for fulfilling our own needs.

If we have attempted to hide our own feelings because they cause pain or shame, we will end up projecting these repressed emotions onto others. It is easier to judge another's feelings, choices, or actions than to take a good look at our own. When we judge, we are often avoiding something we don't want to see within ourselves.

If we deny our feelings, we start accepting limiting beliefs as true about who we are and how our life will be. Then, even as we try to protect ourselves, we will continue negative patterns and keep getting hurt in the same way. As we carry heavier armor and repress more of our true selves, we will feel burdened and then judge ourselves for not feeling good.

You deserve love even if somebody did something terrible to you or you did something bad to someone else. Pierce through your armor and find the innocent little child inside of you who is totally loved. No matter how tragic or horrible your life has been, know that you are not alone. I have read thousands of student autobiographies. Everyone has dealt with adversity, and each person has more resilience than they initially realized. We all have fears and pain, and more people than you probably imagine will love and support you if you open up and share with them. Take credit for the courage and strength that you have already demonstrated in your life. No matter what happens, you can still give and receive love.

What Is Armor?

We all carry armor, a layer of protection. Some carry a heavier weight than others. We will shed it at times, when we feel safe, but then we pack it on again whenever we get hurt.

Armor manifests in different ways. We tend to hold onto our thoughts, emotions, beliefs, and behaviors even if they are no longer working for us. This can show up as playing a certain role, carrying extra weight, being consumed with making or having a lot of money, relationship or sexual issues, the inability to be productive, holding onto unresolved issues or unfinished business, distracting ourselves with technology devices and social media, or numbing ourselves through food, drink, or drugs—all in an effort to hide our painful feelings and thoughts. We often believe that if we hide our suffering we are taking care of ourselves since we are only supposed to feel good. But as we protect ourselves from pain, we only form heavier armor. As we cling to it and get attached, it becomes harder to let go. It takes courage and strength to shed that heavy armor.

We repress feelings because we couldn't deal with the intense emotions when they occurred. We buried them, hoping they would just go away. If we continue to ignore them, they eventually start speaking more loudly—like my body shutting down when it couldn't take anymore. When we repress feelings, we are saying, "I can't deal with this now. I need to protect myself. I will hide it so nobody finds out the real me and dislikes me or, worse, hurts me. If I have to, I will carry it around and deal with it later, when I am ready." Eventually, the time bomb explodes, manifesting as illness, injury, or the loss of a loved one or job. Then we *have* to deal with it.

Another way we use armor is to play a certain role, like putting on a mask or a Halloween costume. Defining ourselves by a certain role might make us feel safe or important. But this kind of thinking limits us. We can be a parent, spouse, athlete, businessperson, "smart kid," teacher, actor—but we also are much more than that. I had always been known as a champion swimmer—that was what made me feel like someone special and important. When I got sick and could no longer swim, I had to learn how to redefine myself, which required me to look deep within to see all the feelings, needs, and desires I had forsaken for so long.

Life is an adventure, with good and bad, heartache and happiness, sorrow and joy. To try to protect ourselves from the ups-and-downs of life is not possible. When we stop separating ourselves from so-called "negative" feelings, we feel whole and connected. As we stop shielding ourselves from the wind and storms that come along, we release stress. We reclaim our spark.

When we face our fears, their dark power dissipates and we find compassion for ourselves and others. We can acknowledge that we needed certain feelings and emotions to survive at some point in our life. But now it is okay to let go of this armor. When we do so, we can start to realize how great we really are. We don't need to fear our own magnificence. We can let go and love what has occurred up until now in our life. As we judge ourselves less, we take better care of ourselves and allow true healing to begin.

Yes, it is nice to feel good, but when we acknowledge, forgive, and accept all of our feelings and actions up until now, we will be at peace. We can figure out what inspires us and see that our soft, warm heart is still there underneath our unraveling layers of protection. We begin to feel connected and have more energy. Our spirit is coming back out.

How Can You Shed Your Armor?

To reclaim your power and shed your armor, you first need to recognize that you have it. Then, become aware of how you pack it on. To start, surround yourself with people whom you trust, so that you can let your guard down. Then be willing to feel bare. Take time out of your busy schedule to pay attention. Initially, the chatter inside your head might say, "I am wasting time—I have a huge 'to do' list," or "I am bored." You might feel vulnerable and exposed, even to yourself. Keep going; as you honor your truth, you will begin to feel lighter and happier.

I worked with Anneke and Dr. Helms to shed my layers of armor. I cried, wrote in my journal, and learned to appreciate and express all of my emotions. As I became more attentive to my sadness about being sick, my frustration about not being able to swim, and my anger about not healing fast enough, I could also experience more joy, even while I was bedridden.

Have the courage to really know yourself. You might not like the new you initially, and you might want to go back to what you were comfortable with. Commit to being true to yourself even as distractions try to pull you back to your old ways.

What can you do today to be more honest with yourself? Be open to new possibilities and try them. You might surprise yourself. Not only will you feel better, you will probably see external results, too, such as weight loss, a healthier body, and happier relationships. You might even be able to stop taking unnecessary medications that you thought you needed.

Exercises to Decrease Armor

#1: Forge a relationship with a part of yourself that you dislike—either in your body, emotions, or actions. Acknowledge how you feel about it, thank that feeling, and then let it go.

#2: If you feel that your job defines you, ask yourself, "Am I really happy in this job?" If not, why are you staying in it? To accumulate more stuff that ultimately does not satisfy you? Does this serve your family? Does this job satisfy the role you are playing, but not you personally? Can you shift how you are living? Stay honest with whatever feelings arise for you.

Stop Protecting Others from Pain

Honor your feelings, and take them seriously. Stop trying to protect others, especially your parents. If you live in fear about how someone else might respond, then trust that you are strong enough to love and accept yourself, even if others don't. When you are real about your experience, it scares other people if they are still denying their own feelings. Remember that it is not personal if they reject you for you speaking the truth. All they are really doing is rejecting their own truth.

Some people benefited from you being numb—if you confront your emotions, then they will have to confront theirs, too. They might decide to change along with you, or they might try to pull you back so they do not have to face their pain. Remember, they want to be accepted, too, and you might unknowingly cause them to feel exposed or confront their fears. Have compassion for them, but stay on your path to becoming your true self.

You cannot mold yourself into what somebody else wants you to be. If you try to, out of your loyalty to that person, you both will suffer. You want to be happy, yet it might seem uncomfortable to feel good if others around you are not happy. Other people might be jealous of your happiness or try to bring you back into their world of unhappiness so they do not have to face their truth. They might project their insecurities onto you: "Look how selfish he is, doing what he wants" or "She's trying to make me feel bad because of her own pain." Yet, helping them to reflect on themselves is the best gift that you can give them. They can choose to be inspired by or annoyed by you. It is not your job to change how they feel about you. Your job is to remain focused and stay on your path, even as others try to distract you.

Surround yourself with people who support you in your journey and inspire you to honor your true self. Be willing to change even if others around you judge you for it. This requires tremendous strength, as friends, colleagues, and family members may try to pull you back to what they perceived you to be. As you release your armor, you will feel lighter and free. Let go, and learn to love your true self.

Honor Your Feelings

> *"Never apologize for showing feelings. When you do so,*
> *you apologize for the truth."*
> *—Benjamin Disraeli, British Prime Minister*

There is so much pressure in our society to only feel happy and not acknowledge other feelings. It is okay to feel happy, but it's best when happiness comes from a place of feeling fulfilled. Know that even if you feel angry or depressed in this moment, you can still feel at peace within.

It is okay to be upset, to feel embarrassed, ashamed, mad, or depressed. When these feelings come up, it is a sign that something is bothering you. Go deeper, and explore the underlying cause of what you are feeling. What is really troubling you? What need of yours is not being met? Are you living the life you want? Learning to listen to our truth can be challenging, as we might worry about our own or others' judgment. As we listen, we will become aware of where these beliefs came from in the first place.

Because you feel loyal to someone and don't want to hurt them, it can be hard to speak up and express your feelings. At first, doing so might provoke other feelings within you, such as guilt or fear, that make you want to keep quiet. You might think, "I don't deserve to be heard," "Others are more worthy than I am," or "What if they get angry at what I say and then hurt me?" Listen to every feeling that comes up, and express yourself as best you can. You might end up screaming, crying, lying in a fetal position, or writing in your journal. As you release your pent-up emotions, you will start to feel better. The key is not to wait until a crisis occurs—start now, and stay committed to your path.

Acknowledge Your Fears

Through focus and meditation, we can recognize our feelings and thoughts, shed our armor, understand what motivates us, and figure out what makes us feel complete. Initially, all these thoughts and feelings might drive us crazy or make us think that we are a mess inside. We can stop having conflict with ourselves, and start being honest. We can acknowledge our shame, mistakes, and fears—of abandonment, rejection, not feeling heard, feeling needy and dependent. As we face them, our fears dissipate, and we honor our truth. Acknowledgment helps us to forgive ourselves, grieve for what was lost, and let go.

You might be afraid that no one will understand you, that you will be alone in your journey. Have compassion for fearful voices that ask, "Who will love me after all I have been through?" or "I am afraid I won't be loved for who I am." Trust that you are not alone. You will be amazed to find how many other people are dealing with similar issues. The details of your experiences might not be the same, but there are others out there who will understand what you are going through. As I started to heal from CFIDS, I realized that many of us have denied our feelings. I was not alone. Knowing this mere fact helped me to face my own pain.

Face Your Dark Side

Like anyone, as I was healing I had moments where I would get distracted or want to numb myself. I tried to swim, but it was too exhausting. I took stimulants and pretended that I was fine, rather than face the fact that I was sick. As I began to listen within, I realized I had a lot of repressed anger about not taking care of my needs. I had been so good at pleasing others and thinking that being "nice" was more important that I had not honored what I really felt.

By expressing the feelings that you had from an experience, you reclaim a part of yourself. Nobody else can take this from you. As I worked with Anneke, I had fun expressing all parts of myself. If I felt depressed, I could throw myself a depression party—dress up in black, make a black cake, and so on. We can all laugh when we imagine this—but it works! I acknowledged parts of me that I had hidden out of shame. I had become afraid of them, and of what might happen if I let them out. But as I let my feelings emerge, through meditation or just being aware, I realized I had compassion for them. I felt sad about what a part of me had gone through as I tried to hide what I had felt.

When we avoid the dark side, we can feel an underlying heaviness, stress, anxiety, or boredom, which manifests in different ways. When we stop distracting ourselves, and attempt to pay attention, we initially feel uneasy. As we decrease stimulation and try to listen to our inner selves, we don't know how to manage our continuous stream of thoughts, and we want them to stop. After all, they can drive us crazy when we first start really paying attention to them.

We experience stress when we are not being true to ourselves. We might feel anxious about acknowledging our dark side, or just plain bored with our life if we have been living inauthentically. To avoid dealing with these feelings, we look for distractions to enliven us rather than putting in the effort to ultimately experience the spirit and life within us.

What is something that makes you feel down, anxious, stressed, or bored? How do you respond to those feelings? Do you need something external to make you feel "up" or alive? If so (and if you are in a good mental place), reflect on something that you are ashamed about, or attached to wanting, such as eating chocolates. Maybe when you are depressed or bored you eat unconsciously. You try to give yourself energy, or a feeling, such as euphoria, that you had once before by eating them. Decide that you will indulge in this, and pay attention as you do this. Buy yourself some of your favorites chocolates and eat them throughout the day.

Notice how your feelings change. What does that first chocolate do for you? How about the tenth? Are you feeling satisfied? Do you want to stop? Often, when we deny ourselves something and try to hide how we feel about it, we become consumed by it, rather than freed by denying how we feel. Notice this, and be willing to have compassion for everything you feel and everything you have done. Remember, it does you no service to beat yourself up. Even with mistakes, you are okay just as you are. It is better to live your truest life rather than trying to hide and act perfect as you dismiss who you really are.

All of us have times when we used a method or action to survive. It might be something we were not proud of at the time, but we didn't know how else to deal with it. For me, I kept pushing rather than stopping. I was afraid to listen inside. Maybe you yelled at someone after they hurt you, or manipulated someone since you didn't know how to honestly and directly ask for what you wanted. You might have lied or been controlling to get your needs met. You still were trying to learn what your needs were and figure out how to satisfy them. Know that you no longer need to feel guilty for directly stating your needs. You can stop playing these old games as you take care of yourself.

Integrate All Parts of You

Human beings tend to play out both their "dark" side and their "good" side. We are sad. We are happy. We succeed and fail, we feel clear and confused, right and wrong, proud and shamed, good and bad. We feel worthy, and then not deserving or good enough. We can be narcissistic as we think we are better than everyone else. On the flip side, we can feel terrible, inferior, like a nobody who needs external validation to feel okay with ourselves. We might experience insecurity deep within as we go to great lengths to be noticed in the business world, athletics, on the stage, or even within our families. We can be very loving and then emotionally hard on ourselves and others. All of us sometimes act from a good place and sometimes from a poor place. The more we can acknowledge both sides, the more we can work on integrating them. We can combine and balance these voices/parts of ourselves by being aware and having a focused mind.

Rather than pushing away what you find difficult, look at it. Own it. Instead of fighting your repressed side, befriend it and dissolve this dualistic struggle. Face the difficulty, and it no longer will control you. All you have to do is acknowledge it, see it for what it is, and forgive yourself for repressing it. When you allow a feeling to surface, you can tell it that you no longer need it. Thank it and let it go. You can change the patterns in your life, integrate both sides of yourself, and live more fully. The following exercise, taken from Gestalt therapy, can help.

Exercise: What Are Your Feelings?

As children, we tend to take in what we hear from our parents. If we often saw and heard them be angry, for instance, we might have taken on those feelings as if they were our own, while disregarding what we actually felt in that moment. This exercise will help you to hear the "voices" from both yourself and your parents and to gradually differentiate which is your voice and which is someone else's that you have believed to be your own.

Set two chairs facing each other. Sit in one, and leave the other one empty. Talk to someone who raised you. Then, move to the other chair and become that person, talking back to you. Let's say it is you as a child talking to your father. Child says to father, "I am afraid to tell you what I feel because you always get mad at me." Father says to child, "I don't have time to listen right now." Child feels unheard and sad. Child says, "I do not feel heard, and I need you." Continue going back and forth, sitting in each chair. Sit with the feeling of each person.

Validate how you, the child, feels as you are not heard, or as someone gets angry at you. Then, notice how you feel being the one who ignores or get mad. Do you feel like both feelings are yours now, or somebody else's? Have you repressed them? Can you have compassion for both parts of you now? What does this exercise bring up inside of you? If you were taught to not show emotion, you now have permission to let it out. Scream, cry, feel it; do whatever you need to do to express it. As you become more aware, you differentiate which feelings are your own and which were actually someone else's. Then you integrate these voices within, and own your true feelings.

Take Responsibility

Many people function from a place where they are reactive to their environment and want to be told what to do. They do not realize their own power. Instead, they prefer, or have gotten comfortable, being victims in their own life as they let other people take control.

Taking responsibility is tough for many of us. It is easier to look for things that were done wrong to us so that we can remain a victim. We blame and judge other people, pointing out their supposed faults rather than dealing with our own. We also like to pretend that we are perfect, as we rationalize that our life is working out just as we had planned, even as we are suffering deeply within.

Don't be fooled: Even if you are older, you still might be looking for someone (your parents, children, siblings, spouse, or friends) to take care of your unresolved childhood needs, rather than owning up to them and taking care of them yourself. The wounded child inside you still wants to be loved, held, and taken care of rather than to grow up.

Now it is time to do your part to meet your own needs. Question your habits and beliefs. Yes, some beliefs may seem silly ("If I say I don't like something, my partner might leave me"); they were probably created while you were in a fearful state. By being willing to change, rather than stubbornly trying to prove yourself right, you will no longer need to justify a position that no longer serves you. You can act on your own behalf rather than on someone else's.

As I learned to ask for help, I let go of my old beliefs about needing support. Rather than feeling shameful or guilty, I felt loved by those around me. I was pleasantly surprised to be so supported by people, several of whom were newer friends. Because I was learning to love and appreciate myself, I could finally accept generosity and care from others.

When you initially admit to all of your feelings, thoughts, and actions, you might feel ashamed. If so, accept that feeling and *feel* it. What does it mean to you? As you observe it and acknowledge it, it no longer has power over you. It is like turning on the lights in a dark house. The gremlins are suddenly gone.

It is time to give yourself what you have been looking for from others. Be your own best loving parent. When you start speaking and living from your true self, you realize that you have a huge source of power and love within. Regardless of your past events, you accept who you are and appreciate this life. You become more clear, decisive, and proactive in your choices. Your happiness comes from within. You do not need to rely on other people or external circumstances—you are in charge of your own well-being.

Taking Care of Your Needs

It was hard for me to accept that I had needs and that I deserved to fulfill them. Being sick made me realize that I could ask for help and still be respected. I didn't have to take care of others in order to get their acceptance and love. It gave me clarity and energy to determine what my needs were and state them clearly.

As you listen within, shed your armor, and are honest with yourself, you will discover your true needs and desires. With as much detail as possible, state your needs (or write them down). What did you always want that you never got? How can you give this to yourself today?

When, as adults, we still seek love and availability from a parent, partner, friend, or child, we are trying to fulfill a need from long ago. We cannot change the past, but we can deal with feelings as they arise now. We can reclaim the needs we had as children. Then we no longer have to react to events that are happening now in the same way we did when we were young. Our goal is to recognize our capacity to love ourselves and to receive love in a healthy way.

As parents, we might feel a sense of importance raising a child who needs us. We want to feel in control rather than helpless and needy. If we don't pay attention, we might try to use our children to meet our unmet needs. We want to be held and loved; yet, it can be scary to ask for this. When we needed it as children, we felt helpless and depended on another person to feel this love. Now, we might look to our children to fulfill this, rather than work on our needs with a therapist, friend, or partner.

It is okay to have needs and wants. We just need to be willing to open up and express them. Often we think we are selfish or not worthy, or that people will judge us if we state what we want. If we repress our needs, we only frustrate ourselves as we manipulate others to get them met (even though another person can't fulfill our needs; only we can). By being clear about what you need, you can ask for your needs to be met in a healthy way, and by doing so, you can give and receive love.

Exercise: Express Your Needs

Ask the little child inside you what he/she needs, and then give it. When I was in college, I made myself a tape telling me wonderful things about myself. I'd listen, but sometimes I doubted my own words since I was not ready to hear them. At times, I would cry as I felt my beauty and radiant power that had been hidden. Listen to yourself like you wanted to be heard as a child. Make a list of your needs, and state what would help you get your needs met. How can you directly express these needs, so another person can understand you and possibly help you?

As you become aware of what you feel inside, you become clear about what you want. You express your feelings and needs, act on them, and feel satisfied with your decisions. When you validate how you feel and what you want, and then do it, you feel your power.

Getting Healthy

By the time I graduated from Cal Berkeley in 1995, I had regained a lot of my health and vitality. Like anyone who has chronically overextended their energy, I had to learn the value of rest, and then I willingly committed to it. I was sleeping through the night, but I still needed fourteen to eighteen hours a day of rest in order to function.

In addition to feeling better physically, I was also on my way to being emotionally healthier than ever. I couldn't exercise yet, and I didn't have the energy or stamina to look for a job as I had planned to before my illness. However, my mind was clearer, and my heart felt open.

I decided to move to Connecticut and attend graduate school for Marriage and Family Therapy and Gestalt Therapy. In graduate school, we were required to seek counseling, to ensure that we were taking care of ourselves while also seeing patients. I developed some enriching friendships with people in my program, and we were open and honest with each other. We were all starting to understand our past and how it affected our current patterns and beliefs. We worked on shedding unnecessary baggage, healing old wounds, and appreciating our strengths. As we became effective therapists, we also became healthier and happier people.

Claim Your Voice and Trust Your Power

To be in your power, honor your vulnerability and resilience. Trust yourself, shed your armor, and have faith in your own ideas. Don't hide your child inside—that child has stories to tell you. Claim your voice and free yourself. It is time to take care of you—by doing so, you will ultimately help others heal, too, and you will make your relationships richer and stronger. No matter what you were told as a child, or what you experienced the "rules" to be, you have the right to speak up and state your needs.

The goal is not to ignore your past. Instead, observe it and acknowledge it without judgment. Have compassion for yourself, and honor all your feelings. Decrease denial, and shed defining roles. Be the true *you*.

Chapter Twelve

Healthy Relationships: Bringing Our Your Best Within Yourself and In Your Relationships

Love begins at home, and it is not how much we do...
but how much love we put in that action.
–Mother Teresa

As you continue to pursue being your best in all areas of your life, you can also bring out your best in relationships. How do you do this? How do you define a successful relationship? What motivates you when it comes to your personal life, sexual preferences, experiences, choosing a mate? How have you experienced love in your own life? What belief system is a pattern for you, and how can you change it for the better?

In the last chapter, we discussed the importance of acknowledging our feelings and becoming clear on our needs. In order to do this, we need to listen, accept what has happened up until now, and honor how we have felt at different stages in our lives. We have to be honest with ourselves, even with the parts of us that we want to forget. As we are honest, we build trust and respect for ourselves. We feel better when we don't hide or have secrets or lies, and we express our true selves. We realize that we can accept who we are and change within, and thus see change occur in our relationships and lives.

When we are honest with ourselves, it is easier to be honest with others, which helps us build trust and respect. When we take responsibility for who we are and what we have done, felt, and experienced, we break toxic habits and form healthy bonds.

We need to pay attention, communicate, and express our needs as we set clear intentions and boundaries. As we learn and understand our own values and beliefs, we can apply these to our relationships. With honest, open communication and healthy boundaries in place, our relationships will flourish, and we will be able to give and receive love and appreciation wholeheartedly.

Setting Boundaries

Are you honoring yourself and the people around you? Do you say "no" to a person who might want more from you than you are willing to give? Are you prepared to lose friends, romantic relationships, or a group of friends if you stand up for yourself and they don't like it? You have the power to choose and create positive changes in your life.

As I continued to work with my therapist, I learned the value of reclaiming my truth in all areas. One of my biggest lessons was learning to say "no" and set healthy boundaries. Before being sick, I had pretended I was fine and never asked for help or even wanted to admit that I had needs. But I eventually learned to speak up for myself and get my needs met. I opened up to my college coach, Teri, and she respected my needs. I felt validated and empowered to keep speaking my truth and setting boundaries. Gradually, I learned to take care of myself in all my relationships.

What is a boundary? It is a limit or border that can refer to our physical or emotional space. Physically, it can define how close we physically are as we talk to someone or whether we let someone touch us, and in what way, and how often. Emotionally, boundaries define what is appropriate to share and what are *our* emotions versus someone else's. Are we overly responsible for another person's feelings? Can we respect their feelings and needs without trying to control how they think or feel? Can we say "no"? Can we directly and honestly ask for what we need? Or do we give up our desires to comply with another's demands? These kinds of questions determine our boundaries.

You need to respect other people's emotional boundaries just as you respect their physical space. In order to have clear boundaries, you must know how you feel and identify what your needs are. As you become aware of what your boundaries are, you can enforce them.

Boundaries can be too closed or too open. Rigidity keeps people out of your life—you don't feel connected, as you probably don't talk about or show emotions or ask for help. It is hard to let someone get close to you. On the other hand, if you have loose boundaries, you will tend to take too much from others or give away too much of yourself. You might allow others to touch you inappropriately, confuse love with sex, or take on others' feelings as if they were your own.

To have a healthy boundary, you want to be firm in expressing and standing by your needs, while being flexible. You respect other people's feelings while also honoring and taking responsibility for your own. Be willing to stand up for yourself while supporting others in expressing their needs.

Initially, stating your needs and standing by them is scary. You might worry what other people will think, or how they will respond to you. If you had learned to repress your anger over being hurt, you might have anxiety as you start expressing anger, especially to others. Be clear about what you need, and do not apologize for it or feel that you have to justify it. Your job is to take care of yourself and be compassionate toward other people. Listen to them, and learn from their sincere feedback, but do not worry if their response is negative. If they no longer want your friendship, know that you'll be okay in the long run. You want friends who respect you and your boundaries, not invade them or try to make you feel bad about them. As feelings come up, acknowledge them, but stay on your path.

Notice your energy—if you feel heavy, anxious, fearful, or angry, you probably need to set a boundary with someone. Yes, this will test you at times, especially if this is new for you. Similarly, when you deal with people who are functioning from fear, it is hard for you to feel uplifted by them. They may try to invalidate your thoughts and ideas, which will bring you down. They are unable and often unwilling to listen, learn, and grow. Your best feedback might be no feedback, or you might want to stop spending time with them. Remain firm. As you continue to do this, you will feel your own power and trust yourself. Your energy will increase as you are true to yourself. The main thing is to honor who you are and what you want.

Let's say you do not want to kiss on your first date. It is up to you to be clear with your date that your limit is holding hands, nothing else. Respect your own needs. If they try to give you a hard time about this, recognize that they are not respecting you—and that it will only get worse if you keep spending time with them.

Also, know you are not in charge of another person's feelings—honor them and how they feel, just as you want to be respected for your own emotions and needs. This will help you have more conscious, mindful relationships. If you have a fear about a friend having a certain feeling, express that to them. ("I'm afraid that if I spend time with Linda, you will get jealous and upset.") When you both trust one another, you each can have compassion for this feeling and enhance your connectedness and understanding of one another.

Focus on how you can set healthy limits. One simple way is by saying no. If you are nervous to do this, ask yourself, "Why am I afraid to say no? What is the consequence that scares me?" Can you imagine another outcome that makes you feel good? If you stood up for yourself, how would you feel? It is normal to fear change. Remember, your whole reason for picking up this book was to be your best. As you stay committed to your path, change will occur, and this is how you will become your best and brightest self.

Being more honest with ourselves alters our relationships. If we have always done what someone wanted, even though we didn't feel good about it inside, we may feel heaviness and resentment. We might fear their anger if we don't give them what they want. We might fear getting hurt. The unknown consequences of actions can be scary, even if we know we are acting in our own best interest, but try to stay true to you. Whatever it is, know that you have the right to claim and use your voice.

Stop fearing the result of "no." Imagine the flipside of what is possible. Even if you upset somebody, you will finally be taking care of you! As you do this, your relationships will shift. Both parties might benefit. If other people can honestly share their feelings and needs, this will serve you well, too! There will be some people who are unwilling to grow or to understand you; one of you might decide to terminate your relationship. If this person is no longer in your life, you might feel sad. So, be sad. Grieve the loss. Then pick yourself up and stay focused on what you can create for yourself. Who do you want to be around? Who inspires and brings out the best in you? Those are the people you want in your life.

Communication

The foundation of any good relationship is communication. Know how you feel and what you need, then express it. This can be verbal or nonverbal. In athletics, a good coach knows how to talk to an athlete in a way that fits with the athlete's personality and style of communication. They know if the athlete needs a hug, certain words of encouragement, or just to be left alone. The main thing is to empower one another. When two people trust each other, it is easier to have a strong relationship and to perform at your best.

It is important to know what works for you, and how you can best feel heard and also understand others. Harmony in communication occurs when you know it is okay to have your differences, but you respect and listen to the other's opinion. Remember: listen, trust, show respect, be honest, have compassion, and set boundaries.

To have effective communication, start by saying "I feel" rather than blaming the other person. State, "When you do this, I feel..." or use "if, then": "If you don't stop, then I will tell the coach/parent." Tell your partner what changes you want to see: "I prefer hearing constructive feedback instead of being blamed." Using "I" statements puts the responsibility on you and will keep the other person from getting defensive. This allows you to communicate your needs and desires in a way that is conducive to better understanding.

Conflict Resolution

Sometimes when we try to share our feelings, it causes problems within a relationship. The first step in communication is awareness. From here, each person can better understand the perceived differences that led to the miscommunication. We view people in a certain way based on our beliefs and perceptions. We can even have conflict within ourselves about what we think is true.

Conflict is a normal part of communication—it is okay to have differences, and it provides an opportunity for growth and learning. Try the following exercise to enhance your ability to listen without interrupting as someone gives you feedback. As you learn to listen, the other person feels heard, and you can both gain from sharing honestly what you experience.

Sit in a circle with two or three other people. Have one person share a story about a conflict and how it was resolved while the others listen. Then have each listener give feedback about what they heard and observed. Did you believe the storyteller? Do you think he/she was rationalizing what happened, or telling the truth? Is he/she playing the victim or owning up to his/her part in the conflict? How would you have handled it differently? What did you like about what he/she did? Try to keep your attachment to the storyteller out of it; you are simply an observer.

This exercise can help us see ourselves objectively. By getting input and feedback from people we trust, we can gain a better perspective about how others see us and how we interact in the world.

It is okay to be assertive in our communication. We might fear speaking up since we have unpleasant memories from experiencing conflict. Maybe our parents had one final yelling match right before they divorced. This could cause us to feel rejected as we deal with change in our original family system. We may not like to tell the truth, since we fear losing an important person in our life. Thus, we avoid conflict since we associate it with pain, even if we know our current situation is not optimal.

On the other hand, we might avoid conflict because we grew up in a home where everyone pretended that everything was fine, even if it wasn't. We might remember an underlying tension of unresolved conflict in the air. It could be each individual's own energy regarding their own conflict, or conflict among two or more people.

Conflict triggers a fear of rejection in many people. But remember, you are never alone—there are always people, whether friends, family, coworkers, or support group members, who will be there to back you up and help you get through difficult times. When afraid, it's easy to protect yourself or pack on your armor. In your adult relationships, especially with a mate, notice your fears and talk about them. Once you stop valuing self-protection over love and honesty, you will be free to assert your true needs.

Exercise: Getting Your Needs Met

In Chapter Eleven, we discussed how to differentiate your own emotions from someone else's. Let's do an exercise to help you express your needs and feelings to an authority figure or friend. It is okay to be honest even if there is disagreement. We grow by understanding someone else's viewpoint.

Imagine being back in your childhood home. What feelings do you have here? As you remember the energy in the home, pretend you are now having a conversation with your caregiver(s). Tell them what you liked about being raised by them, and what you didn't like. What did you want from them that you didn't get? Express your feelings, and then imagine having a positive, loving interaction with them. Maybe you hug him/her/them, or they tell you that they always loved you and are sorry if they hurt you. You also take responsibility for times that you know you reacted in a way that may have been hurtful to them.

Express your needs to your caregiver(s). Imagine them being compassionate and open as they ask you, "How were you hurt as a child? How did you feel or what did you do when I did X?" If a parent was not emotionally or physically available and attentive to you (perhaps they worked a lot or didn't spend quality time with you), you may have felt ignored. If a parent smothered you with love, was nosey, or gossiped about you to others, you might have hidden your true feelings to protect yourself (since they invaded your boundaries).

Honor all of your emotions as you sense both your feelings and the other person's concern (or lack of regard) for your feelings. Pay attention to what you really need. Then imagine telling this person what you need from him/her. Allow yourself to feel good stating what you need. Now act as your own best parent and fulfill your needs in some way today.

How to Change Your Relationships

When we are not clear about what we want, we feel conflicted within ourselves, and that is reflected in our relationships. We might want to learn, be happy, and grow; yet we might also be afraid of the unknown and worried about making changes. The key is to recognize that you can only control yourself, and then take action accordingly.

You might be in a relationship that is stressful. You initially think you need to change the other person. Is that the solution? You can't actually change somebody else. How do you change a relationship then? By not reacting emotionally to them, or by focusing on seeing them as someone you love, even in disagreement, you will be able to work out conflict more easily.

Balance between sharing and listening is also helpful. You can change how you respond to another person and state your needs more clearly. Then pay attention to his/her emotions and needs. As you understand where another person is coming from while also asserting your needs, the dynamic of the relationship changes for the better.

Nobody is going to satisfy you completely. Your goal is to bring out the best in yourself and in your relationships. Envision what you want in a satisfying, loving relationship and work toward making that a reality.

Complete Unfinished Business

As we learn to have healthy boundaries, we become more adept at putting closure on past experiences. We tend to complete unfinished business by bringing past events back up into the present to relive and resolve them. What we needed from our immediate family is likely what we seek from our mate and others today. On an unconscious level, we seek to fulfill our needs through others unless we learn to take care of them within.

As mentioned in Chapter Eleven, it is important to feel pain when it comes up rather than pretend it does not exist. That way, we can learn to express our feelings and needs, and change our interactions with others.

Some of us have gotten comfortable carrying heavy armor. We spend time with people who prove us right that we should be beating ourselves up. We think that if we let our guard down and be our real selves, we won't be worthy. If someone has experienced criticism or, worse, abuse (more people have than you would expect), it is common for them to avoid their own pain but then unconsciously re-create it again in an attempt to re-experience the feeling and emotionally heal from the original trauma. If somebody's physical boundaries were violated (sexually or otherwise), they might seek out many men/women who continue to violate them.

Similarly, if we were abandoned or neglected by a caregiver, we look for attention to make us feel attractive, to be noticed, or be "somebody." We might be promiscuous or jump from one relationship to another as we search for someone to love us. Yet we often lose our self-respect and feel lonely as we get more addicted to needing to find love. We think if we find the person they will give us what we want and we will be okay, but it doesn't work that way. As mentioned in earlier chapters, we must first accept and love ourselves in order to be fulfilled. Nobody else can do it for us.

It is important to understand what is driving us to reinvent unhealthy patterns in our relationships. We need to go back to what motivates us deep within. What are we really looking for that causes us to repeat destructive behaviors? For the person who was neglected, he/she might just want any kind of attention, no matter how bad.

How can you give yourself what you want? How can you have healthy boundaries so you can change a negative pattern into something you feel good about? Take a moment to write in your journal about what feelings come up for you when you reflect on places you get stuck in relationships. What do you really want? How were you valued as a child, and how do you value yourself now? Are you willing to change to honor your worth? What do you tell yourself? How does this get reflected in your choice of friendships and romantic partners? How would you describe your dating experiences? What kind of relationship is best for you? What themes do you notice in your life? Which ones do you like, and which do you want to change? What are you looking for from another person, and how can you give this to yourself? What are your beliefs regarding relationships, and how can you change them to start having different experiences? Are you willing to stand up for yourself? If not, what scares you? Can you imagine a good outcome as you take care of yourself?

If you were (or are) fortunate enough to have healthy role models (parents or others) who demonstrate connection, communication, trust, and willingness to compromise, you will experience love in a different way. If you didn't have this, you can imagine what it would be like and focus on creating it for yourself.

Reactions To Change

As you become more true to yourself, assert your needs, and set up boundaries, people who were used to you being a certain way will either accept the new you or try to pull you back into being your old self. If you used to take care of them, and now you say "no" and establish boundaries, they might respect this or resent this. If they resist, and if you need their approval more than your own, you might give in. Be easy on yourself. At first, you might go two steps forward and one step back. Be aware; notice sensations and emotions that are giving you feedback. Reflect on what these people mean to you, and then mobilize yourself into taking action toward shedding your armor, regardless. If the other person is not willing to support you, then you may have to separate yourself from him/her. If the other person is willing to embrace (or at least recognize) your true self, you both gain, as that usually means he/she also wants his/her true self to emerge.

Within relationships, there are typically two levels of change. Level One is when people find someone else to replace you in their game. If you used to do whatever someone wanted you to, and now you say no, they will find someone else to take your place. They don't grow or change; they just change the players in their game. Level Two alters the pattern. The dynamic either is dissolved, changed, or no longer played out. If you were the family member who focused on helping a sibling or parent (such as enabling them in an addiction) and you start taking care of yourself and changing your behavior toward them, they might actually respond positively. They learn to heal and take care of themselves rather than finding someone else to allow them to go back to their old habits.

Thus, pay attention to change within and around you. When you are avoiding something that is hard for you to admit (such as letting a boyfriend/girlfriend convince you to behave a certain way sexually), you might keep seeking out similar people. Once you become aware and are willing to shift your beliefs and behavior, you will no longer fall into this trap. Your radar will alert you to people who would typically not respect your boundaries, and you will learn to attract people who can honor your needs and feelings.

Forgiveness And Letting Go

When you have expressed your needs and others can't respect them, you often experience an end to a relationship. As this happens, have compassion and thank these people for being in your life. Know that it is okay if they do not like the new you—this is a reflection of them, not you.

If you feel tension with someone, but you do not feel safe (physically or emotionally) talking to them directly, thank him or her from your heart. Ask for their forgiveness for any wrongdoing you might have done, and then forgive him or her for any wrongs they may have committed. Wish them the best, and imagine them being surrounded with love and support as they become their true self. In doing so, you will give yourself peace and help yourself heal. This forgiving, loving energy does not know any boundaries—it travels and can be felt by the other person, even if you do not speak these words directly to them. You do not need to control how that person completes their relationship with you. You can only take care of it on your end. You don't need to be validated by others, only by yourself.

As you forgive others and ask for their forgiveness (even if only within your-self), you can let go of any unresolved energy. This frees you up to respect yourself, to keep growing, and to honor other people's needs and desires.

Learning From Relationships

Often, we do not want to admit that we are not happy in a relationship. We would rather rationalize that we committed to this person or friend and are supposed to stick it out. Or we are afraid of being alone, so we pretend like everything is fine.

We might be going through some unfinished business that this person trig-gers in us. Whether we like to admit it or not, our relationships are our best gurus—mirrors that reflect who we really are. Another person chal-lenges our way of thinking and acting just by being who they are! If we can embrace them just as they are, we will learn the most about ourselves. When we heal and grow, we thrive within our relationships.

The key to any relationship is being honest with one another, and sometimes we have to agree to disagree. The more we can express our needs and work together to try to meet them for each other, the more content and happy we will feel.

Commitment Fosters Growth

Relationships are an opportunity for self-growth and deep connection. The purpose of commitment to another person is to know that you can feel safe enough together to heal old wounds, to share and be honest, and to love one another even as you reveal your full selves.

When we are first in love, many of us imagine a fairytale romance in which our partner fulfills all of our unmet needs. Once we realize they have their own needs, too, we get angry at them because they're not fully attending to us. Over time in a relationship, we get to experience a reflection as our partner allows us to see what we project and how we handle various emotions. In order for a relationship to survive and thrive past the initial "falling in love" phase, each person has to love and care for themselves as well as their partner. When we stop judging others and have compassion, we become more compassionate and accepting of ourselves, too.

All relationships require commitment, honesty, and awareness. If we are not committed to growth and honesty, it is easy to fault our partner and think that ending a relationship will solve our problems. When we have not taken responsibility for how we view the world, and we project our problems onto someone else, we think if we get rid of that person, we won't have problems anymore. There are times when it is healthiest to leave a relationship, but just the act of leaving another person is not the solution to becoming happy.

It is possible that your unhappiness has nothing to do with that person. If you are unfulfilled, you cannot expect another person to make you happy—and just moving on to someone else will simply continue your negative patterns. Using a split in order to grow is not wise if you have not communicated and tried to grow together first. Personal growth happens when you are clear on your intentions and can learn from mistakes and from another's perspective.

When I paid attention, I knew intuitively if I was supposed to be in a relationship or not. My rationalizing to stay, even if I knew it would be best to move on, had caused me (and my partner) heartache and pain. As I justified staying, I'd get confused about what I really wanted. Then I would avoid being honest with my partner and myself. But once I learned to trust my gut, I knew what to do. If I sensed it was best to end a long-term relationship, my partner and I would communicate about what had worked and what we could learn, no matter how painful, before peacefully parting ways.

The key is to learn from every relationship. If we don't understand what motivated our behavior with one person, we will look to satisfy our needs the same way in the next relationship. Typically, patterns show up again and again until we face them.

We all have coping mechanisms that no longer serve us—or the people around us. Take note of your habits, and be aware of when you are treating yourself or others poorly. Keep assessing yourself and your relationships.

It is easy to get busy with work, children, and other activities and avoid really connecting to your partner. When we don't slow down enough to pay attention, we act out old habits. In my marriage, we check in with one another to see how we are feeling. We often end our day by sharing something we appreciate about ourselves, our family, and each other, even if we had a disagreement that day.

Be willing to tell your mate what you like, and express when you don't like something that he/she did. When you hear feedback, trust that your mate has good intentions for expressing his/her appreciation or frustration about something he/she liked or didn't like. We all are here to learn. When you know you are committed to one another, you can feel safe in helping each other bring out your best.

Authority Figures

We often are influenced by other people. As children and teens, we are most affected by adults, coaches, parents, teachers—anyone in authority. We learn from their example and absorb lessons from their words and actions. However, we do not need to assume that anyone, regardless of their position or role, is always right. Wise authority will encourage us to speak up and be ourselves, even if it pushes their buttons.

It is vital to trust our own intuition even as we respect authority. We have the right to stand up for ourselves and voice our opinions and beliefs, especially if there is potential harm involved. When we are working with people who are willing to learn and grow, we can speak from our truth and have a compassionate conversation while having differences of opinion. We both end up gaining from this interaction, as long as we can see that it does not have to be personal and that one of us doesn't have to win.

Everyone is fallible. Even if a coach, teacher, or parent is doing their best, they are not perfect and do not have all the answers. They can still try new ways and innovate, too. If you have an issue with someone, talk about it. If you just leave a relationship, team, school, club, or corporation without trying to deal with a problem, you do a disservice to everyone involved. In any relationship, when we hurt someone else we feel it ourselves. If we can both communicate and learn, everyone benefits.

Also be aware that parents, mentors, teachers, and coaches have their own needs, too. They get tired from working, taking care of children or others, and trying to balance their responsibilities. Trust that their intentions are good and that they want the best for you. That said, be willing to speak up, especially if you feel that someone is abusing their authority.

Parents, it is vital to honor your needs without using your children to fulfill your needs. And know it is okay if you are not perfect. The best way to help your children is to be true to yourself. They will model your behavior more than your words. As you develop your own confident, radiant self, you allow your child to do this, too.

Stay clear about what you need and want. Then express it and take action. Want a night out? Arrange it. If you have work to do, communicate this to your kids so they know you love them even if you seem stressed. This way, they learn to value your feelings as you value theirs. Tell them when you will be there for them (to put them to bed, attend their game or event), and be sure to follow through. If you had a bad day, express this, too. It is normal and healthy to express your feelings—all of them.

Be honest and expressive with your family. Communicate and grow together. You want your connection and love to thrive. Share yourself, and be open to others sharing with you. It is okay to have both good and bad moments (and emotions). As you express yourself and show that you are human, your kids will learn valuable lessons they can use in all their relationships.

A Coach's Influence

My relationship with Coach Shoulberg was an interesting one. Even though I appreciated his heart of gold and the way he pushed me as an athlete, I also recognized that he projected his beliefs onto me. I had the right to my own experience, and it was vital for me to acknowledge how I felt, including loss over what wasn't and appreciation for what was. I was lucky to work with a man who had a normal amount of fear and still let his love shine through for us. This dichotomy is normal in all of us.

Often, we want to pretend that someone is either perfect or terrible. As we understand all parts of ourselves, we more clearly appreciate and have compassion for others, too. Human beings are complicated and complex creatures. If we focus on taking care of our own needs and emotions, we will worry less about defining other people.

I appreciated much about Shoulberg, but I also had had difficulty accepting his obsession with body weight and some of his ideas on training. I didn't always like the way he communicated his thoughts. Yet, over the years, I expressed myself to him, even when it was uncomfortable.

After I got sick with CFIDS and stopped swimming, Shoulberg still checked up on me. After so many years of working together, we had built a relationship based on love and respect that went beyond swimming. In 1994, when I was in the midst of healing, Shoulberg and I talked about our relationship. He acknowledged his mistakes as a coach and a person. I shared my feelings, owned up to my mistakes, and told him what I had learned from him. We discussed our backgrounds, how we perceived the world, and how we were willing to change and grow. This gave us a better understanding of ourselves and of each other.

Shoulberg's influence on me was profound and long-lasting. To this day, we occasionally talk on the phone. I also see him about once a year at a swimming-related event or occasion. A few years ago, we celebrated his fortieth year at Germantown Academy. More than 500 former swimmers attended. Because Shoulberg had always shared wonderful stories about other athletes he coached, we felt like we knew people we had never met. He created a familial bond in generations of swimmers who came through Germantown Academy that made us feel deeply connected to each other.

Moving Forward

Going through ups and downs, not only within ourselves, but also in our relationships, helps us build a stronger love and bond with one another. We develop a rich understanding of our humanity and what drives our spirit. When we honor this, we can forgive mistakes and have compassion and love for one another. We can value the successes and good memories, too. We learn that we all make a difference in this world, and it is vital to shine our light. In doing so, we can inspire others.

As I lived my life without swimming, I found new ways to be fulfilled. I had a serious boyfriend, and we enjoyed learning about ourselves and each other, and working on our relationship. I immersed myself in better understanding myself, and relationships in general. I opened up to family members and resolved old conflicts. I found joy and freedom as I focused on the gifts, power, and potential within us all.

While living in Connecticut, I continued my physical healing as well. I started walking more, and I got acupuncture treatments from Stephen Birch, a colleague of Dr. Helms. I even coached swimmers at the Yale University pool with Yale Coach Frank Keefe (one of the men who had timed me in the infamous 14,000-meter butterfly back in 1987).

A highlight of this time was being asked by the United States Olympic Committee to carry the Olympic Torch in New Haven, Connecticut, for the 1996 Olympics. I was nervous when I found out that the path of my one-kilometer run included a steep hill. Since I was an Olympian, they assumed I could handle it. I started walking one kilometer a few months before and practiced running again. In my training days, I could easily run ten miles. Now, I just hoped I could get through a kilometer. I ended up doing the run in a light jog, and I felt my body getting stronger than it had been in years.

Even though swimming was no longer a part of my life, I had found a new way to feel content. Life wasn't perfect, but I was focusing my energy on what was important to me. As I worked on improving my health, my boundaries and balance became stronger and more defined. My relationships either shifted, or I changed with whom I spent time. I had struggled with setbacks, but I had refocused and moved forward.

PART FOUR

MAXIMIZING YOUR POTENTIAL AND FEELING CONTENT

Chapter Thirteen

Distractions and Refocusing: Getting Back on Track

The successful warrior is the average man, with laser-like focus.
                                                                —*Bruce Lee*

Taking care of yourself physically, mentally, and emotionally is critical in helping you reach your goals. Now that we have discussed how to do that, let's train your mind to stay focused on your dream.

When you get stuck or distracted, how do you refocus on your higher vision and move in the right direction? By using the refocusing techniques and other mental training tools in this chapter, you'll learn to be unfazed by your weaknesses and how to play to your strengths. As you focus on your goals and dreams, you can trust in your inner self to wisely lead you where you want to go.

Distractions

There are many sources of distraction—obstacles and unexpected challenges, your own mind, coaches, parents, teammates, colleagues, competitors, even the performance itself. Your expectations of success or failure, other people's expectations of you, the media, how you feel on any given day, your beliefs, even your finances all affect you and can keep you from focusing on the task at hand. The key is to not let distractions thwart your energy and focus.

You want to be bigger than the circumstances around you. Be aware of them, but know you can either choose to dwell on them or let them go. You can train yourself to see distractions as merely a vague background in your life that cannot hurt you or keep you from reaching your goal. See your distractions as scenery in your movie—while the backdrop is constantly changing, the major character (you!) keeps moving forward with the plot.

As I work with clients, and through my own experiences, I see how similar we all are. We all have typical issues that we go through. Regardless of how minor or severe, we are all affected by our ability or inability to feel at ease and in control of our own destiny.

Some people reach success at a young age and have to deal with being observed, judged, and admired. They must be clear about who they are, or else they will get bombarded with distractions and opinions about who they are supposed to be and how they are expected to live. Injured athletes have to decide whether to get back on track and redefine their plan or stop. After dealing with a loss such as divorce or death, a person must refocus in order to move ahead.

Trust Yourself

How can we stay on track even when such obstacles stand in the way? How can we trust and center ourselves to live the life we want? If we feel loyal to someone or responsible for another, or if we have shoved down emotions and carried that heavy armor, how can we let go enough to perform? By listening to our inner selves, determining what truly motivates us, and working through emotional issues, we will be prepared to tackle obstacles that come our way.

Sometimes a competitor might trigger an issue we have with someone. For instance, if I never thought I was good enough for a parent, and a certain competitor reminds me of this parent, I might have to address my original issue before I can perform at my best against this person. If I was used to giving up my dreams to take care of a parent's emotional needs, I might give up against this competitor to take care of him/her in the same way. The lesson for me here is that I deserve to take care of myself first—and will perform best when I do—and I ultimately help my competitor when I am at my best, as that brings out the best in him/her, too.

Committing to being our best can be a challenge, as we have to face our own fears. We must be clear about what is motivating us to fully live *our* life. It's funny how lessons are available for us everywhere! There really is no place to hide when we pay attention.

It is common to not fully trust ourselves at times. One client I worked with had been told to radically change his approach to swimming, which caused him to lose confidence in his abilities. He had a pattern of being behind for the first quarter in the race. This made him tense, as he thought he was not as good as the other swimmers and always had to play catch-up.

As he learned to retrain his brain to trust *his* own race, instead of feeling tense and frustrated as he focused on others, he learned to relax and trust that he would be where *he* needed to be. His confidence grew, and he became more accepting of himself and his abilities. Then he could race in a way that worked best for him, rather than trying to force his body to rush and catch up. Refocusing mentally altered what he could do physically and changed how he raced. When this young man learned to trust himself, he began to beat swimmers he had never won against before.

Train Your Focus

You can control your focus. Distractions and your imagination do not need to get the better of you. In earlier chapters, we discussed the benefits of meditation and paying attention. But no matter how much you practice focusing and being in the moment, life will throw distractions at you, and some of them might take you off-course for a bit. Whatever happens, keep focused on the present, accept and love yourself, know you are okay, breathe, relax, and try to do your best. You are on track. Now, just trust that you are.

Sometimes you have to get your head in the game, to shift gears so you can focus on what is happening *now*. For swimmers, this starts when they get up on the block, for actors when they step on stage, for a businessperson when they enter a room for a meeting. Focus on this moment; try not to get stuck in the past or future. A swimmer might notice the wet concrete as they step up to the starting block. Someone about to enter a conference room might smell fresh coffee, or look at the chairs around the table and choose where to sit. Focusing on your sensations in any given moment helps to keep you centered and grounded, not thinking about what happened before or fretting about what might happen in the future.

Mind training is powerful. Athletes who have gotten physically injured, but who mentally trained for hours every day, can still perform well. The body and mind are interlinked; the body doesn't know the difference between mentally practicing and physically training—it simply takes in each experience as if it really happened.

On the other hand, you can train and perform so that everything is technically correct, but if you have gremlins remaining in your closet (believing you don't deserve to win, issues with a coach or your parents, fearing the wrath of an angry competitor), your mental state will prevent you from doing your best.

A swimmer I worked with had difficulty training herself to relax. As she swam, she was quite rigid. She focused on what was wrong and felt the need to be perfect. This is how she was out of the water, too. She had to learn to feel "out of control" in order to be her best. She practiced relaxing in every part of her life: with her boyfriend, her family, her coach, and herself. As she let go of trying to control the world around her, she relaxed in the water and improved her races. To make this shift, she had to learn to feel safe and trust that it was okay to let her guard down, "to dance like nobody is watching." The transition challenged her, but ultimately she was much happier.

One of the exercises I did with this young woman was to have her express her fears through guided journaling. Some of the questions included: When was a time you felt relaxed and happy in your personal life? And as a child? Describe the circumstances and how you felt. In swimming, when have you felt this way? When have you allowed yourself to appreciate a whole race, rather than focusing on the things that you were not satisfied with?

Now imagine your performance, and magnify these good feelings. Exaggerate feeling out of control as you move. Relaxation in muscles increases speed. As you relax the mind, practice letting go and not needing to control. Run down a hill at full speed, to the point where you feel like you might fall; relax and keep going. Know that you will be okay if you relax. It is meant to be easy, not so difficult. Know that it is okay to have help. Let someone have an idea for you, especially those who support you. They are trying to help, not hurt you. Trust those who are trustworthy; there are more people like this than you might expect.

When we are perfectionists, it is easy to find something wrong in everything we do. However, it is important to see the perfection within the imperfection. In a performance, it is common for random events to occur that are beyond our control—we need to deal with these distractions, refocus, and continue on. I remember being at an indoor meet when there was a big storm outside. As the starter began the race, the swimmers dove in, and the place went pitch black. The electricity had gone out, and the race had to stop. The swimmers all had to readjust and wait for the power to come back on before they could race again.

What matters is how we deal with the random events that life throws our way. Within a race, there comes a point when we must decide whether or not to push ahead and keep going. Maybe we get distracted by non-sportsmanlike competitors, cheering fans, or an unhappy coach. We cannot control what others do, and if we react to them we might forget our game plan and get distracted. Sometimes these events can enhance our performance and other times they can be a negative distraction. It is important to stay focused within, to know what motivates us and keeps us empowered, and to be flexible.

Getting Unstuck

Whether you have been sidelined by an illness, injury, distraction, excuses, or some other unforeseen negative circumstance, know that this does not have to last forever and it does not define you as a person (You are okay just as you are!). Whether the roadblock is mental or physical, it will slow you down. But keep trying to push yourself forward.

It is important to be aware of what is causing you to feel stuck. Once you understand the problem, you can fix it. Ask yourself: Did I give my best effort? What can I learn about myself from this performance/event/incident that I can use the next time? Is there a pattern regarding where I tend to get stuck, physically or mentally? What can I learn from this? What is the solution? What can I do to change this? What do I feel good about?

Are you limiting yourself with old beliefs that no longer serve you? Are you letting your mind and emotions run wild? Do you have a story that you have told yourself over and over to protect you, or to rationalize and justify your position? Are you willing to alter this temporary roadblock and take a different path than before? Can you be centered and calm and able to create what you want? What problems can you allow the universe to solve for you? When you trust, the details will fall into place.

When I work with clients and we address the source of tension that might have nothing to do with performing (but is affecting their ability to be their best in the actual event), they are then freed up. They find their own voice and power again.

I had a client who was diagnosed with vocal chord dysfunction and anxiety. She was a top college athlete who competed nationally, but she had panic attacks before her races. Her body was stiff, and she tended to carry tension in her shoulders and jaw. She also had shallow breathing. First, we worked on deep breathing exercises. Then, we anchored a positive feeling into her right hand and a negative feeling in the left. This way, she could experience each of these feelings and then release them, illustrating that she had the power to re-create either feeling at any time.

Soon, she was feeling less anxious, and things that used to stress her out no longer fazed her as much. Her voice became stronger as she learned to feel calmer, listen within, and express herself more. She realized that stressful events and feelings would not last forever. She felt better about herself and continued to thrive in her sport.

You can apply these lessons to your own life. If you notice that you get stuck in a certain place or pattern in your life, it is easy to assume that you will get stuck there again. If you are a swimmer, perhaps you get stuck on your turns. Maybe in meetings you always get flustered when you have to lead a presentation. If you're a student, perhaps you do well on papers but then choke on tests. You might assume that "last time this mistake happened, and therefore it's going to happen again." If you recognize that you tend to lose to others at a certain point in a competition, you will continue to create this reality. (We like to prove ourselves right in our beliefs.)

But you can change your patterns by refocusing your thoughts. Allow yourself to visualize how you want the activity or performance to go. Visualize each movement, and—if you can—actually practice them. Be aware of the deliberateness of your actions. Go so slowly that you can practically feel your brain communicating with your body, telling it how to move and how to feel. Shift your focus from the obstacle to this present moment. Trust in your own power, knowing that your body and mind will work together so you can achieve your goal.

If you are a swimmer and tend to have slow turns, pay attention to everything you do. Do you get too close to the wall and then look to see where it is? You can change this habit. Tell yourself, "I will keep my eyes down and trust that the wall is there. Nobody has moved it. I know that I am safe—I will not hurt myself as I'm doing my turn." Then actually practice the movements. Put yourself in position on the wall. Stop where you typically get stuck. Then, change it to the new way. Practice doing it correctly. Allow your nervous system to take it in. Believe that you have overcome an obstacle. Then congratulate yourself for doing it well.

Maybe you keep getting stuck in conflict with a certain person. Rather than feeling angry or frustrated as usual, imagine seeing this person as a little child wanting love. Picture yourself having a successful interaction with this person, coming from a place of compassion.

Be open to having something different occur. Your past does not define your present. You control how you respond to circumstances and how you interact with the people around you. As you trust in your inner wisdom, live in the moment, and allow yourself to change your patterns, your whole life shifts for the better.

Do Something That Makes You Feel Alive

When you get stuck, you might forget to give yourself permission to feel good. What can you do *today* to feel alive and inspired again? Do something you have always wanted to do, something you thought you couldn't or were told you shouldn't do. Let popcorn fly all over the kitchen. Go for a walk by the ocean, and feel the air and wind on your face. Paint, play a musical instrument, fly a kite, or read a good book all the way through. Sign up for a class, call a friend you've lost touch with, start writing a novel, or agree to that blind date. Whatever you do, focus on being present.

We feel most alive when we immerse ourselves into each moment, doing something we love. Whatever endeavor we commit to allows us to find our true selves if we stay with it.

For me, water is always my sanctuary. I can feel whole and be connected to my true self in many ways, but when I am most stressed I feel complete and relaxed once I get in the water. I can let out my anger, my tears, my joy. I can float and rest, allowing myself to be held by the water when I need to feel taken care of. When I have transcended my rational mind and am lucid and attentive, I experience being merged, feeling completely connected with the water. I lose myself fully in the moment, becoming more recharged and refocused. If I had obstacles in my mind, I see the world in a new way.

How to Overcome Distractions

When setbacks occur, we tend to get down on ourselves. If we don't address the issue, we might start to feel burned out, and even consider quitting. Sometimes it is good to take a break, evaluate where you are at, figure out why you keep getting distracted or knocked off course, think about what you want (whether it's the same goal as before or a different one), and make a plan to get you where you want to go. Then, start taking action. Here are some exercises to help you:

Change your reaction: Think of a time that you lost your focus, your ability to perform well, or your temper. Recall the scene. How do you wish you had responded in that situation? Imagine a similar scene happening again. This time, picture yourself rising above it. Maybe even write out all the details as you envision yourself responding in a different way.

Every day, you can practice not reacting to small distractions, such as a car pulling out in front of you, the room temperature being cooler or warmer than you like, or one of your children whining and nagging. In that moment, focus on something that makes you feel good. Clearly state to yourself what you want ("I will stay calm"), and know you can make it happen. When you are clear in your intentions, you are more likely to follow through.

Many athletes get distracted by other people at a performance. They might get stressed out by what they are told, or they might feel conflicted about upsetting someone if they win. We get to protect our space and our energy, so nobody can bother us unless we let them. We cannot control how other people perform or what they choose to say. Similarly, nobody controls us, unless we let them. We get to decide how we respond to distractions. We can take control through training and preparation. When we are prepared, we can focus our energy on doing our best.

Be prepared: Unexpected events and circumstances often show up in the eleventh hour. Realize how circumstances can affect you. Then try to minimize their distracting effect on you.

To stay focused on what you want, write down your ideal performance plan. Then play it over in your mind, so you are clear about what you want to do. Be aware of potential obstacles, create a strategy to overcome them, and then have a backup plan. Be alert, allow your mind and body to be open and flowing, and be ready to shift if and when an obstacle appears in your path.

Write down any possible distractions, and think about how you can handle or reframe them. If you start to worry about others, shift the focus back to yourself. Rehearse what you can control during the race. Picture yourself celebrating. As you rehearse all the steps, it becomes more effortless.

I have kept a journal since the third grade. During my main training years I wrote down what I ate, how I slept, whom I interacted with and how that affected me, what happened in school, my training sets, physical measurements, and how I felt. I wrote up race plans. I used visualization to relive my best races, and I focused on achieving my goals. I learned what worked best for me—and what did not—and adjusted my training accordingly.

Figure out what works best for you: Every person gets focused and motivated in different ways; for example, not everyone learns and performs at their best through visualization. You need to find what works for you.

Get a sense of when you will perform, and with whom (if performing with others). Once you have that information, you can focus on what you need to do to get ready. For swimming, you dress in a swimsuit, goggles, and cap and warm up properly. Maybe you listen to your favorite music, talk to the people who motivate you or calm you down, or spend time alone rehearsing your race.

There is no right or wrong way to prepare. You want to listen to what feels right for you, then do that. Learn what routine keeps you focused, in your zone. Know what tools from your toolbox you can pull from, such as meditation, visualization, breathing exercises, or self-affirmations. Use what is most helpful for you.

Plan ahead, so that if you do lose focus or get off track, you will know what you need to do to refocus. Use the tools that work best for you—and don't be afraid to change them if you find they're not working for you anymore.

Different styles of preparation: Some people learn and feel confident when they visualize—you might watch a video of yourself or an idol, or rehearse your ideal race plan in your head. Some people talk to themselves. You might tell yourself what you want to do or remind yourself how talented or strong you are. If you are kinesthetic, you might be empowered by getting a hug, holding someone's hand, or getting a massage. Even tapping or lightly massaging your own muscles can be effective for this. Or you might find that you need to physically move, to be active, in order to calm yourself down and get ready. Find what works best for you, and then do it.

Do something for another: If you are distracted by your own thoughts, do something for someone else. Cheer on a friend who needs some encouragement. Put your skills to use by volunteering. Focusing on another person will get you out of your head and help you forget about your own problems. Fostering a connection can help change your state of mind, so that rather than moping or feeling down you will feel more confident again. When you allow yourself to be fully present with another person, you no longer feel alone and separate. You get to benefit from someone else's energy. When I was really sick and would go motivate the swim team, their energy and enthusiasm came back to me tenfold.

Stop overanalyzing: When I performed, sometimes I would naturally be ready to go. Sometimes I wanted to be alone, so I could get calm, breathe deeply, and let my mind get quiet. Other times I needed to be around people, to focus on their company, so that I would stop overthinking.

Don't worry about doing things the "right" way. What feels right to you might be different from one day to the next. Listen to what is going on inside of you so that you can attend to your deepest needs. Don't question yourself or overanalyze. In order to be our best, we must learn how to stop interfering with our own needs.

Learn from others, but listen to your inner voice: Remember, everyone gets stuck in limiting beliefs at various times. Even the best coaches, parents, and mentors have their own fears, insecurities, and biases. Share your ideas and goals with them, so they can support you on your path, but stay true to your heart's desires.

If you have a coach, teacher, or mentor who puts their own wishes or demands ahead of yours, pay attention. If something doesn't sit well with you, honor your deep wishes. Know the difference between not wanting to go for something versus not wanting to take someone else's path.

When we take care of ourselves, we feel good about ourselves. Then, we can perform to our potential.

Keep It Simple

It is important to practice and rehearse; however, it is also easy to overthink. If you are running down the stairs and try to think about one knee bending, how your arms should move a certain way, or where your toes should go, you might actually fall. Many swimmers worry about doing a certain number of kicks off of each wall, or following a specific stroke count or tempo. It is good to train to do these things, but once you have practiced an activity over and over, you get to trust that your body knows how to do it. Thus, when you have a race or performance day, you can just be in the moment, trust your body, and allow yourself to shine.

How do you get to this place, or how do you return here if you've gotten distracted? What is something that can help you get back to this moment so you can focus and attend to the task at hand? Initially it might help to have a word or phrase, something you can focus on to snap you back into the present. Or you can lightly touch your thumb and second finger together, or squeeze your fist as you say "yes" to yourself.

Emotions can be a huge distraction. If you are emotionally caught up in your last event, a mistake you made, or what someone said to you, it is hard to focus on your own performance at the same time. Thus, your goal is to refocus so you can be present with what is going on right now.

Try to become detached from your emotions. Think of yourself as bigger than the circumstances around you. Tell yourself that you do not need to listen to anything negative. Focus on exhaling bad oxygen and inhaling good oxygen into your body. Basically, do whatever works for you to get back to being present. Practice these exercises daily, so they start to become automatic for you.

Learn What Motivates You

It is hard to stay motivated if your underlying goal or expectation is outdated or comes from someone other than yourself. When distractions pull you off course, you will be driven to keep going only if you are motivated by your deepest desires. If you are simply trying to please someone else, or trying to achieve something that's not really important to you, it will be difficult to maintain focus because you really want to be doing something else.

How do you let go of other people's expectations and focus on your deepest, truest desires? As discussed before, listen to yourself and honor the voices you hear. Also, spend your time and energy with people who make you feel good, who respect and encourage the real you. Don't get caught up in trying to make someone else's dream come true—only they can do that. Be present in each moment, and act on your own behalf. When your actions are fueled by your own motivation, you feel confident and energized.

By changing old beliefs and patterns, you produce new results. Distractions no longer thwart you as you focus and listen within. You adjust to necessary changes as you become available to all possibilities. In this open space, miracles occur.

Chapter Fourteen

Maximize Your Potential: Mental Training Techniques to Transcend Limitations

Do what you can, with what you have, where you are.
–Theodore Roosevelt

We have discussed health and wellness and how to refocus. Now we'll focus on more techniques to enhance your life and your performances. By trying new ways to bring out your best, you will learn what works for you and become more confident in your abilities. Stay focused on what you want, and allow yourself to be creative. You will maximize your potential and very possibly go beyond what you thought you were capable of.

Act As If

Set the intention of what you want. Assume this desire has already been fulfilled. Imagine it with as many details as possible. Notice how you feel because it is already here. Write, talk, and live it as if it has happened; nothing can take it away from you unless you allow it.

When you focus on what you want as if it is already here, you imprint this into your memory. Your body believes it to be true. Remember, you are the main character in your movie called *My Life*. You are the star. Shine your light. Take responsibility for how you live.

You asked for something to show up in your life, and you have been acting as if was here. When it actually arrives, respect that it came to you, and do something with it. (Don't ignore it; honor it.) Even though part of you might be resistant to having this, relax and allow this wonderful event, thing, or person to be here in your life. You have permission, and you deserve it.

Self-Hypnosis

Self-hypnosis can help you program your mind to actualize your desires. When you go into a deeply relaxed state and suggest what you want to yourself, your subconscious takes it in and feels it as if it is real. This can help you become clear about your performance, and also create the ideal reality inside of you before you perform. You have the power within. You can either feel terrible and create negative outcomes, or you can look at the world in a positive way and bring forth healthy and powerful outcomes. It is up to you.

Some people are more receptive to self-hypnosis than others. To make it work, you must first trust that you are in a safe place and can let go. In doing so, you will allow the conscious mind to rest while you delve into your subconscious. Here you can allow your true desires to surface. It is important to be clear about your ultimate goal. When you bring this intention into your deepest self, your nervous system and your cells take in this information as if it had already happened.

Write Your Script

Before going into hypnosis, write down exactly what you want to hear in your subconscious mind. Make sure you write only what you want, in a positive frame of mind, versus "I should, I need to, or I don't want to." Do not write down things that you *don't* want. Instead of saying, "I don't want to mess up" or "I am done being sick," say, "I can easily do this" or "I am well." Record your script so you can play it back to yourself while you are in the hypnotic state. Then, while you are in hypnosis, your subconscious mind will absorb these messages.

I used hypnosis a few times when I competed in swimming. I laid out each detail of my ideal race plan, and then I had a hypnotist help me to get into a "trance." In this state I was able to absorb information on a deeper level than my intellect would typically allow. On my own, I would get into a relaxed state and listen to audiotapes on which I had recorded my "script." During one particularly rough season, I used hypnosis to help me get back on track. I ended up winning one event in the World Championship Trials and making the World Team in a second event.

Hypnosis does work, but not for everyone. Usually, people are nervous and unsure the first time they try it. You need to be in a safe environment, around supportive people you can trust. From there, you will be more willing to be vulnerable as you go into this "deeper" state. And if hypnosis never works for you, there are plenty of other tools to try!

At some point, you have tapped into your subconscious mind, but you might not have realized that you can create new powerful things for yourself from this place. Your conscious, rational mind might not believe that you can achieve your goals or make your dreams a reality. Thus, you will end up sabotaging your own efforts if you are not careful. By using hypnosis, you can get yourself to believe that you are capable of receiving what you really want. The more you practice this technique, the more confidence you will build in yourself, as you start to believe in your own power.

Steps for Self-Hypnosis

Focus on an object to help clear your mind and calm you. I liked to use a burning candle. I enjoyed watching the flicker and color from the flame. This helped calm my mind and body. Then, once I felt relaxed, I would close my eyes and go into a trance.

Lie down, and close your eyes. Focus on your breathing. You can use any of the breathing techniques mentioned in this book, or one of your own, to help you relax. Feel the air go in and out of your nose. Recognize the sensation of warm or cool air, and allow your body to melt and get heavier and heavier as you go into a deeper state.

Trust yourself. You are safe. Train yourself to relax all parts of your body. You can start with your feet and go up to your head, or go in any order that works for you. As you breathe in, tense up your feet and hold your breath, then slowly exhale out as you totally relax the muscles in your feet. Move on to the next body part and continue until you get to your head. As you go into a deeper state of relaxation, you will sink further into the floor, bed, or whatever you are lying on. Allow your eyes to be closed.

Your self-hypnosis has begun. From here, you can start programming yourself with beneficial suggestions.

If you have recorded your script, turn on your listening device (iPod, CD, or cassette) and listen to the messages. At the end, tell yourself to slowly open your eyes, wake back up, and come back into the room (get back into your conscious mind). This will get you out of the trance and into a conscious state.

You can stay in a hypnotic state as long as you wish. I tended to be in one for about fifteen minutes. It might seem like one minute or an hour, as you might have no sense of time. This is common when you are in your subconscious mind. Also, you might feel sleepy when you are done, or fully refreshed.

To benefit from self-hypnosis, use it consistently. Over time, your subconscious mind will become more receptive to taking in the suggestions. Repetition is the key to planting these ideas in your deeper mind. Be willing to use these tools even when you are not sure how much they are working for you. It can take time to get fully relaxed, or to trust the process. Be open and receptive, willing to explore what various techniques can do for you.

Visualization

"Imagination is everything. It is the preview of life's coming attractions."
– Albert Einstein

Visualization can enhance your performance and help make your dreams a reality. When you imagine what you want, and utilize all your senses, you create a heightened awareness. Your perspective shifts, and you become more empowered. You feel like you have already won. This helps you believe in yourself, since the image in your mind feels as if it were real. When you feel better, more positive experiences will show up in your life, and your confidence will continue to grow.

By imagining all possible scenarios in a performance, you will be better prepared to handle them. Distractions do occur, but when you know to expect them and have practiced how to deal with them, you will react more calmly, which will allow you to stay focused on your ultimate goal. Visualization is also a great way to check in with yourself. As you picture a performance, you might notice a certain place where you get stuck. If you slow down and imagine each sensation (your fingers plucking a guitar, your feet hitting the ground as you run, your posture as you give a presentation), you can "retrain" your mind to send your body different messages.

Your body tends to listen to your mind, not argue with it. If your mind tells your body to "blow it," it will. But if your body hears, "I am fully capable of performing well," it will, regardless of what happened last time. We also need to listen to the body and be aware of how it moves, so we know what to do. Help your mind and body work as a team. Your body doesn't know "awake" versus "dream" versus "past, future, or present." When you recall a past event or imagine a future one, the body receives the information as if it was real right now. The subconscious mind can't tell the difference. Thus, be very careful what you allow yourself to think, believe, and act on.

Visualization Exercises

Get yourself into a deeply relaxed state before you begin these exercises. Even as various distractions go on around you, find your center, your calm place. Feel safe here. Imagine a white bubble of energy around you to protect your space and keep you from reacting impulsively to anything or anyone around you. Once you do this, you can be open and receptive.

Use your breath to fully inhale and exhale, letting the belly rise and fall. Relax your mouth and jaw as you exhale. Count from twenty down to one. As you inhale say, "Twenty," then exhale and say, "Nineteen," and so on. Let go of the tension in your muscles. Maybe tense yourself up as tight as you can and hold it. Then, when you feel like you can't take it anymore, let all the tension go. Or, have a partner or friend hold your arm, and truly let them hold it. Let your muscles go limp. When your partner feels like it, without telling you, he or she will drop your arm. It should fall quickly if you have fully relaxed.

Now you have focused and calmed your mind and body. You are ready to visualize and imagine.

TV Screen Exercise—Feeling Your Own Power: Imagine watching someone you admire on TV doing what you want to do. See them running fast, being confident, expressing joy. How do they move? How do they warm up, or get ready? How do you feel as you watch them? What characteristics do you see, and which ones do you want in yourself? Recognize that they are already within you. Now, keep watching the person...and have the person become you, so that you see yourself on the TV screen. You have just embodied that person and their energy and confidence. How do you feel? You are no longer watching yourself; rather, you are feeling yourself perform. Allow yourself to feel in your power, and enjoy this.

If tension arises, exhale it out. You do not need to analyze why you are feeling a certain way; just notice where you feel the tension and then let it go. If you have a hard time releasing the tension, ask yourself, "Am I willing to let go of the tension?" And then say yes. This helps your ego to be willing. Sometimes we like to hold on, because we are used to feeling the tension and are afraid of what we will feel like if we let it go. Trust that it is okay to let go of the tension, to let go of control, and allow yourself to know you will feel freer and lighter by exhaling and letting go.

Now, let's change the channel. I know it is not fun to bring up a time when you did not feel as good, but this exercise will help you be less attached to the negative emotions. You will see that you can switch your feelings in an instant, as simply as changing the channel or turning the TV off or on. Pretend you are changing the channel. Now you see yourself onscreen but imagine that you are feeling stressed out. What do you notice about the person you see? Is he or she scared, tense, breathing, or holding their breath? Allow your courageous, confident self to help this scared, anxious person. What do you want to say to him or her? Do they need a hug, or reassurance? Go ahead and hug them. Are they starting to feel better? Do you notice any changes in his or her energy since you have helped him/her? Allow yourself to feel good. You have integrated your worries and embraced them with your higher energy (love, acceptance, and confidence).

Change Your Emotions in an Instant: When you are expressing a feeling, you have to let go of any other thought or feeling. You can't have two feelings in the exact same moment. So choose to focus on the positive. Imagine yourself doing something that didn't go the way you had wished. Then re-imagine the same scenario with a positive outcome. Go back and forth. Notice that you can only focus on one emotion in each moment. You truly have the power to shift what you see in the world and how you feel in each moment.

Anchor yourself in your powerful, confident feeling by associating it with a physical movement. Squeeze your fist, raise your arm, and say, "Yes!" Smile—feel happy, good, proud, or excited. Know that you can go back to this feeling whenever you want to.

Being On Autopilot

When you have rehearsed what you want to do mentally and physically, you can perform on autopilot. You get out of your own way as your body takes over—it knows what to do. How can you train yourself to let go and get into a state of flow?

During each physical practice, focus on one new thing you can improve on. Then imagine yourself executing the desired skills. Picture the performance in your mind. When you go out and use your new skills, let them unfold naturally. Practice being attentive in each moment. Do not judge yourself— just re-create the positive feelings you had when you felt at your best. Allow yourself to have those feelings daily. Create a race plan/strategy and then rehearse it through the season, so by the time you perform, your body and mind will have gone through the motions many times before.

Your goal is to practice exactly what you want to do in your performance, and practice it consistently. Your body/nervous system will remember it. You have spent the energy training your mind and body to get in shape and be focused. You have mastered the details involved in your performance. Now the goal is to have it all come together in the same moment so you can experience your peak performance. In psychologist Mihaly Csikszentmihalyi's book Flow, he describes this place as, "The state in which people are so involved in an activity that nothing else seems to matter."

We have all have experienced this state of flow. When you are in the zone, you don't feel self-conscious and yet you are very alert. You might have little sense of time—it can seem speeded up or slowed down as you are immersed in the moment. It is as if the activity is being done to you; it is effortless. You love being able to do what you are doing. Participating is the best reward.

To get to this state, you must first train your mind to stay focused on a task and not become distracted. This is kind of like learning to walk: At first it requires a lot of attention, but then you get to the point where you don't even think about it. The foot just picks up, the leg moves, and then the other one goes. Once you train yourself, it requires little energy to do the task.

As you become more focused and aware, and are able to keep from getting distracted, you will notice that your power really comes from your subconscious mind. If you train yourself to get focused and stay focused, you will be able to let go and be on autopilot. Trust your body and mind, and the power that lies within you. You will be amazed at what is possible.

Face Your Fears (And Then Transcend Them)

What is the worst that can happen? What if you were never any faster or better, and you only got worse? Are you afraid that people will turn against you or abandon you? What if you were always number one, breaking records, and stifling the competition? What pressures would this put on you? How would you feel? Where do these emotions and fears come from? Notice them and let them go.

You might be sad because you did not win. If you let your team down, what will happen because of that? Will the coach be mad at you? Who else gets mad at you like that? How do you feel when someone is mad at you? Maybe you feel ashamed or bad, like you are not worthy and you want to hide.

You can see how one emotion leads to deeper feelings that have gotten buried. It is okay that you have repressed old hurts and feelings, but now you can express how you feel and let go of these burdensome emotions.

Both failure and success stir up feelings in us. We might feel really good about an achievement, but also notice tension associated with it, too. This is normal. We can acknowledge this, pay attention to whatever emotions arise, express them or detach ourselves from them, and believe that they do not have to control us.

Sometimes we have a deep fear associated with getting what we want (succeeding) or having our worst fear happen (failure). We do not need to know where these feelings come from, but we will be empowered by acknowledging the fear and letting it go. We probably created these feelings to help us survive in our past; now we can thank the fear for the purpose it served, and send it on its way.

Other Mental Training Techniques To Maximize Your Potential

Anchoring: You can establish a neurological link between a specific emotion and a stimulus. Then the stimulus will trigger that feeling whenever you want it to. For instance, you can train yourself to associate a physical movement with a certain feeling. You can pick any feeling you want. Now imagine a time when you experienced this feeling. If you never have, imagine someone who has and feel it.

If you performed well and got excited, then jumped up and down, shouting "yes!" exuberantly while clenching your hand in a fist, the emotion and action become linked in your mind. To bring back those feelings, you would "anchor" the physical act of jumping up and down while shouting "yes!" and clenching your fist. As you re-create this moment, you will feel good energy surge through your body. The more you repeat this action and allow yourself to feel the joy of the time you performed well, the more you can tap into this feeling. Even if you are stressed, when you clench your fist and yell "yes!" you will feel a sense of power and excitement since you have rehearsed it.

You can anchor in a feeling through visualization, feeling, touching, tasting, moving, using your voice, smelling—whatever you wish. Anchoring is a form of neurolinguistic programming, also known as NLP. The more you practice creating your trigger to a certain emotion, the easier it will be to create that emotion anytime you want. I often lightly touched my thumb and small finger together when I wanted to calm down. When I wanted to feel excited and in my full power before a race, I would squeeze my fist. I had anchored in these physical movements with a specific feeling. Even if your rational mind doubts what's possible in that moment, you bypass the worries and get into the core of your power by anchoring.

Balance of Relaxation and Excitement: We all have our own personal line between relaxation and arousal. On a continuum, some of us need to be more relaxed before performing, while others prefer to be more excited/aroused/anxious/intense. The key is to determine the point at which you perform at your best. In my swimming days, I found that if I was too hyper, I needed to do some deep breathing to calm down. If I was groggy, I jumped up and down to get my heart rate going and make sure I was alert and focused. Our goal is to be okay with the butterflies in our stomach—when we balance this aroused state and focus it, then we can utilize it.

Notice how you feel, and from there you will know if you are "on," if you need to do some relaxation exercises, or if it would be best to get yourself more aroused. If the stress of your performance causes too much excitement or anxiety, it will be hard to perform at your best—but you need *some* arousal or you won't be able to perform at all. The key is to balance focused intensity with physical and mental relaxation.

Self-Talk/Reframing: Be aware of how you talk to yourself. If you have been thinking negatively about an event (whether in the past or the future), you can reframe it to see it differently. This will change your interpretation of the experience. Instead of saying, "I always mess up" switch it to "I have worked on this, and I am ready." If you tend to say, "I am not good enough. I always fall behind and need to catch up," you will feel stress and then not do well. Instead, tell yourself, "I focus on my own performance, not anyone else's." Then you can be in control of what you do.

Do not blame yourself or expect everything to be perfect. Allow yourself flexibility in whatever might happen. The perfect performance is one in which you are fully present, able to manage any distractions or obstacles that come your way.

Dissociation: In a relaxed hypnotic-like state, re-envision a past experience as if you are an observer watching it for the first time. Just see what happens—do not judge. Rather than re-experiencing the emotions, you are detached from the situation and can see it in a new way. This allows you to work through a troubling situation, get unstuck from a negative pattern, or think critically (but not negatively) about a past performance. You might have had a poor interaction with someone. You can observe it with no emotion. Then, you can adjust what you would want to have happen. By doing so, you will feel differently about this situation.

Advice From Your Friendly Local Therapist

It is important to use these tools consistently. Practice them *before* your main performance so that they become automatic. Physically doing a task is not always the best way to improve your performance. Taking time to sit quietly, imagine, and reflect can have longer-lasting benefits. Review your actions from the past; see what needs to be changed before you put a new plan into place. Be willing to change so your new habits will stick.

We all have potential—we just need to tap into it. When we see glimpses of it through visualization, we realize that much more is possible than we ever imagined. It starts with being willing to dream like a child again! Then as we follow through using exercises from our "toolbox," we learn to trust in our abilities to create in actual physical life, instead of just in our imagination.

Trust the changes you are making. As you change how you see the world around you, so do you change within. This can be scary, and some of the following doubts might start to creep in: I can't get motivated. Even after many successes, I am still not satisfied. I am constantly striving, thinking I need to achieve in order to be okay, to be somebody, to feel successful, to define who I am. I'm not sure if I can stay committed to the tasks I need to complete to reach my goal. I'm afraid I'll upset someone else if I win (or don't win). I feel like I'm not good enough.

Expect to face doubts; be prepared for them. Remind yourself of what motivates you. How can you transcend your limitations? What drives you to excel? How do you feel when you're in the moment, doing something you love to do, that tests you and makes you feel alive? What other challenges or limiting beliefs might be holding you back? How do you overcome challenges? How do you stay focused on what you want—on your dream? When you get distracted, how do you get refocused?

Create A Performance Plan

When I competed, I drew up a race plan that started a few weeks out. I included specifics about eating, sleeping, stretching, and relaxation. I imagined how I wanted my races to go, how I wanted to feel, how many kicks I would do off the wall, when I would breathe, how many strokes I would swim per length, when I would pick up tempo, and when I would rotate more from my hips. I figured out what to say to myself if I got distracted in a race, so I would be able to stay focused and keep going.

Write up your performance plan, starting from a few days or weeks before. How will you rest, eat, sleep, think? How will you use your time? Will you socialize more or less? Will you rehearse your race mentally, and when? Will you practice relaxation techniques? When will you do all of these things? How do you want your perfect day to go? You can make the day of your performance be whatever you want it to be. What do you want to eat that day, and when? How will you get ready for your performance? Which people do you want to have around you, or would you prefer to be by yourself? What will you have packed in your bag? How will you mentally and physically warm up? What are the steps in your actual performance? Describe everything in as much detail as you can, in the present tense. Create the feeling for yourself.

Rehearse your performance with distractions going on around you—this will really train your mind to focus. Try to think of all possible things that could happen, and prepare yourself to deal with them; that way, you do not have to put energy into them anymore.

There is a point in races (especially ones longer than thirty seconds), where we have a choice: to push through and keep going, or not. It is like going into a tunnel and choosing to stay focused on the light ahead. You can practice this in your training sessions so when you get to a performance you will know how to handle distractions. When you get tired and want to give up, test your limits and see what happens.

The same goes for a business meeting: You can set the intention before you actually arrive regarding what you want to happen. If you know who are you are meeting with, allow yourself to see the people in your mind. Imagine how you first greet them, where you sit, and what you plan to discuss. What are your goals for the meeting? What would you like the overall mood and energy to be? If you'll have a tough negotiation, you might anticipate tension and disagreement. Remember, you cannot control what others do, but you can set the intention for what you want. This puts you in a place to influence your colleagues, so they can come from a better place, too (for instance, talking calmly rather than arguing).

High-Centered Energy

When you are grounded and feel good about yourself, you are more likely to have a positive interaction. Similarly, if you are stressed out, tired, or mad at the person with whom you are meeting, the connection takes on a different tone—and most likely the result will, too! Keep yourself centered, and maintain good energy. If someone near you is being negative, make a decision to stay distant from that energy. Envision a bubble of positive energy around yourself. You want to be in your own power, not have it sucked away from you.

Focus on the energy you want in and around you. If you feel down, talk with someone who inspires you, or go out and inspire someone else. You can even draw energy from a crowd. When two or more people come together, a new energy emerges. When I ran cross-country, I imagined being light like a top cross-country runner. One girl who was often ahead of me reminded me of a deer bouncing along effortlessly. I would draw from her energy and imagine myself being like a deer running easily through the woods. I felt light and free and happy.

Brain Integration And Meridian Work

If your left brain and right brain are not functioning together efficiently, this can affect your energy. To keep the meridians open and help energy flow throughout your body, you can do some simple exercises. One way to integrate the left and right brain, so you can be stronger and more alert, is to create figure eights with your arms. Allow your arms to feel light and relaxed as your eyes follow their movement. Breathe naturally and effortlessly; your breath is relaxed so you do not hear it. Have the movement be one continuous motion. As you cross the midline, you are helping to integrate both sides of the brain so that they can work optimally together.

You can also tap on certain acupuncture points to assist in opening up blocked energy. (More information about how energy flows can be found in Dr. Helms's book <u>Getting To Know You</u>.) In general, you cannot go wrong. If you tap above your eyebrows, by your cheekbone, your collarbones, pec area, lower back, down the outside and inside of your legs, or your two feet together, you will open up many channels of energy flow.

How To Prepare For A Performance

Your performance begins well before the actual start. If you are getting ready to perform and worrying about people around you, what can you do? Be an actor in your own movie—act as if you are a strong, confident person. How do you walk out to your performance? How do you feel inside? Everyone has different ways to be relaxed and yet alert and ready. Here are some things I did that might help you get ready to perform:

- Listen to music. When I was nervous I'd play my classical music or Yanni, Enya, chanting music, or Enigma to calm me down. If I was half asleep, some good dance music would perk me up.

- Play a game, such as tic-tac-toe. I liked to do this when my mind needed a positive distraction that allowed me to focus and feel ready to perform but took my mind off the race.

- If I was ruminating in my head, I found it helpful to talk with others, to focus on their inspiring energy rather than feelings of fear. Sometimes you need support and encouragement. One person in particular who helped calm my nerves at national and international events was masseuse Dianne Limerick. I would ask her silly questions such as, "Am I as relaxed as I was a year ago?" She would remind me to breathe and relax, and tell me to say, "I feel great."

- If you are feeling spacey or overly aroused, ground yourself. Plant your feet into the ground, like a tree. Center yourself, and breathe deeply.

- When I made the Olympic Team, I sang ABC's to myself: "A is for Aggressive, B is for Bionic," and so on. Make up your own mantra or song to make you feel good.

- Breathing exercises helped me focus on the moment. By varying my breathing, I could stir up creative energy, focus, and get myself to a happy place.

- Tap/touch yourself—for those of you who love being hugged or touched, this will help you tune in to your power.

- Create a highlight video with clips of your best performances. Watch it, and be inspired!

- Talk to yourself. What we say to ourselves is very powerful, so it is important to be mindful of the words inside your head. Being negative or saying, "Don't do X" will probably cause you to do it. Similarly, don't say you want to "break a minute"—say, "I allow myself to go 59 seconds or faster easily." The "or faster" is important. It allows you to consider beyond the 59…maybe you'll end up going a 57. Tell yourself things you like to hear.

- Remain open to what is possible.

- Enjoy this moment in your life. If you can be present and pay attention right now, you will notice what you need, since you will be listening to yourself and your body. You will know if you are in a good place or if you need to shift gears in order to perform at your peak.

- If you are waiting around before a performance, you might get anxious. This is the time to dig into your toolbox. Know what you need to do, and have exercises handy that will keep you calm and focused.

- Use relaxation techniques, such as breathing in and out as you tense up each muscle and then relax it. Do this for every part of your body.

- Inhale for four seconds, hold for two, and exhale for four. You can also have the exhalation be twice as long as the inhale…forcing a deeper relaxation.

- Practice counting from one to ten to get your thoughts to quiet down. Imagine writing each number, seeing it, and saying it. When your mind gets off track, come back to the number and keep going.

- Regardless of where you are (whether at a performance or in a business meeting) breathe deeply and smile high.

- It is only when we go too far into the future or the past that we feel stress. That is why it is so important to take in your surroundings. Be in the moment.

- Act as if any positive energy you feel is for you to enjoy.

- If there is music playing that you do not like, or you sense negative energy around you, focus on something that pleases you—listen to calming music, or close your eyes for a moment and picture two people in love.

- Establish routines to stay in the moment. When I looked down and saw the scar on my left foot from rope climbing, I was reminded of getting the rope-climbing record. In my mind that meant I could do an amazing performance again right now.

- Be honest with yourself, and realize that you are in charge of you. Nobody can affect you unless you let them.

The goal here is for you to realize that you are control of your energy and your destiny. Even if you are in a stressful environment, you can change how you feel by focusing on positive things, or you can literally leave it (such as a toxic workplace, a college you don't like, or an unhealthy relationship). I have wrestled with making changes even when I knew they were the best thing for me. Each of us gets comfortable, and sometimes the unknown is scarier than an unhappy familiar place. That is why it is important to keep doing the exercises in this book, so you can build confidence in yourself to take the leap and try.

Positive Reinforcement and Feedback

We love to be told we are doing well. It builds our confidence. In childhood, mistakes are seen merely as learning opportunities. They are not personal. Remember that now. It is helpful to receive feedback to know where we are at, compared to only focusing on a desired outcome. If we only think about the end result we become fearful since our ego is caught up in needing to win in order to be okay with ourselves.

When we appreciate each step in the process and stay focused on the tasks and experiences rather than the outcome, we can turn mistakes into opportunities to learn. As we become more aware of our capabilities, we can remind ourselves of what we have done well. By doing so, we feel good about what we are learning and know we are powerful and capable, which makes it is easier to develop intrinsic motivation.

Keep Transcending Limitations

Here are tips and reminders to help you maximize your potential:

1. Keep a higher vision of what motivates you. Review Chapters Two and Four in this book to help you go deeper within and discover what you truly want.

2. Reflect periodically—perhaps every six months, ask yourself: Are you doing everything possible to achieve your dream? Are you taking steps to make it happen? Reflect on what you have done over the past six months, and prepare for next six months.

3. Trust yourself. By making a plan and following through, you build confidence. Celebrate each step of your achievement. Trust that you do as you say you will do. If you say, "I will win" and have followed through on your other action items, you can believe that you will complete this step, too.

4. Stay focused on yourself. If you start to focus on or compare yourself to someone else, remember that you can only control yourself, not anyone else.

5. Know how to refocus easily. Are you someone who talks to yourself? Or visualizes what is going on? Or needs the sensation of touch? Use what works for you.

6. Surround yourself with people who uplift, support, and inspire you.

7. Remember that the medal is a bonus. The journey is what really matters and will have the most influence on your life.

8. Rather than straining, let things come to you easily. Work with your body and mind rather than against them. I spent many years trying too hard, and I didn't need to.

9. Continue to build your confidence. Realize your strengths, and let them shine!

10. Have fun! Enjoy the journey.

Chapter Fifteen

Going Beyond: Discovering Your True Self

To be yourself in a world that is constantly trying to make you something else is the greatest accomplishment.
—Ralph Waldo Emerson

By using tools to help take care of yourself and perform at your best, you have fostered trust within yourself and cultivated your inner wisdom. You have let go of old, unhealthy beliefs or patterns with which you had grown comfortable. As you let go of things that no longer serve you, you are becoming your true self. You can claim your own strength in a whole new way. You have trained your mind. Now let yourself go deeper.

As you move past your comfort zone into uncharted territory, ready to experience enlightenment, you first must be aware of your habits, patterns, and beliefs. As you train your mind, you strengthen your will power. You complete your tasks and build your confidence, enhancing your faith in what is possible. As you strive to be your best, you go deep within, pulling from your depths to do more than you thought possible. In doing so, you go beyond your rational mind into a new realm of connectedness. From here, you feel compassion, love, and peace for all.

You are the only one who truly knows your divine plan or calling in this life. Other people can guide you and help you learn, but ultimately you must decide what you can and will do. You set your goals and create and follow your plan. Along the way, you test what is possible. What are you really capable of? Are you guided by something greater than your human mind?

Doing the mental exercises in this book is a great way to start training your mind and emotions. By doing so, you can alter your level of consciousness, which changes how you see the world. (For more information, review psychiatrist Dr. David Hawkins's book, Power Vs. Force.) You learn to concentrate and focus so you can go beyond the mind and experience the present moment from a deeper consciousness. You see that you are interconnected with everything, so there is no need to fear.

As you go into an alpha brain wave state (bridge between conscious and subconscious) and then theta (subconscious) and finally a delta brain wave state (connecting to universal source energy, not just your own), you have the power to alter how you view the world and what gets manifested for you. You can go beyond your limiting beliefs and see that there is a greater order in place that helps you create your intentions. The choice is yours. You decide. Much more is possible than you ever imagined.

Listen To Your Intuition

More people are studying Eastern philosophies and alternative views on life, trying to understand what is possible. How do we maintain a childlike wonder and innocence and get back to being courageous enough to explore the possibilities in life? Many of us yearn for more connection to life's mysteries and magic. To develop our human spirit, we need a healthy balance of time alone and time with others. The more we open ourselves up to our spirit, the more we can impact the world and help others feel their completeness within, too.

Einstein said, "The only real valuable thing is intuition." When we listen to our inner self—our intuition—answers come that guide us. Sometimes we gain wisdom by focusing on our physical sensations. Often our body knows something is wrong before our conscious mind is willing to hear it. (Muscle testing shows this, as discussed in Chapter Eight.)

Similarly, science shows that our eyes receive information intuitively as well as consciously. When we look at a TV screen for less than half a second, the image is imprinted on our brain, and we feel it even if we are not cognizant of it. We can also learn by paying attention to our emotions. Do we feel happier, excited, and more energetic when we think of a certain topic or interaction? This is feedback that our intuition is giving us. Our insight is our inner truth.

When we take time to slow down, observe, and be still, we find out what really motivates us, and what is best to do in each given moment. We develop an inner knowing. The more we use it, the more it works for us. Paying attention applies to all areas of life—a good example is eating: what we want to eat, when to stop eating, when to get a snack, and so on. If we eat out of boredom or to satisfy an emotional need, we might be eating unconsciously. If we are hungry and pay attention to what our body wants to eat, we will know what is best to feed ourselves in order to feel balanced and alert. Often we intuitively know how our body responds after eating certain foods or if we eat too much. When we are willing to listen, and let ourselves feel good regularly, we will do what is best by honoring what our body tells us.

Using Intuition To Find Your True Self

> *"And remember, no matter where you go, there you are."*
> – *Confucius*

Like dreams, our intuition is constantly processing and utilizing information it collected from the day's events. Our brain also prioritizes the importance of events in our lives; it knows which ones to process first. Trust your own natural instincts, no matter how wild and crazy they may seem. If your gut tells you to take a different route home, you might avoid an accident. If your boyfriend proposes and it doesn't feel right, listen to your instincts and move on.

Bring out your creative genius. Trust your intuition and insights. By attaining inner creativity, you help others to be inspired, too. To foster your creativity, explore. Every day, play a game with your family or friends, draw, paint, sing, or spend time in nature—listen and watch the animals, leaves on a tree, ripples in a lake, or clouds in the sky. As you allow your creativity to grow, it becomes second nature. You easily start seeing the extraordinary in the ordinary. You allow your inner spirit to shine and inspire and guide you to be on your path.

Ask yourself questions: What were you born to do? What is your destiny? What gifts are you ready to offer the world? Are you willing to let go of your fears? What is your vision for your life? Spend some time each day listening to your inner self, and remove any clutter that's getting in your way. As you listen, pay attention to whatever ideas arise. If you feel inspired, follow through on it. If you have an urge to do something, make a plan and do it.

Tap Into Your Subconscious

> *"The subconscious is ceaselessly murmuring, and it is by listening to these murmurs that one hears the truth."*
> – Gaston Bachelard

We function mainly from the subconscious. For example, when we learned to walk, we imprinted how to do this into our subconscious. Our conscious mind no longer had to think about it. We can train ourselves to do this with other thoughts and actions, too. How do we tap into our subconscious mind and increase our energy? How do we live the life we want and focus on actions that serve our highest good?

We often use our rational mind to sabotage our subconscious desires and our intuition. The good news is we can reprogram our subconscious mind to alter these messages and create new habits and actions that will produce results we want. The brain is like a muscle; it can be trained and altered. Neuroplasticity research shows that our neurons are remarkably flexible. Our brain is constantly changing and adapting based on sensory, motor, emotional, and intellectual demands. As Dr. Bruce Lipton, a stem cell biologist, states, "A cell's life is controlled by the physical and energetic environment and *not* by its genes."

Studies show that when we quiet our mind, even if our body is moving, we feel easy effortless power and can create more satisfying results. When we go into deep meditation, visualization, self-hypnosis, or contemplation, we get into a relaxed subconscious state, where it is easier to reprogram our mind. It is like waking up from a dream and wondering if it was real or not. This is the power of our subconscious. In a dream state, we can shift our awareness, and thereby our reality.

Brain-wave activity is altered in these states, primarily while in theta and alpha. Theta waves suggest deep relaxation and awareness. Alpha waves are indicative of wakeful rest, not sleep. Delta waves indicate sleep, and beta waves are more present during typical activities during the day. When we function in beta, the mind and body are active. Energy flow can get stuck between the mind and body more easily, and thoughts get in the way. But when alpha and theta waves are more abundant, we less focused on figuring out a problem and more willing to observe and rest. Somewhere deep within, our spirit takes in information from our life and continues to process it while we are in this more relaxed state. Through the balance of stimulation and reflection, we become clear in our intentions and desires and can achieve our best.

I often used self-hypnosis to delve into this deeper state of consciousness. This helped me to perform my best at meets, and I also practiced altering my beliefs and healing while in a deeply relaxed state.

Reclaim Your Innocence

Life is constantly changing, and we experience excitement about new pos-sibilities as well as anxiety over potential loss. We first experience change as we come out of our mother's womb. There is grieving over no longer being one with our mother in the warm and cozy place we were just in. We also are joyful as we fully begin life in our own body. As we grow from being an innocent baby and become conditioned, we can lose our sense of our true self. As we get older, we can acknowledge parts of ourselves that we had suppressed in order to survive. We can learn to forgive ourselves and accept that we are okay as we are, with all of our feelings and actions that we have had up until now. We can feel complete again, and return to our innocence.

Achieving Bliss

> *"Where there is FAITH, there is LOVE; Where there is LOVE,*
> *there is PEACE; Where there is PEACE, there is GOD;*
> *Where there is GOD, there is BLISS."*
> *– Sri Sathya Sai Baba*

We are in a physical body but also have an ego. Yet we can have moments, hours, or days in which we transcend beyond our ego while still in our body. In these moments, we can reclaim our lost selves. We can do this while living from our spirit and purpose. When we are in this place, we have faith and trust, knowing that we are taken care of.

One of my favorite spots to connect with myself, and everything around me, is at The Esalen Institute in Big Sur, California. The beauty of the ocean and the cliffs come together to amaze and inspire. The sound of the waves crashing into the land and then going back out reminds me of the spaces in between; breathing in, pause, breathing out, pause. Our thoughts, emotions, and interactions are similar to this. Thoughts arise, reaching their true form, and then dissipate, just like the waves in the ocean. When we talk with another person, there is a beginning, middle, and ending to the conversation and then a pause, and possibly a repeat of the same process.

Esalen is named for the Native Americans who originally lived on this land, and the institute has been a rich source of inspiration and transformation for many people around the world. From the meditation hut, I can see a river below me—I watch the water move downstream and reconnect with the ocean. The water easily flows around the rocks. It may stop in spots, but it works with its environment to find the easiest path.

In order to flow like a river or sway like branches bending in the wind, we must learn to adapt to the changes and obstacles that come into our path. We can learn to let our life flow easily, just like water does. As with a river, energy flows and is constantly moving.

We are merely a drop of water in the vastness of the ocean—yet we are also the ocean itself. There is a greater force/power that is invisible and yet everywhere. It manages all of us; we just need to let it guide us. When we feel God, or this universal force, we feel and see the power of love in ourselves and in everyone.

In an enlightened, blissful state we feel formless, while feeling at one with everything around us. When we listen to our spirit, we transcend ego. We can ask and receive more quickly since our energy is enhanced.

We can experience this oneness with everything, anytime. We do not need to do something special, achieve some amazing outcome, or have millions of people watching us to validate that we experienced being in the flow, connected to all. We just need to be attentive to ourselves and allow life to flow through us. This requires trust, faith, and commitment—everything we have been working on throughout this book. When we experience it, we feel at one with all, a pure joy and yet also nothing, as though we are just observing ourselves; there is no "you" or "I." There is no duality—no subject and object. They have merged into one, and there we experience this feeling of utter bliss.

Bliss can happen while playing sports or music, studying, having scx, eating, cooking, engaging in a conversation, or while surrounded by nature. There is no limit to where or when it can happen for you. It requires giving up trying to control what will happen in the moment, as you are purely open to everything and anything. You open yourself up to receive energy and consciousness, and to give it back as well. It is a merging of yourself with whatever is going on around you. It is almost like dreaming while you are awake.

How To Unlock The Wisdom Within

Wisdom is readily available for you once you have trained the cognitive mind. When you let go of distractions and can just be, trust, and have faith, you can easily go beyond. In this state, you answer to your higher inner truth, your wisdom, and your happy, fun, free soul.

Our goal is to get beyond the limitations of the conscious mind in order to allow greater wisdom to work through us. We need to see that our mind and body are not separate—they are one entity. They function greater together than alone.

We can be in a clear, calm state (in which our brain produces more alpha waves, and we are in a deep state of relaxed awareness) while also being active. I enjoy getting to this place when I exercise or perform, being relaxed while also intensely engaged in an activity. I love using physical movement to find enlightenment, even if it only lasts for a few moments. In this place, we can use our full potential. It can happen easily, without having to force it or even think about it.

Through self-awareness, we can merge our small self into our big Self, which allows us to experience going beyond what we thought possible. We can tap into this rich reservoir of energy at any time and go beyond the rational mind. When we open ourselves to the natural flow, we find God within us and are connected with all. As Jesus said, "It is the Spirit who gives life; the flesh profits nothing" (John 6:63, NKJV).

Exercises To Help Foster Your True Self

"The key to the universe lies dormant within the self, waiting to awaken through self-discovery." – Taejoon Lee

1.To connect with your true self, it is best to validate what you feel, say, and do. When you know "I am" instead of "I am not," you feel more energy within.

2.Imagine what you want. Anything that currently exists was once imagined. Do you want to reprogram your subconscious mind? If so, start by training your cognitive mind to be calm. Or use hypnosis to keep your brain from being overly stimulated with more than it can process. Then, tap into your subconscious (theta and alpha waves), and alter what happens for you in your life.

3.Before you go to sleep, set up your subconscious mind to receive only what you want it to focus on. Review what you appreciate about your day or yourself. Or ask yourself a question that you want answered as you sleep. At night, your subconscious works on what is most important.

4.Visualize with a guide. If you prefer not to work with another person, *pretend* that you have a guide, a wise mentor, who can help you connect with the wisdom that lies hidden within you. Get quiet within and ask this wise person to speak to you. When you communicate with this wise guide, you do not need to search outside yourself. Your higher self speaks to you, and guides you.

Tap Into A Higher Level Of Consciousness

The tools and exercises in this book will help you strengthen your mind and manifest your intent. But the ultimate goal is to tap into your higher level of consciousness.

When you get sick, have problems, or feel stuck, you are functioning from a certain energetic frequency. When you change your energetic state—the frequency that functions around your body—you can more easily heal your issues and fears. Live from spirit rather than ego desires. This will help you to follow what you really want versus what you *think* you want.

When we were young, we wanted X, and as we got older, after we received X, we realized it was not X that actually fulfilled us. Some of us got disillusioned and depressed; others sought out Y, hoping maybe Y would be fulfilling. Eventually, if we were lucky, we realized that neither X nor Y could make us happy. We discovered that peace was already within us. When we allow ourselves to go deeper within, we transform our intentions and insight and, therefore, our lives.

When we are challenged to give our best, we constantly find ways to improve on what we are doing. We learn to cultivate a calm mind and body while in motion. Then, when outside distractions occur, we can remain mentally composed and precise in our movements. Since we have trained our body and mind to focus, be attentive, and listen, now we can go beyond and let a higher consciousness take over and perform for us.

After a performance where we experienced going beyond, we often do not recall how the details unfolded, just that we enjoyed it and felt like we were observing ourselves as the experience happened. We were totally engrossed in the activity and paid no attention to the past or future; we only experienced one thing in each moment. No distractions. We did not have to force it—it happened for us. In that state, we love everyone around us, including ourselves. There is no "other," no duality, in this moment.

When we are no longer preoccupied with trying to be "somebody," we can expand beyond our "self" and experience a bigger sense of our true *Self*. We transcend our mind and body and experience a oneness with everything, where there is a singular merged experience. The goal is to go beyond the boundaries of our own body and mind, to not focus on anything else except being immersed in this moment. From here, it is though things happen to and for us, rather than us having to try. As long as our conscious mind stays alert and open enough (we need to be present and have an innocent heart so we do not limit ourselves with small beliefs), we can allow deeper experiences to happen for us. I easily found this deeper place when I swam or meditated. While swimming, it was as if the water moved me. What works for you?

Creating The Life You Want

Once you get in the flow, you can get beyond the part of yourself that is constantly trying to determine who you are, what you mean, and why you act the way you do. Your requests unite with universal energy to manifest them for you.

When your vision is clear, you can make a big difference in the world. If your ego wants something that is not for the good of all, the universe might not allow it. Thus, when an answer comes to you in your own life (like a divine calling) or something inspires you, respect it and thank it for showing up by taking action.

You can have true peace and satisfaction if you go deep within. Once you no longer rely on external outcomes or approval for happiness and fulfillment, you get to experience your true self. So what do you really want? Will your wishes bring temporary or lasting happiness? You can have both. Being your best is about finding your power and radiance deep within. From here, stress decreases since you do not have to live up to someone else's expectations or be somebody you are not. You are free to be yourself. You accept the perfection within.

Chapter Sixteen

It's Not About The Medal: Finding Peace Within

*Better indeed is knowledge than mechanical practice. Better than
knowledge is meditation. But better still is surrender of attachment
to results, because there follows immediate peace.*

- Bhagavad Gita

In 2003, when I started exercising again after a decade, I was reinvigorated. I felt at home in the water; it was easy for me to connect with my spirit there. Swimming reminded me of who I was deep within: a little girl who just wanted to play and feel good inside. I reclaimed my true voice—and my power—and felt alive again. My focus was no longer on winning—just on the joy of swimming and of life. I had missed my time in the water, and I was bursting with joy that I was finally able to swim without being knocked out for days afterward. For years, I had not known if I would be able to do this again.

Nineteen years after my first international competition, with almost a decade of illness behind me, I walked out onto the pool deck at the 2004 Olympic Trials in Long Beach, California. Throughout my life, I had wanted to earn a gold medal at the Olympics. I had accomplished many things, but not that. Amazingly, though, it didn't really matter anymore. Even though I was in the second-slowest heat in lane one, and far from winning the overall event, I experienced pure joy just from being immersed in something I loved.

*****

Just as I had done years before, I followed my standard routine as I prepared for the 2004 Olympic Trials. Before I left the hotel room, I gathered my swim gear together: two pairs of goggles, two caps, two racing suits, my warm-up suit, and two towels. I felt content inside, and I was excited for the opportunity to participate in this meet. Ross Gerry, my coach and boyfriend, who was a 2000 Olympic Coach and former Stanford Coach, drove the few minutes with me to the swimming complex built for this meet. (Many top meets nowadays set up temporary pools just for the competition which are taken down after the meet.) There were two outdoor fifty-meter pools, one for the competition and one for warming up and cooling down.

I put on my turquoise swim cap, which said "Swim Craft," the team name that Ross and I had created. I remembered how we had chosen that name—to remind ourselves that swimming is a craft. It's not about filling up time with "garbage yardage" or numb thinking, but about moving with gratitude like an art form in the water. My goal was not about getting a medal; it was to refine my craft in the water and in my performance. My focus had been to train physiologically, prepare mentally, master the perfect technique, and know my race strategy.

I warmed up, did some short pace work, and rehearsed my start into the water. I got out, dried off, and smiled at Ross. I was so happy to be here. I changed out of my swimsuit into my Speedo full-body racing suit and put on my warm boots and USA parka (at meets I liked to maintain my energy, so I often wore a warm hat, boots, and maybe even gloves). Ross and I hugged, knowing we had experienced a wonderful journey over the past year. We had worked together to get to this moment, and we wanted to take it all in.

I walked to the ready-room area, where we could see the racing pool. Heat one had just marched out to swim, and an official was lining up my heat. We were next. I breathed in and out, and smiled. The blue sky and light clouds were a nice backdrop for the sea of color in the stands. I could hear the cheer of the crowd for the heat walking out before mine. Once that heat was behind the blocks, my heat began to walk out. My heart burst open, and tears welled up in my eyes.

I thought, "This is it. This moment is it." My mind went quiet and I felt at one with everything. All of the years of being sick flashed through my mind, the years of swimming for the US team, the years of joy and struggle that had shaped and molded me. I appreciated it all.

When I first started swimming with Ross in December 2002, I swam 500 yards three days per week. I didn't know how my body would respond, as I had not exercised that much in years because I had been bedridden and healing from CFIDS. I gradually built up to swimming 3000 yards five days per week, and I also did dry-land work (stretching and strength training). I trained differently than I had in my past, doing much less yardage and alternating more intensity with rest. We erred on the side of not doing as much out of fear of an illness relapse. I was thrilled to be able to train at all.

At the Olympic Trials, my heat walked halfway around the pool to the twenty-five meter mark. We stopped and waited for the first heat to start. My teammate and friend Dr. George Tidmarsh was in the first row of the stands by this halfway mark. He leaned over and gave me a high five and a big smile. He and a couple other guys, Brad Howe and Bart Wells, had been my main training partners over the past year, and I was grateful to them for helping me get here.

Heat one started to race, and we walked the remaining twenty-five meters to the starting blocks. I walked to my lane and heard the announcer state the winners and their times for heat one, but that was all a blur to me. I was in my own world. I looked down my lane at the clear blue water. The scoreboard was high above the turn end of the pool. The stands near me on my right were full of cheering fans; I could feel the vibration of the noise. But all I really heard was the music of Yanni playing in my headphones. I did my last few stretches, rubbed my hands on the blocks to stimulate them, and smiled. The announcer introduced me, and I waved to the crowd. I put my headphones away as he continued introducing the other seven swimmers in my heat.

The starter blew his whistle. We got up on the blocks. I heard, "Take your marks! *Beep!*" Off I went. I had a clean entry into the pool and started with a relaxed tempo as I built my way toward the fifty-meter mark, which was the halfway point. I was in the lead. I had a quick turn and good streamline, and I picked up my tempo coming home. I won my heat, but it was not my best time. Yet, I was happy. I just enjoyed the race. I heard some people call out my name and congratulate me. I smiled at several people I recognized.

Even though I would not make it to the semifinals, I felt good being able to do what I loved.

I saw Ross when I got back to the cool-down pool, and we both smiled and hugged each other. My time was not what we had hoped for, but this whole journey had been fun. I had not done this to prove anything. I had swum to feel alive and for the mere fact that I could.

A couple days later, I swam the fifty-meter freestyle. I just missed making it back to the top sixteen semifinals by two people. I decided to do a time trial, as I believed I could go faster and I didn't want to be done yet. I was having too much fun!

By the time we started the time trials, most of the stands were empty and the warm-up area was quiet. I had about twenty minutes before my race. I walked to the Porta Potties and saw one with a green vacant sign on it. When I opened the door, I almost fell over—Coach Shoulberg's bare butt was staring me in the face! I quickly shut the door and burst out laughing. Shoulberg finished, came out laughing, and gave me a hug with his big twinkly smile. He said in his goofy way, "Go kick Aaaaasssssssss, ROCCCKKK-KYYYY!!" All I could do was smile.

***

I had experienced a lot with Shoulberg, and we had both grown and learned while creating many fun memories along the way. He used to joke that I should have been a courtroom lawyer because I could defend myself better than anyone with him, which kept him on his toes. Shoulberg had been like another parent figure to me. As I accepted myself, I had learned to accept all of him, too, including both his mistakes and his strengths. I knew that when I swam my time trial, I would once again hear his bellowing voice, still cheering for me after all these years.

I went to do my time trial with a few other swimmers. I swam the fifty-meter in 25.89 seconds, which would have placed me eleventh going into semifinals (top sixteen). Jill Sterkel, a four-time Olympian and my friend, said, "Nice swim!" and smiled, knowing that would have been fast enough for me to swim again. I laughed, knowing that I would have loved to swim again that night in the semi-finals. Since the prelim swims determined who swam in the semi-final, my time trial swim counted as an official time, but not for bumping someone out of the semi-finals.

Sometimes life has a mysterious way of giving us what we need. I didn't need to do this swim with thousands of people watching, or earn a gold medal, even though I would have enjoyed both of those things. For me, it was enough that I swam my best time, even with very few people around. I had been immersed in my body, feeling my speed in the water...and the experience alone was a triumph for me.

These Olympic Trials gave me a sense of closure and showed me how much I had grown. I learned humility and was content that I was able to take part. My deeper Self was just pleased to race. I'd already had a fabulous career, and the ultimate blessing was still being able to swim. It felt like a gift. I was healthy and able to do something I loved. Participating became my success.

This event was also important to me in terms of my relationships. Both of my parents were at the Olympic Trials to cheer me on. Instead of being excited about my latest success, they were happy for me and proud of me even though I was not the fastest. Feeling their love and support meant a lot to me. Also, my oldest brother and his daughter had flown out from the east coast to watch and support me. He had rarely acknowledged my swimming successes in the past, but that was behind us now. I felt and appreciated his love and support. My high school coach, Shoulberg, and I had come full circle in valuing our relationship and what we had learned along the way. And I had fun being with Ross, my boyfriend and current coach, who I had fallen in love with and who would eventually become my husband.

I had also learned to appreciate the moment. I enjoyed experiencing the peace and freedom that comes when the mind and body are fused with motion, being moved by the water. Even though I did not make it to the finals, not reaching my external goal didn't matter the way it would have years before. I had experienced being in the moment, doing what gave me joy, and I felt immense love and support from my family, Ross, and old friends. I felt complete.

I appreciated my journey over the past several years, and I had a newfound respect for what I had accomplished, not just in swimming but in all aspects of my life. I knew what it meant to experience my energy at its best, and nothing else mattered. No medal could ever compare with this feeling of bliss.

My spirit did not know how old I was. I felt young at heart, especially when I swam. It seemed to me like I was ten years old again—an innocent, energetic young girl just playing and enjoying life. By being able to swim and perform after years of illness and struggle, I realized I could thrive after CFIDS. My body and mind were well. Now I hope I can be an inspiration for others who have battled a chronic illness, and give them hope that their lives can improve, too.

One day I might receive a bronze medal from the 1988 Olympics, since it is known that the first and second place finishers (East Germans) were using steroids. However, even if I were to receive the medal now, it does not matter. Over the years, I have realized that joy is in the process, not the outcome.

What experiences can you recall where you have immersed yourself in the process of whatever you were doing? When you got caught up in the outcome, how did you get back to staying in the present? When you go deeper within yourself, you feel free. This part of you knows that even when you get what you thought you wanted, the deeper experience of being immersed in the present with a quiet mind gives the most long-lasting fulfillment. We see that what we wanted all along was the feeling of true bliss we create in each moment. We can feel content even through life's ups and downs. We can be at peace within. Ultimately, true bliss is available in each moment.

Questions To Ponder

How do you define success? Has it changed as you read this book?

I define success as finding something that you love to do with your time and immersing yourself in it. When you can be present doing something you love, you no longer worry about what you gain by doing it, since you are enjoying the beautiful opportunity to be in the moment, doing what you love, testing and fulfilling your potential. In this place, there is bliss. You experience what people call "no mind"—peacefulness and oneness with all. When you are in this place, amazing miracles show up for you. You put together the perfect race and win that medal, though it's the enjoyment of the experience that's the real reward. You gain other opportunities from it, too. Yet, you know that you are still you, even as new possibilities present themselves to you.

What does attaining "the medal" mean for you?

The "medal" can represent anything that you have wanted to attain, such as a title, a role, a certain amount of money, the perfect relationship, or anything else. The medal also has a deeper meaning. We might enjoy recalling how we stayed committed to our path even when we had doubts and felt unsure, with no guarantee that we would receive exactly what we wanted. We had to trust, surrender, and have faith that our goal was possible, even in the face of uncertainty. By taking on the challenge and continually testing ourselves along the way, we discover what we are capable of. When we exceed our own dreams and realize that we had more power than we knew, we experience the wonder of this world and this life. This is a magical place to be.

You can relive that magical experience and feel good from it. Yet, if you do not find this joy inside on a regular basis, the happiness that comes from winning, doing well, and getting approval from others will only be temporary. Once you are no longer winning, or you lose a certain title, you might doubt who you are, and people who used to adore you might not pay attention to you anymore. But when you are clear about your motivation and feel content within, others' opinions won't matter anymore.

After an amazing experience, an athlete or performer will often say that they love everyone. They are experiencing a blissful feeling of oneness with all. After achieving her best time in a local meet, a swimmer that my husband and I had been coaching—who had struggled throughout the season—said, "I don't know what it's like to win a gold medal, but I feel like I just got one." This swimmer had experienced a breakthrough within herself. She expanded her horizons and saw the world through new eyes. It does not matter what level we attain in sports, career, or life. What matters is how we feel doing it.

Has any external pleasure fully satisfied you? For how long?

Yes, we enjoy having money, medals, and other nice things—they bring us pleasure. We feel good when people tell us how good we look or recognize how successful we are. We just need to make sure that we do not get too attached to needing or wanting these things, because then they will no longer satisfy us. Rewards and compliments are fun to receive and can make us feel good. They key is to remember that other people adoring us or telling us how great we are is only powerful if we already believe it ourselves.

We need to know that we are still okay even if we don't win the medal. Losing might motivate us to be more focused in training or try a new approach to see if that can help us win next time. The process itself brings us joy. We learn that winning or losing cannot determine our confidence unless we let it. We are great regardless of whether we reach our goal or not. Just in trying, by giving our best and not quitting, we are winners.

It is easy to focus on what to improve for the next time. However, it is also important to enjoy the moment of alert focus that brings out your best, regardless of when and where it happens. I experienced this when I was really sick with CFIDS and in so much pain that I rarely felt alert. My therapist told me to enjoy feeling great whenever it happened, even in the middle of the night. I often did not sleep well at this time, and I would experience being alert at odd hours. I learned to appreciate having these moments, even if they were at 2:00 a.m! By feeling pleasure even for a short time, we allow ourselves to attract more of it. Eventually this becomes a habit.

Is doing your best enough, or does the place you get to matter more?

When you watch a sport, do you notice how some athletes are mentally rehearsing their performance before they start? The more our performance becomes automatic, the easier it is to have it take on a life of its own, with our mind out of the way. Rather than overthinking, our body is in control. From this place we can get in a zone and execute our events as planned. It is exciting to do our best in any given moment.

Whenever we finish an event or performance, it is thrilling to know that we overcame obstacles, whether mental or physical, and that we did our best. Athletes usually know how they did even before finding out their time or place. When we watch some events (such as skiing and skating), we can see the athletes celebrating before they even know what place they ended up in. In other words, it is not about the medal. They know they have done their best and given it their all, and the rest is out of their control. They can only wait and see what place they get. Of course, they will have another moment of ecstasy if they earned a place that was better than they expected. Yet, even if they don't get the place they wanted, they can still feel great about how they performed.

When do you feel most content? Most complete? When do you go beyond your rational mind and allow yourself to feel free?

"A gold medal is a nice thing—but if you're not enough without it, you'll never be enough with it." – From *Cool Runnings*

If we do what we love and give it our best, the process alone will make us feel great. Amazing things can occur when we are in this state. We can experience joy more easily, and have that feeling of greatness within without needing outside validation to make us believe we are "somebody."

If we do not like who we are, can't accept all of ourselves, and feel stressed about never being good enough, we might think "the medal" will make us okay. We become attached to needing to win in order to feel good about ourselves, get noticed, or feel accepted and loved. When we attain our wish we feel good for a while, but then we wonder, "Is this all there is?"

When we do what we love for the joy of it, we decrease ego and increase spirit, which enhances our energy. We commit to our goals to experience this oneness, this blissful state of flow. We enjoy just being able to participate. We are present and not attached (though not apathetic). We break free from the need for certain outcomes, and we feel liberated.

When you experience this, you want it daily. Even when sick, I loved exploring what was possible in training, in school, and with people. This fulfilled me and brought me joy. When you know you are okay regardless of the outcome, you enjoy the process of each activity. When you take pleasure in the activity itself, rather than doing it solely in the hopes of a certain outcome, you will feel centered and grounded no matter what happens. When you lose yourself (ego) in your favorite activity such as music, sports, work, art, you feel like you *are* the musical notes, the playing field, the color on the canvas. You feel complete.

Even if you become a success in the eyes of others, you will not be fazed. Regardless of how others see you, whether you "win" or "lose," you will not be affected in your core. You will be clear about yourself and your intentions, not relying on others to validate you. When you are true to yourself, you inspire others to discover their true selves. You will have a positive impact on your sport, business, family, or community. External glory is short lived. But the sweetness of the journey and of inner satisfaction can last forever.

What is *your* best? What motivates you, really?

When you challenge yourself, train your mind, and have faith, you allow your best self to emerge and blossom. The most we can try to achieve is being present and doing our best in any given moment. When we accept ourselves fully, knowing that we might make mistakes, we allow ourselves to expand our knowledge and wisdom. As we grow and learn, our awareness and consciousness expands. We become more loving and compassionate toward ourselves and others.

Initially the medal or achievement might be what you seek. Once you attain it, appreciate your accomplishments. You can go on to achieve more without being attached to the outcome in order to feel good about yourself. You do not need to wait for a big event—such as the Olympics! — to have this chance. You can commit to something and allow yourself to enjoy life *right now.*

What have you really been seeking? Our ultimate goal is inner peace and freedom. To find this, penetrate the subconscious and go past limited perceptions, beliefs, and impulses. Trust your instincts. What is guiding you? Find the driving force at your core and allow your motivation to propel you.

What brings you the most satisfaction?

My favorite part of watching performers is seeing the joy they exude doing something they love and giving their best effort, especially after many years of hard work. It's inspirational! Being able to participate in the Olympics is a thrilling and satisfying achievement. It is a fabulous experience to participate with focused athletes from all over the world who test you and inspire you to bring out your best.

When we live our dream, no matter what the outcome, we get to experience the divine within us. In those moments when an inner calm comes over us and life seems to go in slow motion, the mind is quiet and the world is miraculous. Everything is happening just as it should. In such moments, we experience ultimate peace and perfection.

When we are doing what we love, giving our best, and appreciating our efforts, we uncover the deeper nature of our true selves. Once we experience deep love of ourselves and others, have that feeling of fulfillment, and appreciate our gifts, we see that external gains are small in comparison. We get to claim our inner prize of peace and happiness that comes from doing what we love and loving ourselves. Our ultimate medal is the treasure of our Self.

Chapter Seventeen

A New Way To Live: Being Your Best Without The Stress

Thousands of candles can be lit from a single candle, and the life of the candle will not be shortened. Happiness never decreases by being shared.
–Buddha

The whole process of success, illness, and recovery back to health, performing, and serving others has made me wiser and richer. The wisdom I gained is not something tangible that I can hold onto, like a medal. My inner experience is deeper and more valuable than that.

In moments of being fully present, we stop suffering and receive inspiration. We feel complete, as we are immersed in the now. We appreciate our entire selves and accept what is. Our confidence builds, and we feel good. We love ourselves and stress less, knowing that we have committed to being our best. Life is all of this: love and acceptance, give and take, learning and growth, happiness and peace, finding satisfaction and our ultimate truth within.

How have you grown and brought out your best as you read through this book? Now that you are living from a deeper place within yourself, if you were to go back and do some of the earlier exercises, how would your answers change? As Buddha said, "There are only two mistakes one can make along the road to truth: not going all the way, and not starting."

By picking up this book, you made a decision to start a new process for yourself, to take action in your life. Now that you have begun this journey, I hope you are clearer about what you want and can take action to do what you love.

By dreaming big and committing to your goals, you are training your mind to be strong and resilient even in the face of change. Your faith about what is possible in your life is growing. This process is helping you define who you really are; you can see what you are made of.

As you accept even your darkest moments or hidden parts of yourself, you gain compassion for yourself and all living beings. As you go deep within, striving to maximize your potential, you will find what you ultimately have been searching for: true peace and satisfaction. You know that no external outcome that gives you temporary happiness can totally fulfill you. As you strive to be your best, you realize that this is its own reward. In these moments, you feel your radiance and power, and you experience complete satisfaction. From here, stress is not a factor since you are truly living the life you are meant to live. You are free to be yourself.

Balance

In order to maintain this feeling of consistent peacefulness, consider the importance of maintaining balance. I discussed this in various chapters, but I want to emphasize that without it we are prone to get stuck, sick, injured, or stressed. It is important to have a steadfast will that keeps us focused and energized for the long haul, but we also need downtime to regenerate. After moments of inspiration we need recuperation and time to digest. With training, we need rest and relaxation. As we stimulate and challenge ourselves, we also need to restore our body and mind so we can process what we have done and allow for new ideas to emerge. We want to train the mind while also giving it a chance to be free-floating as we immerse ourselves into dreamland. By getting into our subconscious, we can allow our creativity and intuition to appear and guide us.

Balance is like a symphony. There are fast movements and slow ones, louder and softer tones. The music would not be as beautiful if it was only quick and loud. The flow and timing of the whole piece makes the music enjoyable. A well-placed rest can be as vital as any note.

Balance applies to everything. As our society becomes more fast-paced, we need the balance of rest—from activities, technology, information, etc.—so we can recover from stressors and rejuvenate not only our minds but also our bodies and spirit. Even as you get excited about applying principles in this book, stay focused on the idea of balance. Keep from getting overly committed; you don't want to become overwhelmed. We all have experienced feeling burdened by too many external pressures (from work, school, sports, family) and internal pressures (ones we put on ourselves). It would be ironic for "getting healthy" to be another pressure rather than a pleasure.

If you find yourself getting pulled in too many directions, prioritize and decide what is most important. Remember, you are in charge of your life—nobody else is. Decide what is important to you, and focus on that. Delegate (a task I have had to learn!) and know it is okay not to do everything right now. Take time to rest. Be honest about how you feel, and honor your feelings even when others doubt you. Keep coming back to your breath. Focus on living in the moment.

To help you maintain balance, write down three things that you could do to unwind every day. Do not include abusive actions such as numbing yourself with food or drink, too much TV or screen time, or some other addiction, including sex or working out too much. Focus on three things that will help you relax and calm your mind so that you can eventually feel refreshed—activities such as taking a bath before going to bed, stretching, or deep breathing. Then, let yourself do these three things each day.

Keep focused on your dreams. Regularly ask yourself, "If I could do anything I wanted, what would it be?" By doing this, you will be inspired to keep dreaming bigger and truly create the life you want. By feeling good, you will have a newfound energy!

Keep building your own trust. Trust in yourself is the number-one priority. Allow yourself to be completely immersed in whatever you are involved in. Be present and open, willing to learn from the experience. From here, you will become clearer about how you feel, what you enjoy, and when you can push yourself to reach your peak potential versus times you need to take a break. When you listen to yourself, you build trust and faith in what is possible. You ultimately know what is best for you and what makes you happy—pursue that!

Bigger Vision

Many of us have gone through life searching for answers and seeking what we thought we wanted by traveling the world, earning accolades, spending money, and choosing certain kinds of relationships. When we realize that what we have been searching for has been inside us all along, we find our peace. As Lao Tzu said, "Be content with what you have; rejoice in the way things are. When you realize there is nothing lacking, the whole world belongs to you."

When we can really experience feeling okay within, we are empowered to pursue what we want. Ironically, we also attain it more easily. Yet, the medal is not what we are striving for; the ultimate goal is much deeper. As we search for contentment, purpose, and joy, we experience going beyond the rational mind, into the zone of oneness with everything. When we immerse ourselves in something we love, we are in bliss. We experience each moment as a gift, the perfect present.

The ancient Olympics understood this. They gave out laurel wreaths to the winners, symbolizing that victory is fleeting. The wreath itself would wither and die; only memories and feelings about the events would linger on. Everything is impermanent. When we realize that life is constantly changing and evolving—and so are we—we can appreciate each moment without getting too attached to it. We can flow easily through life, like the water through a river. We can create the life we want and feel content deep within.

As you find this contentedness within yourself, you will inspire others. By finding ways to manage your energy and magnify the spark within your heart, you can dedicate your life to something or someone bigger than yourself. Just as the Olympic Creed ("...not to win but to take part...") provides a message to the world, how do you want to make a difference in your own life and others'? How big can you allow yourself to imagine? Can you shift the thinking at your local school? Impact the way people view training for sports? Alter the way movies are created? Are you willing to share what you learned from your mistakes? How can you help shift the consciousness of people's thoughts without manipulating them? Can you inspire others to realize their own greatness? What is one way you can reach out and be of service to someone around you, starting today?

Let Your Light Shine

You are here to share your gifts. Yes, even if you still doubt whether you have them, you do! Even when I was sick, I was valuable, and so are you.

Sometimes you are given a path that seems daunting, but it has its own lessons for you to learn and share. Life is full of surprises and miracles. If you allow yourself to see them, amazing things can materialize in your world even when your conscious mind did not think it was possible.

As you are true to yourself, you help others be true to themselves, too. What you become in the process is the reward—surprise yourself by learning who you are and what you can create in your life.

Be open to everything and attached to nothing. You can't give away what you don't have. You are God and God is you; God is not definable and can't be confined to a word or a thought, as God is everything. Be the presence within you, and live from this place. Allow yourself to be greater than you ever thought possible. Feel your divine power. In this place is always peace, not stress.

You are no ordinary person—you are extraordinary. Treasure your magnificence; sometimes it just gets buried. There is nothing you need to do; you are already worthy of love.

In Conclusion

I always loved swimming, and felt at peace in the water. In many ways, I had been living my dream life, even though I became very sick. Now I have begun to live my dream in a new way by being healthy, balanced, and taking care of myself. I am married, have children, and help others feel content while also maximizing their potential in sports and in life.

I can let myself shine, share my gifts, and fulfill my potential while serving others.

Listen to your own inner voice and honor your deeper needs and wishes, so that you may get the best out of yourself and your journey. Let your life be balanced and peaceful. Release superficial needs, and experience deeper fulfillment. Live in each moment. Enjoy testing and surprising yourself in regard to what you thought was possible. As you trust and know that you are okay right now, listen to your deeper wishes, beyond the goal of attaining your "medal." Then, your dreams will happen more easily for you.

I hope that you have gone through a transformation in your own life and recognize greatness within that does not have to be defined by other people's version of success. Most important, I hope you will continue to follow your higher vision of what is possible for you now and in your future, so that your whole life flourishes.

Ultimately, when we do what we love, we are stirring the divine in us. We can all realize that the sacred is in the ordinary. We can have it all right now, just by being who we are.

Friendly Reminders From The Book

- Be the director and actor in your movie, called *My Life*.

- Be willing to change your beliefs.

- Dream big!

- Know that you can be happy and achieve.

- Be honest with yourself about how you are doing. Are you on track to reach your goals? Are you surpassing them? Do you need to create new ones?

- Take responsibility for your actions up until now. This puts you in the driver's seat.

- Reflect on what you can do to improve. Then create steps to do so immediately.

- Be a focused dreamer. When you feel stuck, stay committed to your plan. Follow your daily action steps to help you achieve your goals.

- When obstacles arise, deal with them and then refocus on your bigger vision.

- If you feel stressed, listen to what is causing the stress, and give yourself what you need.

- Take care of your health, eat well, exercise, and manage your mood and energy.

- Acknowledge and accept what you feel inside. Honor it without getting too attached.

- Focus on appreciating and accepting all of you.

- Forgive yourself and others.

- Feel lighter and freer by shedding your armor.

- Maintain balance in your life to feel energy and joy.

- Continue to learn about your areas of interest. Seek out mentors, and soak up as much information and experience as you can.

- Examine your strengths and weaknesses, and spend more time making your weaknesses into strengths.

- Meditate, and listen to what inspires you. Then do it.

- Allow yourself to experience happiness and bliss regularly.

- Most important: Enjoy your pursuit, and feel good about doing something that you love. As Buddha said, "Your work is to discover the world and then with all your heart give yourself to it."

- You have permission to be your best, feel good in the process, and have no stress.

- Life is short. Enjoy it!

References are available at www.katrinaradke.com

CPSIA information can be obtained at www.ICGtesting.com
Printed in the USA
BVOW031412250512

290835BV00004B/3/P